A World of Difference

Readings on Teaching Young Children in a Diverse Society

Carol Copple, Editor

National Association for the Education of Young Children
Washington, DC

A World of Difference was provided as an NAEYC Comprehensive Member benefit in May 2003. Besides having all the benefits of Regular NAEYC membership, Comprehensive Members receive 5 or 6 new books a year as these are released. For more, see www.naeyc.org/membership/benefits.htm or call 800-424-2460 and ask for Member Services.

Front cover photographs © Jean-Claude Lejeune; back cover © Jonathan A. Meyers.

National Association for the Education of Young Children
1509 16th Street, NW
Washington, DC 20036-1426
202-232-8777 or 800-424-2460
www.naeyc.org

Through its publications program the National Association for the Education of Young Children (NAEYC) provides a forum for discussion of major issues and ideas in the early childhood field, with the hope of provoking thought and promoting professional growth. The views expressed or implied are not necessarily those of the Association. NAEYC thanks the contributors.

NAEYC would like to thank Elizabeth Jones for her able assistance in crafting the "For Reflecting, Discussing, Exploring" section.

Library of Congress Control Number: 2003103873
ISBN 1-928896-09-X
NAEYC #261

Printed in the United States of America

Contents

About This Volume

As the world grows smaller, we are living more and more in a world of difference. We encounter a profusion of cultures, languages, ethnic backgrounds, religions, perspectives, and ways of living—far more than did our parents or grandparents. Certainly our children are encountering a far more diverse world than most of us did. Boundaries that were usual even a few decades ago no longer exist. For instance, children with and without disabilities are now learning in the same classrooms.

As our experience of other people widens, we can also find fundamental commonalities and shared purposes. Both the diversity and the commonalities contribute to our society's strength and add rich new threads to the tapestry of our daily lives. Yet, clearly there are challenges too.

As teachers encounter a wider variety of children and families than ever before, dealing with all the differences can be very demanding.

"The children in my class speak nine different languages!"

"Now when we talk about families, I don't know what may come up from the children—and what do I do with the information?"

"How do I establish communication with parents who have serious problems, like drug or alcohol abuse?"

"Sometimes a parent and I are really at odds about what's best for the child—am I supposed to do whatever the parent wants?"

"I was going to ask two class dads—a paramedic and a firefighter—to come to our class. But then I thought

about the kids with unemployed dads and I wasn't sure how they'd feel."

"Some parents passionately want us to do Christmas activities, and others wouldn't like it at all."

These are not easy questions and situations. Today there are many areas where teachers feel uncertain and out of their depth. Teachers are deeply committed to the children and families in their programs, and many enjoy the opportunity to get to know different kinds of people and learn more about them. At the same time, teachers are likely to feel overwhelmed by the broad range of differences to which they must respond.

The purpose of this book is to help teachers and prospective teachers respond to these challenges and opportunities. Of course, no single book can come close to preparing individuals for all the situations they will experience in the course of their teaching journeys. Neither do we presume that we have addressed each type of variation that may be significant. Our hope is to give readers the opportunity to hear from scholars and experienced practitioners who devote much of their professional lives to these issues. Through these selections, readers may learn about, reflect on, and discuss the challenges and issues they will encounter in their work, as well as find useful ideas for approaching them.

NAEYC's 1989 publication of *Anti-Bias Curriculum: Tools for Empowering Young Children,* by Louise Derman-Sparks & the A.B.C. Task Force, stimulated a great deal of thought and discussion in the early childhood field and beyond. The animated discussion about how to educate children to resist bias is far from over. In considering principles and guidelines for developmentally appropriate practice, too, the early childhood community has engaged in an ongoing conversation—sometimes heated and always lively—about how cultural differences affect what is appropriate for children at different points in development. Most recently, in 2000 the NAEYC Governing Board challenged the Association to work toward becoming an even more high-performing and inclusive organization. Essential to this goal is continuing reflection and discussion of the kind we hope this volume will encourage.

In recent years, scholars, practitioners, and leaders in the field have completed more research, put ideas into practice, and refined concepts and ways of expressing them. From that rich vein of work, we have drawn this collection of readings. Because NAEYC has been a forum for much discussion and writing about antibias education, inclusion, relating to families, and responding to cultural and linguistic diversity, we found many useful readings in recent NAEYC books and in our journal, *Young Children*. Other selections included here are from books that NAEYC has copublished or distributed. The rest of the readings are drawn from other excellent resources that we find ourselves turning to again and again. We thank all of the contributors for allowing us to include their works here.

Using this book

When constructing this book, we envisioned it primarily as a collection of supplemental readings for courses, typically for individuals preparing to work with young children and their families. It is also useful as a resource for further professional development for teachers, directors, and other early childhood professionals.

Although it certainly can be perused from start to finish, we also anticipate *A World of Difference* being used in component form. We have grouped readings into eight sections reflecting some of the most lively debate and important issues regarding diversity and early childhood. The sections can be read in any order, and each opens with a brief overview to help show how all the pieces in a section fit together. Some instructors may want to select readings from one or more sections for students to focus on, rather than assign an entire section. To facilitate all these uses, the table of contents provides a description of each reading to help everyone quickly find selections to meet specific needs.

Finally, we have included a **For Further Reading** resource list and a set of questions (**For Reflecting, Discussing, Exploring**) that instructors and staff development leaders can use to engage learners in reflecting on the readings and to jump-start group discussion.

—*Carol Copple and Natalie Cavanagh*
NAEYC Publications

viii

Teaching in a Multicultural, Multilingual Society

To build a rich multicultural program, educate children effectively, and build good relationships with families, we need to continually learn about and respond to cultural, ethnic, and linguistic differences. As teachers, our knowledge and understanding of differences should affect the decisions we make about curriculum and teaching practices (Evans). Linguistic diversity, rapidly increasing in classrooms across the nation, presents a host of challenges and opportunities (Tabors). From research and classroom investigation, we now know quite a bit about children's understanding of race, class, and culture; how these concepts are shaped by children's experiences; and how we can stretch and challenge children's ideas (Ramsey). Also important are interactions with families and respectfully listening and responding to what families communicate about their cultures, perspectives, and practices (Okagaki & Diamond; Garcia; Gonzalez-Mena & Bhavnagri).

Approaching these challenges and opportunities as early childhood educators, we must take care not to think in simplistic terms—"This culture equals these characteristics." Any cultural group has many variations within it. There are also many children whose heritage includes not a single cultural or ethnic identity but two or more. Supporting these children and their families requires us to get beyond monolithic categories to think in more complex, multidimensional ways about children's backgrounds and experiences (West; Wardle).

1

Kathleen Evans

Holding On to Many Threads
Emergent Literacy in a Classroom of Iu Mien Children

Excerpted from *The Lively Kindergarten*

All but seven children in my classroom were members of the Iu Mien (ee-mee-EN) culture, a tribal people from the highland provinces in South China and Laos. Looking over my class list before school began, I realized that this new year, working with children from a culture so far removed from postindustrial influences, would require my making some adjustments in the classroom.

The name list was unlike any I had ever received. A few different first names were repeated in a variety of ways; nearly all last names began with the prefix *Sae*. There appeared to be six or seven different root surnames. Although a naming system was apparent, it didn't seem to be based on gender. Naming became the first of many Mien customs I would learn about from these children and their culture.

Beginning with children's vision

During the first days of school, I invited parents to stay to help ease the children's adjustment to school. De-

spite a few children's tears and my gesturing to extend this invitation to Mien parents, none of them came inside. Later in the month at the back-to-school night, the parents stood in the middle of the room smiling at me. The younger-age parents, those who have been educated in this country, helped translate my description of what we were doing in the classroom and the questions other parents had about what the children would be learning. My assistant, who is Mien, explained to me that most parents, because they have not been to a school, feel unsure about their roles in the classroom and at meetings.

I didn't speak the language of the Mien parents, and they didn't speak mine. I quickly learned that written communication to most parents was ineffective. Any message I had to get to the class was efficiently transmitted if I asked my assistant or one of the English-speaking Mien parents to stand at the door and relay it to the parents when they came to take the children home.

As a group, the Mien children, who seemed at the first to be unnaturally quiet and compliant, stared up

at me from the rug, and I wondered just how I was going to provide a curriculum that engaged and stimulated all the children. I had a lot to learn about them, what they were interested in, and what they thought about. I wondered how I could create a curriculum that would reflect their culture and provide a supportive transition into American culture—a completely different way of looking at and being in the world.

In reflecting on that beginning, I realize there had been the option to carry on and conduct a traditional type of class. This was the kind of structure the children's big brothers and sisters had prepared them for. I'm sure the children would have been good and also happy about doing worksheets and coloring pictures. I had observed Mien children in other classrooms, with the teacher as the center and the children appearing to work happily in whole-group activities and doing what they were told when they were told.

But I had never taught this way, and I felt that the spirit of these children—or any child—was too precious to waste on meaningless, empty work. The group of

Mien children in my class seemed so curious and thoughtful. I was confident they would thrive in a classroom in which action, talking, and thinking were expected.

Becoming culturally aware

The Iu Mien families I was learning to know were undergoing a drastic acculturation shift, given the differences between village life in Laos and an American urban setting, plus the trauma of life as refugees and their adjustment to inner-city, northern California living in general and an urban public school in particular. To me it seemed very important to have a classroom that both reflected Mien cultural values and prepared the children as much as possible for success in school beyond kindergarten.

Because the Mien culture's language is spoken, not written, I felt I needed to be clearer in my mind about how the Mien oral tradition and other cultural practices could support literacy learning. The children still lived in group settings in which families shared childrearing, food preparation, and religious ceremonies.

Hence I felt I must be very conscious of the ways my teaching promoted collaboration and cooperation and be careful not to undermine cultural values by creating unnecessary competitiveness. The broad differences in Mien and American traditions and values as well as the fragility of the Mien culture as foreign within a hostile, dominant culture, made me wary of any undermining actions on my part. A Mien colleague, Tom Schao, wrote to me, "The Mien have really just boarded a train that carries a technological and educational advancement that is at least two hundred years ahead of their time, and they are beginning to feel a bumpy, but progressive ride toward an American destination."

Through Mien culture classes offered by the school district, my associations with Mien teachers (two in the district at that time) and instructional assistants from the Mien community, attending all cultural functions I was invited to, and reading whatever I could find, I learned about the culture of the children I was to teach.

Who are the Iu Mien?

The Iu Mien, the Hmong, and other hill tribes have been referred to as Yao ("outsider" in Chinese) in China and Laos, where their status has been not unlike that of Native Americans in the United States. In Asia the Mien were slash-and-burn farmers most noted for their elegant dress and intricate cross-stitch needlework. During the Indo-Chinese wars, Mien soldiers were collaborators, first with the French and later the United States. They were fierce, brave fighters whose acts of courage won their commanders' great respect.

When it became impossible for the Mien people to continue inhabiting the regions of Laos where they had settled, they crossed the Mekong River into refugee camps in Thailand. Later the U.S. government, designating the Mien as "guests" in gratitude for their help in the war, relocated them to the United States and provided welfare assistance and low-income housing in inner-city neighborhoods. In some ways this level of support eased their transition from tribal life to a wage economy. In many more ways, however, the lives of the Mien people were transformed and disrupted profoundly.

Bringing Mien culture into the classroom

Mien storytellers believe that in the days when the Iu Mien lived on the land, the elders would go into the forest to commune with the spirits before selecting a site for a new village in order to decide if the children would be safe in that place from evil spirits. So it is with ghosts that my classroom story here begins.

Around the time of Halloween, in most kindergartens across the country, there is much talk of ghosts. Artwork, stories, and conversations often center on ghosts. Each year at our school a rumor would develop among the first- and second-graders that a ghost resided in the custodian's closet next to our classroom. Bloodcurdling screams and the scampering feet of the older children escaping from the closeted ghost often interrupted us.

At circle time one day following such a ghostly visitation, I asked the children what they would do if a ghost came into their houses. "No problem," said Sarn, one of the Mien children. "All we have to do is call the priest." Thereafter, the children attributed any unexplained occurrences to the spirit world. A cloud passing in front of the sun and casting a shadow on the rug was noted as a significant event. Likewise, a classroom problem was often given a spiritual or supernatural explanation. When one of the favored penlights used for chart reading turned up missing, the children, sensing my distress, suggested that I imagine the missing light and then I would surely be able to locate it. "Do you really think this will work?" I asked. "It might," they offered.

Once when a great flood was prophesied by the shamans, each Mien child wore an amulet to protect her from danger. My assistant thought perhaps I might find this custom strange. But I told her I came from a very devout Catholic family, and I brought in the brown felt scapular my mother had given me at age 7 to protect me from harm. As a child I had an unwavering belief in my guardian angel, and I still pray to St. Anthony whenever I lose my keys. The beliefs of the Mien children resonated with my own recollections of being 5 and still secure in the protection of my mother and her saints.

Near our school is a beautiful park, rich in the history of our city and named after the patron saint of lost keys—San Antonio. In California's early days there was a corrida for bullfights. The trees are old, and the gentle slopes provide for views of the bay, the freeways, the trains, and the downtown skyline. In the morning the Chinese elders come to the quiet of the park to do tai chi chuan. On weekends Spanish-speaking soccer leagues hold matches from dawn to dusk. There is a Head Start program and recreation center as well as an organized tennis program.

But some of the bad things happening in the neighborhood also went on in the park—drug deals, drug users shooting up in the bathrooms, homelessness, violence, sex. Over the years the children have told me stories of the bad things they've seen happen there. It seemed reasonable for the community's elders to believe there were evil spirits in the park, for indeed there were. Still, the children navigated these streets every day. The park was part of their world and belonged to them. If we went there in a large enough group, we could be safe from the evil. So we did go to the park as often as we could, usually with many parents and even many of the elders.

On one trip to the park, Donna ran out of the bathroom shouting, "There's a monster in the bathroom." I went in with her to check, hoping to reassure her but being aware that it was certainly possible someone might have eluded our careful surveillance and slipped in unseen. Finding the restroom empty and remarkably tidy, I said, "See, Donna, there's no monster here." "No, Ms. Evans, it wasn't really a

The beliefs of the Mien children resonated with my own recollections of being 5.

monster. It's a ghost." I certainly was not about to deny the existence of ghosts to someone as convinced as Donna. About this time Kao and Scott entered our conversation. Kao said, "There is a ghost. See, it is moving your hair." "But, Kao," I said, "perhaps it is just the wind." In an instant he licked his forefinger, raised it, and pronounced gravely, "There's no wind." An imperceptible breeze moved the swings ever so gently. And Scott, without saying anything, pointed to them.

In a way, the children in our Room 2 lived in a world not so unlike the one I inhabited at age 5, one full of spirits, both good and evil, guarding our safety *and* tempting us into dangerous places. Last year when one child's preschool-age sister was killed by a car, the children said, "It was not that lady's fault. The spirits put their hands over her eyes, and she just couldn't see Linda."

But urban public schools are not very magical places. And more and more American children are pushed to abandon magical beliefs for the sake of efficiency, technology, and progress. In contrast, spiritual life is a strength and one of the special gifts the Mien children brought to our school. Holding on to it is one of the struggles they must take up to survive in this society.

A conflict of visions

When I observed the Mien children at play, cultural difference was obvious. It was not unusual to see two or three boys collaborating, with very little conflict, to build one car out of Legos. Children rarely played alone. And until a Mien child had been at school for a while, he would not draw himself alone on a page but always depicted a child surrounded by others.

Unfortunately many teachers appear unable to grasp a cultural context in which sharing, taking turns, and cooperative effort are the norm and don't have to be taught at school. Teachers in upper grades complained that Mien children chattered constantly, were unable to work independently, and cheated by giving the answer to children who were having difficulty. The children saw many problems as having an explanation in an unatoned past bad deed or perhaps a curse.

American concepts of blame and fault are not considered in resolving issues. The Mien reach decisions through the consensus of wise people, following discussion that continues until most can accept the reasons. A vote about which nearly half the group is unhappy hardly seems a very sensible way of determining rules for living together. Membership is regarded as the benefit one receives from living in accord with the customs of the community.

So many of the discipline procedures in schools, such as stickers and points for good behavior, would seem quite silly to the Mien community, for whom rules are clear and simple. The community decides on the rules, which mutually benefit the members. If a member is unable to abide by these rules, the community is offended. The offending member must fix the problem if he or she wishes to continue to enjoy the reward of living in a supportive community.

As I learned more about how the Mien community works, I saw more clearly the obvious and subtle ways in which competition is inherent in our schooling in this country and how destructive winning and losing can be to developing a community of learners. Most non-Mien children who came into our group fit naturally into this cooperative way of being in the world.

Into the world of print

The challenge for me was providing children with what Lisa Delpit (1995) calls "the culture of power" while supporting them in retaining what is beautiful and useful about the Mien home culture. The greatest challenge centered on literacy. Historically, since the Mien people had no written language, the priests, who traditionally were the only ones to read and write, did so in Chinese. According to legend, however, the Mien language once was written, but because of Chinese domination the women hid the writing in their needlework where its form was lost or forgotten.

In the Mien's homeland, education involved teaching children the community work of the tribe, the traditions, the stories of the people, and spiritual beliefs. From my observation of the ways the Mien children approached new learning, the teaching method children experienced before must have consisted of watching, chatting among themselves about how the task was to be done, and attempting the task when feeling confident to try without failure. The body of knowledge taught by the Mien has effectively withstood years of oppression, domination, war, and dislocation. For the Mien it maintains a strong, vibrant bond with the past, strengthens their solidarity today, and provides a common foundation as they look cautiously to the future.

Reading and writing is something very new for the Mien people. Many parents can only sign their own names, and they do this with great difficulty. After I posted the class chart of children's names (our main tool for teaching beginning phonics), including each child's picture, Yang Ta's mother spent each morning practicing the names of the letters in her child's name, so she would be able to help Yang learn to write it.

Nai Chow's struggle to learn to write her name illustrates the Mien approach to learning. On the first day of school Nai Chow's older sister made it quite clear that she wanted me to get the spelling of Nai's name corrected—the office had Nai Chao instead of Chow. Next she brought up her concern about Nai's letter reversals and mirror writing. It was obvious to me that every person in Nai's family was working with her on name writing. One day I observed Nai at the name chart very carefully tracing and retracing her name with her finger. By December she had perfected her name.

Cultural conflicts

Supported by family values, quite a few younger Mien parents have graduated from an American high school and have attended community college. A very few have university degrees. But young children's strong sense of place in the family more often is eroded as Mien youth move into middle and secondary school, where dropout rates are very high. Within families and the community some divisions develop as Christianity, materialism, loss of respect for elders, and exposure to rational, logical beliefs about the cosmos become more widely accepted by the young people. Disaffection with school and the estrangement of adolescents from the tribe— "bicultural ambivalence" (Krashen 1993)—are serious problems in the Mien community. I wondered, given these influences and forces of change, if literacy was a positive or destructive force for this culture, for my students?

Further confounding this dilemma of acculturation are widely held popular beliefs that good readers come from homes in which they have "spent over a 1,000 hours actively engaged in some kind of reading and writing" (Cunningham & Allington 1994, 22) before entering kindergarten; that literate children come from homes full of books and magazines; and that the mystery of print has been explained to them. Since these conditions are seen by many schools as the only way children become literate, this leaves little room for children from the Mien culture to become members of the community of readers and writers.

Rather than give in to this deficit model of needing more, I tried to support the literacy strengths I saw embedded in the Mien culture and to build on those. I saw a group with a rich oral tradition, and children with the ability to memorize and recall long and complicated stories. I saw a group of children whose involvement in art and music and with math materials indicated a complex understanding of pattern and the ability not only to re-create but also to create. I saw a group of children who worked together well, so the strong foundation necessary to create a community of readers and writers already existed. Valuing these competencies and taking care to plan my instruction in ways that reflected how children learn at home, I tried to re-create in the classroom the environment of a literate home. In this way I was able to dispel literacy beliefs built on a deficit model.

Many of the activities we engaged in during this school year focused on the importance of the children's Mien culture, the stories about home and family transcribed in their journals and class-made books, their descriptions of activities on the documentation boards posted in the halls outside the classrooms, the little rituals at the ends of our themes, and the big performances to celebrate special events. These all served as cultural bridges. Such passages back and forth between the culture of home and the culture of school—the Americanizing institution—demonstrated that both traditional beliefs and the requirements of modern culture can coexist in one person. I believe a curriculum that is generated from the cultural values of the community and that offers insight and skill necessary for survival in the dominant culture supports young people struggling to find ways to become bicultural.

© Kathleen Evans

Creating curriculum— The threads are time and structure

How is it that seemingly opposing needs and demands became coordinated in a meaningful program for 5- and 6-year-olds? The clearest way for me to explain how this happened is through the idea of an emergent curriculum. Through my observation of the children, chats with them, group discussions in the classroom, my alliances with Mien adults, and my own reflections, I searched for ways to bring both the children's home culture and the skills of empowerment into my classroom. An added challenge was doing this without violating sacred things that rightfully do not belong outside the boundaries of home and tribe.

The beginning of the year, even the beginning of a new phase in the school year, started with reflection, chats, and a review of observation notes, children's portfolios, and other work samples. I also considered the developmental scales and district curriculum expectations, which are part of my practice. To me it seemed most logical to begin with

the familiar and move into the exotic as the children became more grounded and better skilled.

Veteran kindergarten teachers begin by focusing on the child and family, moving to the larger community, and then finally exploring larger topics such as ocean life or dinosaurs. The validity of such practice is in needing to create a functioning community of learners, and to do so it is essential that each child feel valued for his or her unique contribution to the community. Even children whom the class may view as troublesome feel they have talents and skills to contribute.

If my Mien children were going to view membership in the tribe/community as worthwhile and if the rest of the tribe/class were to accept them, then all had to spend time getting to know each other. I had found this practice of moving from familiar to exotic even more useful in working with English-language learners whose vocabulary and usage were constantly evolving from the everyday things they were able to name to the more abstract subjects they would yet learn.

When planning any curriculum, I now have a rule for myself: proceed

thoughtfully and very carefully. Before I followed this rule my teaching was harder work and less successful. Once I would brainstorm elaborate webs around interest areas, with many activities in every subject area and all selectively and obviously connected to each and every other activity planned for the week. My knowledge of every topic I covered during the year was great in breadth and depth. My theme boxes and binders bulged with materials and content. But I was so exhausted and the children so overwhelmed that the joy of learning was lost.

Planning became more of a shared process with the children, although probably not as obvious as when a group would ask, "This year can we learn more about snakes?" Although at times I chose the theme, planning was shared in the sense that I divined a topic that seemed of great interest through observation, chatting, and reflection. I field-tested ideas by putting out a tub of books on the subject, reading aloud other books on the subject, and displaying pictures or posters and watching for a response. If there was enough conversation (in Mien or English or both), if there was noticeable curiosity or interest, then perhaps this could become a community project. After this preliminary engagement, I began the planning process—still checking responses, extending invitations, and making adjustments for the best fit.

Creative emerging ideas

Ghosts and spirits, fishing, sewing, caring for babies, cooking, and constructions all emerged as curriculum areas to include that reflected the Mien children's home culture. The office, bookstore, hospital, shampoo factory, as well as space exploration, all emerged prominently as aspects of learning to share in the culture of power. Our reading and writing, including even children's artistic representations as sign systems, became ways for us to explore, document, and preserve Mien cultural activities. As I watched and listened to the children and collected documentation, I decided what were the recurring cultural themes and confusions.

Fishing

From Mien children's drawings, dictated stories, and chats with the children, I found out how important fishing was to the families. At the water table I added fishing poles, magnetic fish, rubber sea creatures, rocks, shells, and tin buckets. This became an engaging, important place to play. Unfortunately it only had room for three, and many more wanted to fish. So, from construction toys the children invented fishing poles—the long, deep-sea kind. On pillows, which functioned as the bank, they sat, fished, laughed, and joked for an extended period of time.

The playhouse

The way I set up and stocked the playhouse provided some interesting insights into the Mien children's culture. I had included a high chair, even though I had never seen a high chair in a Mien home or a Mien child sitting in one. I just didn't think this through. Before I knew it the children, not the dolls, were sitting in the high chair. And before I thought to remove the chair, it was as broken as the wee bear's chair.

More successful accessories in the house were the Chinese dishes. Toward the middle of the year a group of children had taken to carefully arranging the dishes, the flowers, and artificial fruit into a shrine and then kneeling to pray. They did this without self-consciousness, in a most natural way, completely unaware that my team teacher and I had noticed them.

Sewing

This was something I initiated, and Mrs. Saelee, my assistant, supervised the activity. On small burlap squares the children drew designs, which they then stitched by hand. I had observed the Mien mothers using this same sewing technique as they did traditional stitchery—something they often engaged in as they chatted with each other and watched the children.

At first this was an activity chosen by girls, although the non-Mien boys also chose it. After a few of these boys risked trying, some of the Mien boys thought it might be interesting, though none pursued the sewing very long. The mothers were very pleased with the small, fine stitches the children made. I was truly amazed at the fine motor skills they demonstrated and the beauty of this first needlework. Mien mothers fear that the younger generation will lose this skill, and they appreciated this connection between home and school. I regret that I didn't take the opportunity to discuss why the boys had abandoned the activity so quickly.

Conclusion

The only way I saw for our classroom to manage the very complicated challenge of acculturation was to provide an emergent curriculum. The Mien culture sustained its people for a very long time through some very difficult struggles, but Mien children needed to learn how to function in modern America. They needed to become fluent in English; they needed to read and write well. Most of all, I believed it was best if they continued speaking their native language.

So the question becomes, Who owns the learning process? If teachers and children bridge cultures carefully and thoughtfully, if the curriculum emerges from the needs, questions, and requirements of the individual situation, then it is the learner who owns the learning. As teachers we can still meet standards and expectations and work within guidelines and frameworks. But the topics, ideas, and questions we pursue must emerge from the community of learners, grow out of the interactions among children, and expand between teacher and students. This is the only curriculum that can be culturally relevant.

References

Cunningham, P.M., & R.L. Allington. 1994. *Classrooms that work: They can all read and write.* New York: HarperCollins.

Delpit, L. 1995. The silenced dialogue: Power and pedagogy in educating other people's children. In *Other people's children: Cultural conflict in the classroom,* 21–47. New York: New Press.

Krashen, S. 1993. *The power of reading.* Englewood, CO: Libraries Unlimited/ Children's Books.

Adapted from K. Evans, "Holding On to Many Threads: Emergent Literacy in a Classroom of Iu Mien Children," in *The Lively Kindergarten: Emergent Curriculum in Action,* E. Jones, K. Evans, & K.S. Rencken (Washington, DC: NAEYC, 2001), 59–74. Copyright © 2001 NAEYC.

Lynn Okagaki and Karen E. Diamond

2

Responding to Cultural and Linguistic Differences in the Beliefs and Practices of Families with Young Children

Sophanara stands in the doorway holding her mother's hand. They are next in line to enter the Head Start classroom. Sophanara has watched other 4-year-olds enter the room with their mothers or fathers. But she hesitates. Miss Miller, the teacher, smiles and says hello. Sophanara looks down at her shoes. She doesn't understand what Miss Miller is saying. Sophanara's parents are from Cambodia. Although her father has learned a little English where he works, no one speaks English at home.

Miss Miller invites Sophanara's mother to come into the classroom and gestures her welcome with her hands. Her mother has had very little experience with people outside of the Cambodian community. Although she had only two years of formal schooling in Cambodia, she believes that education is important for her daughter. She expects the school to do what is best and believes that the school is responsible for making sure that her daughter

does well. Sophanara's mother listens to Miss Miller but doesn't understand what the teacher is saying. After a moment's hesitation, she nods and brings Sophanara into this new world with her.

൬

In the United States in 1995, an estimated 60 percent of the young children (birth to 5 years) who were not yet in school spent some time each week in early childhood education and care programs (West, Wright, & Hausken 1995). These young children reflect the great racial, ethnic, and cultural diversity of our society. They are members of families that speak languages other than English, families that have social customs different from those of the mainstream culture, and families that hold different beliefs about child development and different expectations for their children. What are the implications of this diversity for teachers of early childhood classrooms? It is impossible here to cover all of the variations in

beliefs and the sometimes subtle nuances that distinguish beliefs and practices across cultural groups in the United States. In this review we provide illustrations of the ways in which cultural differences in parents' beliefs and practices may affect children's adjustment to early childhood settings, and suggestions for working with young children who bridge two cultures as they transition between home and the early childhood classroom.

Cultural values, beliefs, and socialization goals

All parents have some goals and expectations for their children. Differences in parental goals and expectations arise in part because parents have children for different reasons (Hoffman 1988) and because societies have different expectations for the members of their communities (LeVine 1988). For example, in many Western societies, including European American traditions in the

United States, there is an emphasis on people being independent, self-reliant, and self-assertive and a focus on individual achievement (Spence 1985; Triandis et al. 1988). In contrast, in many Asian and Latin American cultures, interdependence, cooperation, and collaboration are widely held values (Harrison et al. 1990). Differences in these general cultural values or expectations for members of communities can lead to differences in the socialization goals and strategies that parents adopt for their children (Ogbu 1981; Garcia Coll 1990).

We begin this section by discussing examples of the ways in which cultural values are translated into parents' expectations for their children. Then we highlight cultural variation in parents' beliefs about development.

Goals and expectations

First, let's consider parents' ideas about the characteristics most desirable in children. Harwood (1992) asked three groups of mothers of 12- to 24-month-olds what qualities and behaviors they would like and not like their child to develop. Compared to Puerto Rican mothers from lower-class families, European American mothers from both lower- and middle-class families were more likely to indicate desirable traits that relate to personal development (for example, self-confidence, independence, talents, and abilities) and self-control (for instance, restraining oneself from being greedy, aggressive, or selfish). Thirty-five percent of responses of the middle-class European American mothers emphasized some aspect of personal development.

By contrast, the Puerto Rican mothers were more likely to talk about characteristics that focus on being respectful (for example, politeness, obedience) and loving (friendliness, getting along with others). In fact, nearly 40 percent of the characteristics spontaneously mentioned by the Puerto Rican mothers had to do with respectfulness. Less than 3 percent of the traits mentioned by the middle-class European American mothers fell into this category. Thus, parents considered different characteristics to be most important to their children's development, and these differences appear to reflect general cultural orientations toward individuals and relationships.

Another example of cultural variation in parents' goals for their children is seen in a study of a diverse sample of immigrant and U.S.-born parents of kindergarten and first- and second-graders (Okagaki & Sternberg 1993). In this study the parents from four immigrant groups (Cambodian, Filipino, Mexican, and Vietnamese) rated developing obedience and conformity to external standards as more important for children's development than developing independent thinking and problem-solving skills. In contrast, the parents born in the United States (European American and Mexican American) rated developing independent behaviors as more important than developing conforming behaviors. In particular, the parents who were born in the United States believed that creative-thinking skills were the most important skills.

Finally let's focus on the way cultural values and socialization goals shape parents' interpretations of their children's behaviors. As in the previous examples, an individualistic cultural orientation is contrasted with a collectivist or mutual interdependence orientation. In this example, the attitudes of Canadian parents of European origin, who have held a more individualistic orientation, and Chinese parents, who have traditionally valued mutual interdependence, are considered.

In any group of infants or toddlers, there is variation in children's responses to novel objects and unfamiliar situations. Some children are relatively relaxed when confronted with an unfamiliar situation and show little indication of distress. Other children react with high anxiety. They want to stay close to their mother or other primary caretaker. They do not readily explore novel objects or easily interact with unfamiliar people. These actions are indicators of behavioral inhibition.

Researchers have found that the meaning that parents place on these behaviors varies across cultural groups (Chen et al. 1998). In Chinese families, behavioral inhibition in toddlers was positively associated with maternal acceptance of the child and maternal belief in encouraging children's achievement. In contrast, in Canadian families, behavioral inhibition was negatively associated with maternal acceptance and encouragement of children's achievement. Similarly, among Chinese families, children who displayed *higher* levels of behavioral inhibition had mothers who were *less* likely to believe that physical punishment is the best way to discipline the child and were *less* likely to feel angry toward the child. However, in Canadian families mothers whose children displayed *higher* levels of behavioral inhibition were *more* likely to believe that physical punishment was the best discipline strategy.

In short, behavioral inhibition was associated with positive attitudes in Chinese mothers and negative attitudes in Canadian mothers. Although these perspectives on behavioral inhibition are quite opposite from each other, each perspective is consistent with the broader values of its culture.

Beliefs about development

In addition to the general orientation toward individualism or collectivism influencing parenting, other culturally based beliefs undergird parents' beliefs about child development. For example, in their study of immigrant and nonimmigrant families, Okagaki and Sternberg (1993) found that parents have different ideas about what constitutes intelligent behavior. Latino and Asian parents held implicit theories of intelligence in which noncognitive aspects are as important as or more important to the meaning of intelligence than cognitive skills are.

In other words, they seemed to have a view of intelligence that does not rely as heavily on cognitive skills, such as creativity and verbal expression, but rather incorporates and emphasizes other attributes, such as motivation and social skills. For the Latino parents, social skills constitute a relatively important aspect of intelligence. For the Filipino and Vietnamese parents, motivation was a very important characteristic of intelligent first-graders; to be intelligent is to work hard at achieving one's goals. This is different from the Western psychological model of intelligence that focuses on innate cognitive abilities.

In a review of research on the caregiving of minority infants in the United States, Garcia Coll (1990) observed great variation in parents' beliefs about numerous aspects of child development. For example, among some Native American peoples, infants may be restricted in their movement during the first several months of life because they are carried on cradle boards (Garcia Coll 1990; Joe & Malach 1992). In contrast, many European American parents find playpens to be too restrictive and want their infants to be able to explore and move around their environments with greater freedom.

Implications for teachers and caregivers

These examples of distinctions in cultural groups' beliefs about

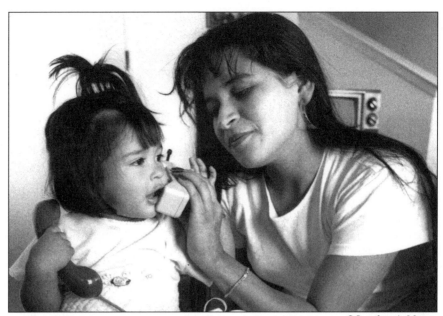

© Jonathan A. Meyers

children's behavior and development suggest that teachers cannot assume that everyone holds the same template for what constitutes an ideal child. For the child whose parents' expectations are congruent with the teacher's expectations for behavior and development, the transition to the early childhood setting may be relatively easy. But when there is a lack of congruence between parents' and teachers' expectations, children may have the additional burden of determining the implicit rules and expectations that govern the early childhood classroom.

What might teachers do to help children make a successful transition from their families' expectations for their behavior at home and the rules and expectations in their classrooms? An important first step for teachers is understanding parents' perspectives and parents' goals for their children. This requires that parents and teachers get to know and trust each other. It also involves more than traditional strategies in which teachers educate parents about the "best" strategies for encouraging children's development (cf., Powell & Diamond 1995).

We must talk with parents about our own experiences, beliefs, and values, and listen when parents talk about their perspectives. Understanding parents' perspectives and the ways in which they are similar to, and different from, our own provides the basis for working together to support the development of each child. Ramsey (1998) offers a variety of strategies teachers can use to develop collaborations with the parents of children in their classes.

Parental roles

What does it mean to be a *good* parent? What are the attributes of a good parent? Cultural groups differ in the ways in which they understand parental roles and responsibilities. In a study of immigrant Chinese mothers and third-generation or higher European American mothers, Chao (1994) observed differences in the ways in which mothers define their roles. For example, in contrast to European American mothers, the Chinese immigrant mothers believed that young children should be cared for only by their mothers or by some other family member.

Also in contrast to European American mothers, the Chinese

immigrant mothers placed a strong emphasis on training and teaching children. To them, being a good mother meant that one started training as soon as the child was ready to learn. The Chinese immigrant mothers endorsed the belief that the primary way in which mothers express their love to their child is by helping the child succeed, especially in school. From this perspective early childhood programs that emphasize play and a constructivist approach might be viewed with suspicion if the parent does not see a clear academic focus in the curriculum.

Among Native American nations, the role of the parent is often defined in ways that are distinct from Western models of parenting. For example, in some Native American communities, responsibility for the care and nurturing of the child extends beyond the parents; grandparents, aunts, or uncles may have primary responsibility for the discipline of the child (Machamer & Gruber 1998). Tribal elders may need to be consulted on matters regarding the care of the child (Joe & Malach 1992). The parent does not have sole authority for making decisions about the child. An implication of shared parenting responsibilities is that the parents may want to include other people in meetings in which decisions about the child will be made or they may want to delay giving a response to the teacher until they can consult with others.

In addition, cultural orientations affect how individuals view themselves in their parenting role. In a cross-national study of mothers of 20-month-old infants from Argentina, Belgium, France, Israel, Italy, Japan, and the United States, researchers (Bornstein et al. 1998) found, for example, that Japanese mothers were more likely than other mothers to attribute parenting successes to their children's behavior and parenting failures to their own

lack of effort. Although the Japanese mothers rated themselves high in their investment in parenting, they rated themselves low in terms of their satisfaction with their parenting and their competence as parents.

This pattern of beliefs fits with the emphasis Japanese culture places on being modest and on the importance of working hard. When parenting is going well, the Japanese mother attributes the success to her child and not to her own ability. When something is wrong, it is because she has not put enough effort into her parenting.

U.S. mothers, however, rate themselves as relatively competent and satisfied with their parenting skills. When U.S. mothers feel something is wrong in their parenting, they are much less likely than Japanese mothers to attribute the problem to something that they have (or have not) done.

Implications for teachers and caregivers

Why should these differences matter to early childhood teachers? As Ramsey (1998) notes, we often expect parents and schools to share common philosophies and practices about young children. Yet our teaching practices reflect our own, and our culture's, goals for children's development and education.

Understanding the ways in which parents (mothers *and* fathers) view their parenting roles and responsibility for their child's behavior provides us with another way to understand parents' behaviors and interactions with us. For example, teachers want children to learn to get along with each other and to solve disputes without fighting. Western understanding of typical development suggests that we can expect 2- and 3-year-olds to resort to hitting and pushing, rather than more reasoned conversation, to get what they want.

We intervene in these disputes, but as Western teachers and parents, we see the source of the behavior as growing from children's individual characteristics, and we act accordingly (by teaching children more appropriate behaviors). Our response to behaviors such as fighting will be different from that of parents whose cultural beliefs suggest that parents bear more responsibility for children's behaviors. For these parents, a logical response would be to call the parents of the children involved in a dispute to inform them of their children's (mis)behavior and to suggest that the parents need to do a better job teaching their children.

Even though we may disagree with parents' suggested responses in situations such as this, understanding the different ways in which adults think about parenting and children's behaviors enhances our collaborations with parents.

Language

Language is one of the most noticeable sources of diversity in early childhood classrooms. Although the type of language spoken in the home is not a parenting practice per se, home language usage can have a profound effect on children's adjustment to early childhood programs.

In 1991, 38 percent of the 3- to 5-year-old preschoolers in our country who lived in homes in which a language other than English was the primary language participated in center-based early childhood programs (Hofferth et al. 1994). Kagan and Garcia (1991) estimated that by the year 2000, about five million preschoolers in the United States would be from families speaking a language other than English.

Not only do children enter early childhood programs speaking (or having primarily heard) a language other than English, but they also have been exposed to varying amounts of language and socialized to use language in different ways. For example, in a longitudinal study focusing on the ways in which parents in 42 midwestern families interacted with their young children, Hart and Risley (1995) observed a vast range in the amount the parent talked to the child, from a low of about 50 utterances per hour to a high of approximately 800 utterances per hour when the children were 11–18 months of age.

Because the amount the parent talked to the infant was highly correlated with the amount the parent talked to the child at age 3, the consistency in parenting behavior results in an important cumulative difference in children's environments. If a child hears 50 utterances an hour for an average of 14 waking hours per day, that child will be exposed to about 700 utterances each day. On the other hand, if a parent addresses the child 800 times per hour, the child will hear more than 11,000 utterances each day.

Thus, children entering early childhood programs at age 3 or 4 already may have experienced great differences in their exposure to language. Hart and Risley (1995) found that greater diversity in parents' language was associated with more rapid growth in children's vocabulary. Consequently some children in our early childhood education and care programs may have a greater need for language exposure than do other children. Some young children may function at a lower level not because of any inherent cognitive limitations but because they have heard less language.

Cross-cultural studies identify numerous ways in which language socialization varies across cultures. For example, Fernald and Morikawa (1993) observed mother-infant interaction in White, middle-class American families and Japanese families temporarily residing in the United States. Although the mothers adapted their language to the abilities of their infants in similar ways (for example, simplifying their speech and adding interesting sounds to attract their infant's attention), several differences emerged in the ways in which the mothers spoke to their infants.

American mothers labeled target objects more often and were more likely to use the adult form of the target label (for instance, *dog* instead of names such as *doggie, woof-woof,* or *Mr. Doggy*). Japanese mothers were less likely to identify the object with a name. Whereas American mothers were more likely to talk about the object, Japanese mothers used the object to involve their infants in social interactions. "*Hai buubuu.*(Here! It's a vroom vroom [car].) *Hai doozo.* (I give it to you.) *Hai kore choodai.* (Now give this to me.) *Choodai.* (Give me.) *Hai arigatoo.* (Yes! Thank you.)" (Fernald & Morikawa 1993, 653).

The Japanese mothers also encouraged their infants to be warm and empathetic toward the toy. For example, as a mother helped her infant gently pat the dog, she would say, "*Hai wan-chan.* (Here! It's a doggy.) *Kawaii kawaii shi-te age-te.* (Give it a love.) *Kawaii kawaii kawaii.* (Love, love, love.)" (653). While the American mothers emphasized teaching their children about the objects in the world around them, the Japanese mothers focused on socializing their children's interpersonal skills.

Implications for teachers and caregivers

One implication of learning to use language in different ways is that some children may be less familiar with standard classroom uses of language.

For example, Heath (1983) observed young children in a community in the Piedmont Carolinas in which children did not often take the role of information givers. In particular, young children were not asked questions to which the adult already knew the answer (for example, "What color is this?"). When teachers asked children these types of questions, the children were confused. They did not understand that the purpose of this type of question asking was for them to demonstrate what they knew—not for the teacher to learn something. Similarly, children in this community did not understand that teachers were giving them directions when they made indirect statements ("Someone else is talking now; we'll all have to wait.") or asked certain questions ("Is this where the scissors belong?") (Heath 1983, 280).

Language reveals cultural differences. It is not simply that the child and the teacher may speak different languages. They may both speak English but may be accustomed to using the language in different ways.

How can teachers respond to such diversity in language among the children and families in their classrooms? We need to develop strategies to communicate when parents are not fluent English speakers and when we are not fluent speakers of their home language. This may mean that we need to locate a translator for meetings with the entire class as well as with individual families. Translators may be people we know in the community or they may be friends (or family members) of parents whose children are in our

© Elisabeth Nichols

schools. Although speaking through a translator makes conversation more stilted, it provides a beginning way to bridge the gap between home and school.

Developing sensitivity to parents' beliefs and practices

Given the great diversity in our country, it is virtually impossible to know what parents from each cultural group believe about child development and parenting practices. Even if it were possible to learn what each cultural group believes, great variation always exists within each group in terms of what individuals value and practice.

What can early childhood teachers do to enhance their ability to work with all families of children in their classrooms? Most important, we should not make assumptions about a family's practices. Within any cultural group—be it ethnic, racial, socioeconomic, or religious—individuals and families vary in their beliefs and adherence to the social conventions of their community.

Listening to parents and sharing our own perspectives is one way that we can begin to understand individual families' goals for their children and the ways in which they try to help their children achieve these goals. Asking parents how we can complement their efforts, rather than telling them what they ought to be doing, supports this type of communication.

This also requires that we understand that some families' beliefs will be quite different from our own and that we learn to appreciate these differences. For example, in one family

we know, the parents' (culturally based) values often reflect goals of interdependence, rather than independence, for their young children. One way that is expressed is in mealtime activities; in this family, the mother feeds her 12-month-old rather than giving him the opportunity to feed himself. Imagine this child's surprise when he entered an infant/toddler classroom in which children had the opportunity to finger-feed themselves Cheerios and drink from sippy-cups! The child sat quietly watching other children eat, then he whimpered for a teacher to feed him.

How might the teacher respond? Is it important that this little boy learn to become more independent (a goal of many parents and teachers)? To what extent should the teacher (and the school) change her ways of feeding this child to reflect the family's values at school?

When the teacher and a child speak different languages—whether in a classroom in which several children speak the same other-than-English language, several children speak different languages, or only one child does not speak English—the teacher can do several things to help the child adjust to the classroom. The first of these, of course, is learning how to pronounce children's names. Tabors (1997) suggests that teachers also learn a few useful words in the child's language (for example, *bathroom, eat, stop, listen*). Using sheltered English strategies—gesturing, using objects and pictures to help convey ideas—gives children additional cues to help decode the message.

Activity choices (for instance, manipulatives) which the child can enter without having to negotiate interactions with other children offer the child who is learning English a safe haven (Tabors 1997) or respite from having to constantly work hard to try to understand other people

A World of Difference

and to make other people understand her. From the child's perspective, observing and following what other children are doing is one of the most useful strategies for coping in the classroom. If teachers include the child in a small group so that there are models to follow, the child who is learning English will have a better chance of understanding the teacher's instructions (Okagaki & Sternberg 1994). Similarly, if the teacher establishes consistent routines for the class, the child who is learning English can more easily participate in classroom activities.

Asking parents to share their child's favorite songs (in the child's home language) provides a way for teachers to share the linguistic diversity of the classroom with all children. This also provides the child an opportunity to be an "expert," teaching classmates something that is familiar to him.

Even in a classroom in which all children share a similar cultural, ethnic, and linguistic background, family experiences are different for each child. Providing children and families opportunities to share their own family cultures with other children is a way to bring a child's experiences from home into school.

There are a variety of ways in which this might be accomplished: by having small and large group activities where children (and teachers) have the opportunity to share something special about their family and their life at home; by using photographs of children's and the teacher's families for a bulletin board or classroom book; by asking parents to provide copies of their children's favorite music or stories for use during free-choice and group activities; by inviting parents into the classroom to share a family activity with the other children. Teachers can use many more strategies to understand and reflect the beliefs and values of families and children (see

Derman-Sparks & the A.B.C. Task Force 1989; Lynch & Hanson 1992; Tabors 1997; Ramsey 1998).

Reviewing our teaching practices and thinking about ways to change our classrooms to be more accommodating and empowering to a wider range of children and families is an important task. As we become more successful, we reflect and appreciate the diversity in our communities.

References

Bornstein, M.H., O.M. Haynes, H. Azuma, C. Galperin, S. Maital, M. Ogino, K. Painter, L. Pascual, M-G. Pêcheux, C. Rahn, S. Toda, P. Venuti, A. Vyt, & B. Wright. 1998. A cross-national study of self-evaluations and attributions in parenting: Argentina, Belgium, France, Israel, Italy, Japan, and the United States. *Developmental Psychology* 34 (4): 662–76.

Chao, R.K. 1994. Beyond parental control and authoritarian parenting style: Understanding Chinese parenting through the cultural notion of training. *Child Development* 65: 1111–19.

Chen, X., K.H. Rubin, G. Cen, P.D. Hastings, H. Chen, & S.L. Stewart. 1998. Child-rearing attitudes and behavioral inhibition in Chinese and Canadian toddlers: A cross-cultural study. *Developmental Psychology* 34 (4): 677–86.

Derman-Sparks, L., & the A.B.C. Task Force. 1989. *Anti-bias curriculum: Tools for empowering young children.* Washington, DC: NAEYC.

Fernald, A., & H. Morikawa. 1993. Common themes and cultural variations in Japanese and American mothers' speech to infants. *Child Development* 64: 637–56.

Garcia Coll, C.T. 1990. Developmental outcome of minority infants: A process-oriented look into our beginnings. *Child Development* 61: 270–89.

Harrison, A.O., M.N. Wilson, C.J. Pine, S.Q. Chan, & R. Buriel. 1990. Family ecologies of ethnic minority children. *Child Development* 61: 347–62.

Hart, B., & T.R. Risley. 1995. *Meaningful differences in the everyday experiences of young American children.* Baltimore, MD: Brookes.

Harwood, R.L. 1992. The influence of culturally derived values on Anglo and Puerto Rican mothers' perceptions of attachment behavior. *Child Development* 63: 822–39.

Heath, S.B. 1983. *Ways with words: Language, life, and work in communities and classrooms.* New York: Cambridge University Press.

Hofferth, S.L., J. West, R. Henke, & P. Kaufman. 1994. *Access to early childhood programs for children at risk.* National Household Education Survey. U.S. Department of Education, Office of Educational Research and Improvement. NCES 93-372.

Hoffman, L.W. 1988. Cross-cultural differences in childrearing goals. In *Parental behavior in diverse societies*, eds. R.A. LeVine,

P.M. Miller, & M.M. West, 99–122. New Directions for Child Development Series, ed. W. Damon, no. 40, summer. San Francisco, CA: Jossey-Bass.

Joe, J.R., & R.S. Malach. 1992. Families with Native American roots. In *Developing cross-cultural competence: A guide for working with young children and their families*, eds. E.W. Lynch & M.J. Hanson, 89–119. Baltimore, MD: Brookes.

Kagan, S.L., & E.E. Garcia. 1991. Educating culturally and linguistically diverse preschoolers: Moving the agenda. *Early Childhood Research Quarterly* 6: 427–43.

LeVine, R.A. 1988. Human parental care: Universal goals, cultural strategies, individual behavior. In *Parental behavior in diverse societies*, eds. R.A. LeVine, P.M. Miller, & M.M. West, 3–11. New Directions for Child Development Series, ed. W. Damon, no. 40, summer. San Francisco, CA: Jossey-Bass.

Lynch, E.W., & M.J. Hanson, eds. 1992. *Developing cross-cultural competence: A guide for working with young children and their families.* Baltimore, MD: Brookes.

Machamer, A.M., & E. Gruber. 1998. Secondary school, family, and educational risk: Comparing American Indian adolescents and their peers. *Journal of Educational Research* 91 (6): 357–69.

Ogbu, J.U. 1981. Origins of human competence: A cultural-ecological perspective. *Child Development* 52: 413–29.

Okagaki, L., & R.J. Sternberg. 1993. Parental beliefs and children's school performance. *Child Development* 64: 36–56.

Okagaki, L., & R.J. Sternberg. 1994. Perspectives on kindergarten: Rafael, Vanessa, and Jamlien go to school. *Childhood Education* 71 (1): 14–19.

Powell, D.R., & K. Diamond. 1995. Approaches to parent-teacher relationships in U.S. early childhood programs during the twentieth century. *Journal of Education* 177 (3): 71–94.

Ramsey, P. 1998. *Teaching and learning in a diverse world: Multicultural education for young children.* 2d ed. New York: Teachers College Press.

Spence, J.T. 1985. Achievement American style: The rewards and costs of individualism. *American Psychologist* 40: 1285–95.

Tabors, P.O. 1997. *One child, two languages: A guide for preschool educators of children learning English as a second language.* Baltimore, MD: Brookes.

Triandis, H.C., R. Bontempo, M.J. Villareal, M. Asai, & N. Lucca. 1988. Individualism and collectivism: Cross-cultural perspectives on self-ingroup relationships. *Journal of Personality and Social Psychology* 54: 323–38.

West, J., D.A. Wright, & E.G. Hausken. 1995. *Childcare and early education program participation of infants, toddlers, and preschoolers.* National Household Education Survey. U.S. Department of Education, Office of Educational Research and Improvement. NCES 95-824.

Eugene Garcia

3

Respecting Children's Home Languages and Cultures

Effective early education curriculum, instructional strategies, and teaching staffs recognize that development and learning have their roots in sharing expertise and experiences through multiple avenues of communication. Further, effective early childhood education for linguistically and culturally diverse children encourages them to take risks, construct meaning, and seek reinterpretation of knowledge within the compatible social contexts. Within this nurturing environment, skills are tools for acquiring knowledge, not ends in themselves, and the language of the child is an incredible resource. The curriculum recognizes that any attempt to address the needs of these students in a deficit or subtractive mode is counterproductive. Instead this knowledge base recognizes, conceptually, that educators must be additive in an approach to these students.

Here are five practical applications that teachers can use to meet the challenges of acknowledging and responding to the importance of the child's home language and culture:

• Know the linguistic and cultural diversity of your students. Like an ethnographer, be very observant and seek information regarding the languages and cultures represented by the children, families, and communities you serve. Learn to pronounce your student's name as the family pronounces it. For each student write down linguistic and cultural information so it becomes as important as the other things you write down.

• Take on the new challenge of serving linguistic and culturally diverse children with resolve, commitment, and

ganas (high motivation). Children and families will appreciate your willingness to learn their language—even small phrases of their language. They will also recognize paternalistic attitudes—attitudes that convey the notion that their children should negate their native language and culture.

• Be up-to-date on the new knowledge base. We know so much more now about how better to deal with diversity. Most of us grew up or received our formal training in eras when diversity was not an issue. Incorporate personal and formal stories, games, songs, and poems from various cultures and languages into the curriculum.

• Share the knowledge with the educational and non-educational community. There is so much strong feeling among educators and the general public that diversity is a problem and must be eliminated. Be clear about how you deal with diversity in ways that respect the need for common culture, shared culture, and individual integrity.

• Above all else, care about and be an advocate for our linguistically and culturally diverse children and families by nurturing, celebrating, and challenging them. They do not need our pity or remorse for what they do not have; they, like any individual and family, require our respect and the use of what they bring as a resource.

Adapted from E. Garcia, "The Education of Hispanics in Early Childhood: Of Roots and Wings," *Young Children* 52 (3): 5–14. Copyright © 1997 Eugene Garcia. Reprinted with permission.

Patton O. Tabors

4

What Early Childhood Educators Need to Know
Developing Effective Programs for Linguistically and Culturally Diverse Children and Families

One day at the water table in a preschool classroom, two 4-year-olds—Naoshi, whose home language is Japanese, and Byong-sun, whose home language is Korean—were playing side by side. They were building a structure with two plastic bottles with a tube running between them. At one point the tube flipped out of one of the bottles, and Naoshi started to help Byong-sun put it back together. But as he lifted one of the bottles, Byong-sun protested, "Stop! Stop!" and when Naoshi didn't stop, Byong-sun took the tube out of the bottle himself. Then Naoshi picked up the tube and again tried to insert it in the bottle. Byong-sun started to help him, saying "OK?" When the structure collapsed again, Byong-sun said, "Uh-oh." As they continued their play, Byong-sun called Naoshi's attention to what he was doing by saying, "Hey." And Naoshi replied, "OK, OK, OK, OK, OK, OK."

०३

This vignette captures an important moment when two second-language-learning preschoolers

have developed enough useful terms in their new, mutual language—English—so they can communicate with each other during play.

But this did not happen in the first, second, or even third month in their preschool classroom. In fact, it didn't occur until the children had been attending the preschool for five months. During the intervening time, both Naoshi and Byong-sun had participated in a lengthy and complicated process of getting used to a new culture and a new language before they could begin to feel comfortable and included in their preschool classroom.

During that time I was able to observe and audiotape in their preschool classroom, so I could see the process as it unfolded. In this article I explore the second-language-learning process from the point of view of what early childhood educators need to know to understand and help young second-language-learning children. Throughout I will refer to young children who are learning English as a second language as second-language learners or as children from homes where English is not the primary language. In neither of these

cases is the terminology meant to imply that I do not value the home languages spoken by the children and families. In fact, I believe it is critically important that young children maintain and continue to develop their home languages (see Tabors 1997, Chapters 8 and 10).

A growing population of second-language learners

There is a growing population of children in the United States whose primary language is not English. Most early childhood educators are aware of this fact, but statistics are difficult to find. One source of information is the bilingual/multicultural survey of Head Start programs that was conducted under the sponsorship of the Administration for Children, Youth and Families in 1994. This survey found that 91 percent of the responding programs reported an increase in at least one cultural or linguistic group in the last five years. The survey reported that 74 percent of Head Start children spoke English at home, 22 percent of the children spoke Spanish at home, and 4 per-

© Jean-Claude Lejeune

cent of the children came from families who spoke any one of 139 other languages (SocioTechnical Research Applications 1996).

The Head Start population, of course, is only a fraction of the young children in preschool programs in the United States. One estimate (Kagan & Garcia 1991)—that may well be an underestimation by now—is that there will be 5.2 million preschoolers in the United States by the year 2000 whose dominant language is other than English.

Programs for children whose home language is not English

There are three main types of programs: first-language classrooms, bilingual classrooms, and English-language classrooms (see table opposite).

A first-language program is one in which the child's home language is the only language used in the classroom. This type of program helps develop the child's first language without exposing the child to English in the classroom. Supporters of first-language classrooms (Wong Fillmore 1991) believe that they play a critical role in helping children maintain their first language at an age when language loss is a real possibility. This type of classroom is the least frequently available.

The second type of classroom—bilingual classrooms—may involve a wide range of different configurations, but its main feature is that there is a match between the home language of the children and the language spoken by at least one of the adults in the classroom. For a classroom to be truly bilingual, however, there should be a plan for the use of the two languages—home language and English—so that children are exposed to appropriate language models in both languages. This type of classroom is available in communities where there are children and educators who come from the same first-language background, such as Spanish.

By far the most typical classroom situation for children from homes where English is not the primary language, however, is their being placed in an English-language classroom. Here there may be children from a variety of first-language backgrounds, and children who share the same first language may use that language when they play together. However, for the most part, English is the main language of interaction for both the children and the teachers. In this type of classroom, children from homes where English is not spoken will not have their home language maintained or developed within the context of the classroom.

Social isolation and linguistic constraints

Children from linguistically and culturally diverse backgrounds may face social isolation and linguistic constraints in the classroom. Particularly in an English-language classroom, the child who does not yet understand or speak English may find it difficult to interact appropriately with children and teachers because of the lack of a mutual language. This often results in the child being treated as nearly invisible or like a baby by other children, leading to frustration or withdrawal. Adding to their difficulties is the fact that children in this situation have very few options for communicating, except nonverbally.

They are caught in what I call the double bind of second-language learning: To learn a new language, you have to be socially accepted by those who speak the language; but to be socially accepted, you have to be able to speak the new language. Fortunately, most children develop strategies for escaping this double bind, but early childhood educators need to be aware that social isolation and linguistic constraints are fre-

A World of Difference

quently a feature of young second-language learners' early experience in a setting where their home language is not available to them.

The developmental sequence of second-language acquisition

There is a specific developmental sequence for second-language acquisition in early childhood settings.

Home language use

Children may continue to speak their home language with those who speak that language. They may also continue to speak their home language with others who don't speak their language, because they have not yet discovered that there is a new language being used in this new setting. For these children it may take time to come to an understanding that this language that they are hearing is, in fact, a different language from the one they hear and use at home.

Nonverbal period in the new language

When children realize their home language doesn't always work, they give up using it with those who don't understand them, but they don't stop communicating. Crying, whimpering, whining, pointing, and miming are all nonverbal requests used during this period. These techniques are, of course, most effective with understanding adults.

To become full members of the classroom, children will need strategies for moving beyond the nonverbal period. Most children do this by using the nonverbal period to start collecting information by watching and listening intently (spectating) and talking to themselves (rehears-ing) in preparation for going public in their new language.

Telegraphic and formulaic language

For most young children learning a second language, breaking out of the nonverbal period means using a combination of telegraphic and formulaic language. Telegraphic language is concise, often one-word usage of the language, such as naming people or objects or reciting the alphabet and numerals. When a child uses catchphrases for getting into and out of social situations, like the ones used by Naoshi and Byong-sun (*no, yes, uh-oh, OK, hey, mine, lookit, bye-bye, excuse me, I don't know*), this is an example of formulaic language. The use of these two types of language helps children get into the flow of the activities in the classroom. They begin to sound like members of the group.

	First-language classroom	Bilingual classroom	English-language classroom
Teachers	Native speakers of L1*	Bilingual in L1 and English *or* native speaker of L1 paired with native speaker of English	Native speakers of English
Children	Native speakers of L1	All native speakers of L1 *or* mixture of L1 and English speakers *or* bilingual speakers of L1 and English *or* mixture of bilingual speakers and English speakers	Native speakers of L1 *or* native speakers of different L1s *or* either of above and English speakers
Language of interaction	All interaction in L1	Interaction split between L1 and English	All interaction in English (except between children with common L1s)
Language outcomes	Development of L1; no development of English	Maintenance or development of L1, while also developing English	Development of English; little or no maintenance or development of L1

Types of Early Childhood Education Settings for Children Whose Home Language Is Not English

L1= Any language other than English

Source: *One Child, Two Languages: A Guide for Preschool Educators of Children Learning English as a Second Language* by Patton O. Tabors, p. 4. Copyright © 1997 by Paul H. Brookes Publishing, Baltimore, MD. Reprinted by permission of the publisher.

Productive use of the new language

A child begins the process of building her own unique sentences by combining formulaic phrases and the names of objects. She describes an activity ("I do a ice cream"), an idea ("I got a big"), or a need ("I want a playdough"). Because she is no longer using memorized phrases ("Hey, what's going on here?"), it may seem that her language ability has actually decreased because there will be many more mistakes ("Me's doctor") as she figures out how English works.

A cumulative process

As children progress through the developmental sequence outlined above, they will not give up earlier phases as they move into new ones except for giving up the use of their home language with those who don't speak it. In other words, second-language-learning children will keep aspects of previous types of communicative use, even as they move on to the next phase. For example, I was building a house out of plastic blocks with Leandro, a 5-year-old whose home language is Portuguese, and had the following conversation (A is author; L is Leandro).

L: I need help.

A: OK. What do you need help with?

L: To—to building a house.

A: Well, I have to start with a wall.

L: I make them apart.

A: You're making a what?

L: Part.

A: Apart? You're going to *take* them apart? OK. Let's see if we can get this door here.

L: How?

A: We have to go up to the top here. . . . We need the . . . lintel (pushing pieces around).

L: And what is for that (showing me a piece)?

A: That's for the corners.

L: For the what?

A: Corner. To go around a corner. Oh, look at this nice big long one. I'm looking for something to go on top of my door.

L: Look at one like that (pointing to a piece), and one like that (pointing again). (Pause) Lot of windows . . .

A: You need a lot of windows?

L: The house has a lot of windows. (Pause) I know what, why have windows.

A: Why?

L: Cuz to we can see outside.

A: That's true.

L: It's tru-u-u-e.

A: You couldn't see outside if you didn't have a window, right? (Pause) Do you think it would be very dark inside, Leandro, without a window? It would be dark, wouldn't it?

L: Yeah. . . . (Pause) And we have to do it like that (pointing to the picture of a house).

A: Really big?

L: Yeah.

A: We'll have the world's biggest house, huh?

L: Like—(gesturing with his hands like a roof).

A: You mean with a roof?

L: Yeah. . . .

A: OK. That looks like it's going to be hard.

L: Yes. How we going to put it . . . ?

A: I don't know.

L: I think we're going to do it with windows.

A: OK. We'll have a solar roof.

In this sequence, Leandro uses nonverbal communication (pointing to the picture and to the pieces, as well as indicating *roof* nonverbally), as well as formulaic ("yeah," "like . . . ," and "I need help") and telegraphic ("windows") communication, although he is operating almost entirely in productive language (making whole sentences even if they are not totally correct English). Note that his questions are not completely or always formed correctly and there are vocabulary items (*apart*, *corner*) that he doesn't understand.

However, Leandro's English skills are advanced enough so that he is able to deal with these problems easily and continue the conversation. The sequence in which he asks the rhetorical question "why have windows?" shows the level of sophistication that he is capable of even in this language that he is just learning.

This conversation with Leandro demonstrates what an adventure it can be to communicate with second-language learners, as it is always a guess as to what language forms and vocabulary they may or may not understand. This is why I think of young second-language learners' abilities in their new language as extremely volatile. If they have both the language forms and the vocabulary to express themselves, they can seem extremely advanced. But missing pieces can make communication difficult. High-pressure situations—such as being called on in front of a group—or emotionally charged situations—when they are upset or excited—can make even the most confident second-language learners unable to communicate effectively.

Individual differences

Leandro was the child who gained the most control over English during the year I was an observer in his preschool classroom. His achievements illustrate the individual differences that children bring to the second-language-learning process.

• Leandro's *motivation* to learn English was high because his parents and two older brothers were already bilingual in Portuguese and English and he had many English-speaking playmates.

• He had considerable *exposure* to English, both at the preschool he attended five mornings a week and in his neighborhood.

• He was one of the *older* children in the classroom, therefore he was able to bring more advanced cognitive and social skills to the second-language-learning process.

• Leandro had a very outgoing *personality* and quickly attracted input in English both from adults and from other children.

It is important to think about how these four factors—motivation, exposure, age, and personality—may affect an individual child's progress in acquiring a second language. Some young children are not motivated to undertake the task of learning a second language at all if, for instance, they know that they are only visitors in this country and will be going home soon. Younger children may move more slowly through the process because they have less well-developed social and cognitive strategies. Or, like Leandro, a child may have all factors working in combination to help speed the process of second-language acquisition.

Support for second-language acquisition in the classroom

There are ways early childhood educators can support and facilitate the second-language-acquisition process in the classroom. The developmental sequence outlined earlier can be influenced by how the teachers in the classroom organize the physical space, how they and the English-speaking children in the class interact with the second-language learners, and what types of activities they choose to present to the class.

Classroom organization

Two aspects of classroom organization can help second-language-learning children. The first is to have a set routine for activities so that second-language-learning children can

Bill Geiger

catch on and get into the flow of events. This will help them feel more comfortable and look like members of the group more quickly, aiding in their social integration.

The second is to provide safe havens in the classroom. These can be a table with manipulatives, a quiet house area, or a puzzle corner that is available at all times. Second-language-learning children can spend some time away from the communicatively demanding activities and develop competency in other skill areas besides language. Also, having a safe haven will help the children feel less pressured to communicate in a language they don't yet know and will give them a vantage point from which to watch and listen until they are ready to join in.

Language techniques

When teachers interact with young second-language learners they automatically use a variety of techniques to help get their message across. These include (1) using lots of

nonverbal communication, (2) keeping the message simple, (3) talking about the here and now, (4) emphasizing the important words in a sentence, (5) combining gestures with talk, and (6) repeating certain key words in a sentence. One teacher has characterized this type of communication as "toddler talk," or the kind of communication that a teacher would use with preverbal children. Using this kind of communication with second-language learners helps them begin to understand what is being said in the new language.

Teachers can also enlist the English-speaking children in the classroom to help with this process (Hirschler 1994). In many classrooms, English-speaking children do not understand why a particular child is not eager to join in their play, so they leave that child out of the group. If the teacher explains that this is a child who comes from a home where he has learned another language, it will help all the children develop understanding about lan-

One of the first questions a teacher should ask herself is, "Am I assessing the child's cognitive, emotional, and physical abilities, or her language abilities?"

guage. Suggestions about how the children can help will develop prosocial skills. A buddy-system setup can pair an outgoing English-speaking child with a second-language learner. Engineering the seating arrangement at snack or lunch, so that English-speaking children and a second-language learner are seated together, will help the child get into social contact more quickly.

Classroom activities

How classroom activities are structured can also make a difference. In most developmental programs there are activity times when a teacher works closely with children and materials. The teacher can use a running commentary technique: "Now I'm going to put the flour in the bowl" or "Byong-sun is putting the cheese on his pizza." During reading time the teacher can choose predictable books, which are particularly useful for second-language learners, and organize times when work with a small group of children makes it easier to tailor the book to the audience.

At other group times, using the same songs and movements repeatedly can help second-language learners tune in. This is often when a second-language learner first finds her "voice" in her new language and feels comfortable in a group situation.

Outside time also has potential for helping second-language learners link up with English speakers, using partners in noncompetitive games

(see Tabors 1997, Chapters 6 and 7, for more suggestions on how to facilitate second-language acquisition).

Working with parents

Teachers will need to develop ways of communicating with the parents of second-language learners. Of course, the first step in this process is to find out about the linguistic and cultural backgrounds of the families. A questionnaire for all parents concerning language and cultural practices, eating habits, child care arrangements, and parents' expectations about their child's experiences in the classroom can begin the process of gathering the necessary information. If the questionnaire is in English, some parents may need time to get help answering the questions. It is important to remember that their answers may not reflect their own facility in English (see Tabors 1997, Chapter 6, for a sample questionnaire).

The collected information can be used to help parents become true contributors to life in the classroom. A parent can be asked to share an activity that he enjoyed as a child or one that he enjoys doing with his own children. If parents of second-language learners are willing to use their home language during an activity, the English-language children can also learn what it feels like to be a second-language learner. Bringing home languages into the classroom will be highly affirming for the children who speak those languages.

Many parents from homes where English is not the primary language are very concerned about what language they should speak with their children. Educational research has found that children who maintain their home languages as they learn a second language do better in school later on (Collier 1987). But children will often make the decision to stop using their home language once they are exposed to English. So it is important to work with parents on these issues and help them develop strategies for home-language maintenance. This is also an important part of building communication with the parents of second-language learners.

Developing new methods of assessment

Developmentally appropriate assessment, in which systematic information is collected during typical classroom situations by the teacher who works most closely with a child, is a good place to start when thinking about the assessment of second-language learners (Bredekamp & Rosegrant 1995). However, if the teacher and the child do not share a language, it will be necessary to expand the types of observations that a teacher is used to doing. One of the first questions a teacher should ask herself is, "Am I assessing the child's cognitive, emotional, and physical abilities, or her language abilities?"

To understand a child's cognitive, emotional, and physical abilities in language-free situations, or as demonstrated in the flow of classroom activities, will be an important part of the assessment process. Teachers will also need to know how a second-language learner is doing in first-language development—here a

A World of Difference

home visit may be crucial—and how he is doing in second-language acquisition (McLaughlin, Blanchard, & Osanai 1995, as discussed in Tabors 1997, Chapter 9).

Developing new understandings about language and culture

All teachers bring belief systems into the classroom, often without knowing what those beliefs are. To develop effective ways of working with linguistically and culturally diverse children and families, teachers will need to examine those beliefs in relation to new information about bilingual/bicultural development. Teachers need to acquire information about the developmental sequence of second-language learning and think about the cultural differences that will be significant to the child. As Bowman and Stott (1994, 131) have written, "Educating all children will require the will and commitment to understand and respond to cultural difference. To the extent that teachers know and understand how children's past experiences have been organized and explained, they are better able to fashion new ones for them."

By providing a classroom setting that is based on a holistic, individual-focused, and developmental-interactionist framework (Genishi, Dyson, & Fassler 1994), early childhood educators will have taken the first step toward providing second-language-learning children with an ideal setting for the necessary interactions that can help them tune in to and begin to understand and use their new language. However, as pointed out in the position statement "Responding to Linguistic and Cultural Diversity: Recommendations for Effective Early Childhood Education" (NAEYC 1996), there are more steps that need to be taken, particularly in the area of working closely with parents to support the home language and culture. The recommendations in the position statement add new dimensions to the definition of what an effective program is in light of the changing demographics of early childhood programs.

Clearly, this is an ongoing process that will continue over time as teachers gain experience and expertise. Business as usual in early childhood classrooms serving linguistically and culturally diverse children and families is no longer possible, and it is certainly no longer preferable. Responding appropriately to culturally and linguistically diverse children and their families will require new information, new attitudes, and new practices on the part of early childhood educators.

References

Bowman, B., & F. Stott. 1994. Understanding development in a cultural context: The challenge for teachers. In *Diversity and developmentally appropriate practices: Challenges for early childhood education*, eds. B. Mallory & R. New, 119–33. New York: Teachers College Press.

Bredekamp, S., & T. Rosegrant, eds. 1995. *Reaching potentials: Transforming early childhood curriculum and assessment*. Vol. 2. Washington, DC: NAEYC.

Collier, V. 1987. Age and rate of acquisition of second language for academic purposes. *TESOL Quarterly* 21 (4): 617–41.

Genishi, C., A. Dyson, & R. Fassler. 1994. Language and diversity in early childhood: Whose voices are appropriate? In *Diversity and developmentally appropriate practices: Challenges for early childhood education*, eds. B. Mallory & R. New, 119–33. New York: Teachers College Press.

Hirschler, J. 1994. Preschool children's help to second-language learners. *Journal of Educational Issues of Language Minority Students* 14 (Winter): 227–40.

Kagan, S.L., & E. Garcia. 1991. Education of culturally and linguistically diverse preschoolers: Moving the agenda. *Early Childhood Research Quarterly* 6: 427–43.

McLaughlin, B., A. Blanchard, & Y. Osanai. 1995. *Assessing language development in bilingual preschool children*. George Washington University. Washington, DC: National Clearinghouse for Bilingual Education, no. 22, June.

NAEYC. 1996. Position Statement. Responding to linguistic and cultural diversity: Recommendations for effective early childhood education. *Young Children* 51(2): 4–12.

SocioTechnical Research Applications. 1996. *Report on the ACYF bilingual/multicultural survey*. Washington, DC: Head Start Bureau.

Tabors, P.O. 1997. *One child, two languages: A guide for preschool educators of children learning English as a second language*. Baltimore, MD: Brookes.

Wong Fillmore, L. 1991. When learning a second language means losing the first. *Early Childhood Research Quarterly* 6 (3): 323–46.

Reprinted from *Young Children* 53 (6): 20–26. Copyright © 1998 NAEYC.

Patricia G. Ramsey

5

Growing Up with the Contradictions of Race and Class

As our society becomes more ethnically diverse and more economically polarized, teachers face the challenge of how to present and explore issues of diversity and inequality in meaningful and hopeful ways with young children. Different classrooms and communities pose a range of challenges. In a classroom with children from different social classes and ethnic groups, creating bridges between children who speak different languages and have different play and conversational styles may be a priority. Teachers working with relatively homogeneous groups of middle-class White children need to prepare them to live in a diverse world that may seem very distant to them.

Over the past few decades, researchers have studied the development of children's awareness and feelings related to race and class, sources of some of the most profound divisions in our society. Many of their findings can be applied to teaching practices and curriculum. This review will address some of the questions that teachers who engage in trying to transform their teaching and their curriculum often ask:

• How much do children notice race and class?

• How does their understanding of race and class change during the early childhood years?

• How do children feel about racial and social-class differences?

• Do these differences affect children's intergroup relationships?

• How can teachers prepare children to value diversity and to challenge the divisiveness and inequities that often accompany it?

Children's awareness of and feelings about race

"Race" in this review refers to groups that share visible physical attributes that traditionally are defined as "racial." Although often used as a biological distinction, race is, in fact, a socially constructed label, as is evident in the inconsistent and biased ways in which racial terms are often applied (Smedley 1993). At the same time, a person's race profoundly affects her or his status and prospects in this society (Ogbu 1991). The contradictions of race have become even more apparent with increasing numbers of interracial births, transracial adoptions, and immigrants with mixed racial heritage (Root 1992).

One question that parents and teachers often ask is, "Do young children notice racial differences?" The answer is an emphatic yes. Contrary to popular beliefs (and possibly hopes), children are *not* "color blind." Infants notice racial cues, and by the age of 3 or 4, most children have a rudimentary concept of race (Katz 1976) and can accurately apply socially conventional labels of "Black" and "White" to pictures, dolls, and people. However, race does not necessarily dominate children's reactions to others. Both Black and White preschoolers categorize others according to sex more readily than race (McGraw, Durm, & Durnam 1989).

How prominently race figures in children's perceptions of themselves and others depends, in part, on their majority or minority status in their local community and on the extent and quality of contacts that they have with other racial groups (Rotheram & Phinney 1987; Ramsey & Myers 1990; Ramsey 1991a). During their elementary school years, children develop more complex racial views as they begin to associate social information, such as the status of different groups, with their physical attributes (Katz 1976). As this shift occurs, children see race less in terms of purely physical differences and begin to grasp the social meaning of racial terms (Alejandro-Wright 1985) and learn the prevailing stereotypes. Children who have difficulty forming flexible and multifaceted categories in general more readily acquire rigid stereotypes and are more resistant to changing them (Bigler & Liben 1993).

Children develop their racial identity during preschool and elementary school years. Preschoolers are often inconsistent when asked whom they look like and frequently make distinctions on nonracial attributes such as hairstyle or clothing. As they get older, children consistently identify themselves with their racial group. The development of racial identity may be affected by current attitudes in one's own group as well as in society at large. Studies done in the 1940s and 1950s suggested that African American children had less clearly defined racial identities, but more recent studies show that African American children develop a clear and unambiguous Black reference group orientation (e.g., Cross 1985, 1991; Branch & Newcombe 1986). In a recent Canadian study, Black elementary school children expressed stronger racial identities than did their White peers (Aboud & Doyle 1993).

Given that young children notice race and are beginning to identify themselves by racial group, the next obvious questions are, How do they feel about different-race people in general and different-race classmates in particular? When children in multiracial classrooms are asked who their friends are, they choose same-sex classmates, and there is little evidence of same-race prefer-

ence during preschool years (Jarrett & Quay 1983) and elementary grades (Singleton & Asher 1977). According to some researchers, children's same-race preferences become more consistent and elaborated during the elementary years (Goodman 1952; Porter 1971; Katz 1976; Schofield 1981, 1982; Asher, Singleton, & Taylor 1982; Milner 1983). This trend, however, is potentially offset by children's increasing cognitive capacity to understand the perspectives of other individuals and groups (Davidson 1976; Aboud 1988). Whether or not children become more or less own-race biased may depend, in large part, on their social environment and the values that they are learning.

From preschool to adolescence, White children consistently show stronger same-race biases and preferences than do their African American classmates (Fox & Jordan 1973; Stabler, Zeig, & Rembold 1976; Rosenfield & Stephan 1981; Newman, Liss, & Sherman 1983; Ramsey & Myers 1990). Conversely, Black children are more accepting of cross-race peers (Hallinan & Teixeira 1987). These findings suggest that White children are more at risk for developing own-race bias in their friendships.

Only a few researchers have studied how young children actually behave with same- and cross-race peers, and their findings present a mixed picture. Porter (1971), Singleton and Asher (1977), and Urberg and Kaplan (1989) saw few signs of cross-race avoidance or antagonism. Finkelstein and Haskins (1983), however, observed that kindergartners showed marked same-race preferences, and the researchers speculated that the roots of these preferences were developing or present during the preschool years. Consistent with their verbalized friendship choices, young White children in some racially mixed settings play

more with their same-race peers than do their peers of other races (Howes & Wu 1990; Ramsey & Myers 1990). However, in one study, the opposite was true, with the Hispanic and African American children forming more same-race groups (Lederberg et al. 1986).

During the elementary school years, racial divisions often intensify as children absorb more of the prevailing social attitudes, and the awareness of "us" versus "them" becomes more established (Katz 1976). However, Howes and Wu (1990) found that in a very diverse setting third-graders played more with their cross-ethnic peers than did the kindergartners, suggesting that increasing racial cleavage with age is not inevitable. Some interventions, such as racially integrated cooperative learning teams, seem to have a positive effect on interracial friendships (Slavin 1980; Rosenfield & Stephan 1981) and may help to counteract the tendency to divide by race.

Children's awareness and feelings about social class

Disparities in wealth and resources profoundly affect all aspects of children's lives (see Huston 1991 and the 1994 *Child Development* Special Issue on Children and Poverty). However, the dynamics and causes of these inequities are difficult for young children to grasp (Harrah & Friedman 1990). Thus, most studies of children's understanding of social class have focused on older elementary school children and adolescents. The research that has been done with young children has explored three areas: (1) children's awareness and understanding of social class differences; (2) their feelings about people in different social class groups; and (3) their ideas about whether or not it is fair that some people have more money than others.

Many indicators of social class distinctions, such as education and occupational prestige, are quite invisible to young children, but they do notice more concrete manifestations and implications of social class. Preschool children can sort rich people from poor people based on clothing, residences, and possessions (Ramsey 1991b). Their ideas about wealth and poverty, however, are quite rudimentary, and they tend to associate being rich with gold, crowns, and treasures. Early-elementary school children are likely to describe and explain poverty and wealth in observable and concrete terms, such as number of possessions and types of houses (Leahy 1983). Young children also are concerned about possessions and possession-related rules (Dawe 1934; Newman 1978; Ramsey 1987a) and are learning that ownership is a source of power and control (Furby 1980).

In our consumer-oriented society, children are exposed to a lot of information about available goods and the role of money in acquiring them. Although they do not have an understanding of social class, they are beginning to grasp the advantages of wealth and the disadvantages of poverty. Finally, young children are beginning to develop a sense of fairness and to notice inequality, especially if they are at a disadvantage (Damon 1980).

Young children begin to absorb prevailing attitudes about the desirability of wealth and assume that rich people are happier and more likeable than poor people (Leahy 1981; Naimark 1983; Ramsey 1991b). When asked whether it is fair that some people have more money than others, many preschoolers do not have an answer; however, those that do often comment that it is not fair (Ramsey 1991b) and say that the rich should share with poor people (Furby 1979). Likewise, elementary school children often say that every-

one should get equal amounts of money and that people with more should share with those who have less (Furby 1979; Leahy 1983). However, as they approach adolescence, children begin to justify inequalities and say that poor people get what they deserve (Leahy 1990), even though adolescents are capable of seeing the role of social and economic structures in perpetuating inequality (Leahy 1983). For many children in our society, the ideals of democratic equality give way to the rewards of economic competitiveness and individualism.

Conclusions and implications for teaching practice

Collectively these findings suggest that children are grappling with the contradictions of our society. On one hand, they are learning to value equality and justice; on the other hand, they are beginning to accept racist ideologies and the unequal distribution of resources. Although race and social class are treated separately in this article and in most research, they are inextricably meshed in reality and in the images children see (Rex 1986). Thus, children quickly learn to associate power and privilege with White people and poverty and subordinate status with people of color.

Teachers and schools play a crucial role in the course of children's attitudinal development; all aspects of practice are potentially affected. Although this discussion focuses on what individual teachers can do, authentically grappling with these issues requires a schoolwide and systemwide commitment to transform perspectives and practices.

As teachers, we need to understand the dynamics and contradictions of our society that relate to atti-

tudes about race and social class and how these attitudes get played out in particular communities and families. Teacher preparation programs should include courses in economics and sociology to provide the background for this work. As practicing teachers we must constantly examine our own backgrounds and perspectives and be aware of how they influence our assumptions about society and about individual children and families. In particular, White teachers need to be aware of how their position of privilege limits their awareness and understanding of social stratification and discrimination (Sleeter 1991) and struggle to push beyond these constraints.

We need to learn as much as possible about the dynamics of our local communities and the messages that children are absorbing in their daily experiences (Ramsey 1987b). School staffs can collaborate with parents and with local agencies to learn about the community and the history and current status of the relationships among the racial, cultural, class, and religious groups in that community. By knowing the local situation, teachers can anticipate some of the issues that children and parents might raise and deal with them effectively.

At the classroom level, teachers can assess each child's knowledge and feelings about issues related to race and social class. A book, a picture, or an event—in the classroom or in the community—can often stimulate these discussions. In particular we should try to identify children who are feeling marginalized because of their background or those who are developing rigid assumptions about particular groups. In conversations with parents, teachers can learn about families' experiences and views related to race and class. With this information teachers can plan and implement classroom activities and involve parents more effectively.

As teachers, we can address these contradictions of race and class along two dimensions: planned curriculum and spontaneous conversations. We can develop activities with books, pictures, music, art, and so on that affirm children's own racial and class groups, support their sense of solidarity with all people, and contradict their stereotypes. Stretching and challenging children's ideas about the world is especially crucial in classrooms that are relatively homogeneous in terms of class and race. In more diverse classrooms, teachers may want to focus on groups that are represented and to support the connections among children from different groups and between families and school. Cooperative activities potentially foster children's interpersonal and intergroup relationships and begin to challenge our society's pervasive emphasis on individualism and competition. Teachers can also plan activities that help children think about what is fair and why some rules and the status quo in our society are unfair (Derman-Sparks & the A.B.C. Task Force 1989).

Children's questions and, therefore, many of our ongoing conversations with them often reflect the contradictions and injustices in our society. We do not need to explain all these complexities to children, but rather to puzzle along with children and provide appropriate information as they try to understand specific events. For example, the images of the Rodney King beating and aftermath of the verdict were confusing and disturbing for young children. Why did the police, who are often portrayed as helpful, beat someone? How can important grownups who are judges and members of juries be so unfair?

Some holidays give rise to these discussions. My 5-year-old son recently—and indignantly—asked me why, if Columbus was mean and

© Hildegard Adler

cruel to the Indians, we celebrate Columbus Day. Why don't we have Native Americans' Day instead? As teachers we can help children think about these questions in ways that they can understand. Local strikes or layoffs, reductions in municipal services, a stereotyped book, or exclusionary play during recess are examples of the many "teachable moments" when children may be open to challenging the status quo and the easy answer of blaming the victim.

In planned and spontaneous activities and conversations, we need to provide children with hopeful and empowering experiences and images so that they are not overwhelmed and discouraged. Children can experience the power of collaboration by writing or dictating class letters to officials and newspaper editors about local problems or to publishers about stereotyped books. They can collect food for families who do not have enough or raise money to provide scholarships for extracurricular activities so that all children can participate.

Many biographies about people who have taken risks and have made a difference are now available for young children. These stories can help children think about how

people can overcome their fears and act to make a difference, whether the action is making a speech, refusing to change a seat, leading slaves to freedom, leaving family and friends, or joining a school or team where no one wanted them. Hearing or reading these accounts may stimulate conversations about being strong and brave in ways that children can understand. These stories also provide a compelling antidote to the violent images of power and strength that dominate the television and toy market.

If we as teachers participate in movements for social change and justice (Sleeter 1991), we provide another authentic and encouraging model for children.

To make these changes in our hearts and minds and lives, we all need support and time. As we teach children to see and challenge the contradictions and injustices of our world, we need to work with colleagues and communities to expand our own understanding and to reflect on our teaching practices. In particular, we must stay attuned to how our children's understanding and feelings about these issues are evolving and use their questions, concerns, and insights to support them in becoming strong, critical, caring citizens.

References

Aboud, F.E. 1988. *Children and prejudice.* New York: Basil Blackwell.

Aboud, F.E., & A.B. Doyle. 1993. The early development of ethnic identity and attitudes. In *Ethnic identity. 1, Formation and transmission among Hispanics and other minorities,* eds. M.E. Bernal & G.P. Knight, 46–59. Albany, NY: SUNY Press.

Alejandro-Wright, M.N. 1985. The child's conception of racial classification: A sociocognitive development model. In *Beginnings: The social and affective development of Black children,* eds. M.B. Spencer, G.K. Brookins, & W.R. Allen, 185–200. Hillsdale, NJ: Erlbaum.

Asher, S.R., L.C. Singleton, & A.J. Taylor. 1982. Acceptance versus friendship: A longitudinal study of racial integration. Paper presented at the annual meeting of the American Educational Research Association, New York.

Bigler, R.S., & L.S. Liben. 1993. A cognitive-developmental approach to racial stereotyping and reconstructive memory in Euro-American children. *Child Development* 64: 1507–18.

Branch, C.W., & N. Newcombe. 1986. Racial attitude development among young Black children as a function of parental attitudes: A longitudinal and cross-sectional study. *Child Development* 57: 712–21.

Cross, W.E. 1985. Black identity: Rediscovering the distinction between personal identity and reference group orientation. In *Beginnings: The social and affective development of Black children,* eds. M.B. Spencer, G.K. Brookins, & W.R. Allen, 155–71. Hillsdale, NJ: Erlbaum.

Cross, W.E. 1991. *Shades of black.* Philadelphia, PA: Temple University Press.

Damon, W. 1980. Patterns of change in children's social reasoning: A two-year longitudinal study. *Child Development* 51: 1010–17.

Davidson, F.H. 1976. Ability to respect persons compared to ethnic prejudice in childhood. *Journal of Personality and Social Psychology* 34: 1256–67.

Dawe, H.C. 1934. An analysis of two hundred quarrels of preschool children. *Child Development* 5:139–57.

Derman-Sparks, L., & the A.B.C. Task Force. 1989. *Anti-bias curriculum: Tools for empowering young children.* Washington, DC: NAEYC.

Finkelstein, N.W., & R. Haskins. 1983. Kindergarten children prefer same-color peers. *Child Development* 54: 502–808.

Fox, D.J., & V.B. Jordan. 1973. Racial preferences and identification of Black, American Chinese, and White children. *Genetic Psychology Monographs* 88: 229–86.

Furby, L. 1979. Inequalities in personal possessions: Explanations for and judgments about unequal distribution. *Human Development* 22: 180–202.

Furby, L. 1980. The origins and early development of possessive behavior. *Political Psychology* 2 (1): 30–40.

Goodman, M.E. 1952. *Race awareness in young children.* Cambridge, MA: Addison-Wesley.

Hallinan, M.T., & R.A. Teixeira. 1987. Opportunities and constraints: Black–White differences in the formation of interracial friendships. *Child Development* 58: 1358–71.

Harrah, J., & M. Friedman. 1990. Economic socialization in children in a midwestern American community. *Journal of Economic Psychology* 11: 495–513.

Howes, C., & F. Wu. 1990. Peer interactions and friendships in an ethnically diverse school setting. *Child Development* 61: 537–41.

Huston, A.C., ed. 1991. *Children in poverty: Child development and public policy.* New York: Cambridge University Press.

Jarrett, O., & L. Quay. 1983. Cross-racial acceptance and best friend choice in racially balanced kindergarten and first-grade classrooms. Paper presented at the biennial meeting of the Society for Research in Child Development, Detroit.

Katz, P.A. 1976. The acquisition of racial attitudes in children. In *Towards the elimination of racism,* ed. R.P. Katz, 125–54. New York: Pergamon.

Leahy, R. 1981. The development of the concept of social inequality. I, Descriptions and comparisons of rich and poor people. *Child Development* 52: 523–32.

Leahy, R. 1983. The development of the conception of social class. In *The child's construction of inequality,* ed. R. Leahy, 79–107. New York: Academic.

Leahy, R. 1990. The development of concepts of economics and social inequality. *New Directions for Child Development* 46: 107–20.

Lederberg, A.R., S.L. Chapin, V. Rosenblatt, & D.L. Vandell. 1986. Ethnic, gender, and age preferences among deaf and hearing preschool peers. *Child Development* 57: 375–86.

McGraw, K.O., M.W. Durm, & M.R. Durnam. 1989. The relative salience of sex, race, age, and glasses in children's social perception. *Journal of Genetic Psychology* 150 (3): 251–67.

Milner, D. 1983. *Children and race.* Beverly Hills, CA: Sage.

Naimark, H. 1983. Children's understanding of social class differences. Paper presented at the biennial meeting of the Society for Research in Child Development, Detroit.

Newman, D. 1978. Ownership and permission among nursery school children. In *Studies in social and cognitive development,* Vol. 1, eds. J. Glick & K.A. Clarke-Stewart, 213–49. New York: Gardner.

Newman, M.A., M.B. Liss, & F. Sherman. 1983. Ethnic awareness in children: Not a unitary concept. *Journal of Genetic Psychology* 143 (1): 103–12.

Ogbu, J.U. 1991. Immigrant and involuntary minorities in comparative perspective. In *Minority status and schooling: A comparative study of immigrant and involuntary minorities,* eds. M.A. Gibson & J.U. Ogbu, 3–33. New York: Garland.

Porter, J.D.R. 1971. *Black child, White child: The development of racial attitudes.* Cambridge, MA: Harvard University Press.

Ramsey, P.G. 1987a. Possession episodes in young children's social interactions. *Journal of Genetic Psychology* 148 (3): 315–25.

Ramsey, P.G. 1987b. *Teaching and learning in a diverse world: Multicultural education of young children.* New York: Teachers College Press.

Ramsey, P.G. 1991a. Salience of race in young children growing up in an all White community. *Journal of Educational Psychology* 83: 28–34.

Ramsey, P.G. 1991b. Young children's awareness and understanding of social class differences. *Journal of Genetic Psychology* 152 (1): 71–82.

Ramsey, P.G., & L.C. Myers. 1990. Young children's responses to racial differences: Relations among cognitive, affective, and behavioral dimensions. *Journal of Applied Developmental Psychology* 11: 49–67.

Rex, J. 1986. *Race and ethnicity.* Milton Keynes, England: Open University Press.

Root, M.P. 1992. *Racially mixed people in America.* Beverly Hills, CA: Sage.

Rosenfield, D., & W.G. Stephan. 1981. Intergroup relations among children. In *Developmental social psychology,* eds. S.S. Brehm, S.M. Kassin, & F.X. Gibbons, 271–97. New York: Oxford University Press.

Rotheram, M.J., & J. Phinney. 1987. Introduction: Definitions and perspectives in the study of children's ethnic socialization. In *Children's ethnic socialization: Pluralism and development,* eds. J. Phinney & M.J. Rotheram, 10–28. Beverly Hills, CA: Sage.

Schofield, J.W. 1981. Complementary and conflicting identities: Images and interaction in an interracial school. In *The development of children's friendships,* eds. S.R. Asher & J.M. Gottman, 53–90. New York: Cambridge University Press.

Schofield, J.W. 1982. *Black and White in school: Trust, tension, or tolerance.* New York: Praeger.

Singleton, L.C., & S.R. Asher. 1977. Peer preferences and social interaction among third-grade children in an integrated school district. *Journal of Educational Psychology* 69: 330–36.

Slavin, R.E. 1980. Cooperative learning. *Review of Educational Research* 50: 315–42.

Sleeter, C.E. 1991. *Keepers of the American dream: A study of staff development and multicultural education.* Washington, DC: Falmer.

Smedley, A. 1993. *Race in North America.* Boulder, CO: Westview.

Stabler, J.R., J.A. Zeig, & A.B. Rembold. 1976. Children's evaluation of the colors black and white and their interracial play behavior. *Child Study Journal* 6 (4): 191–97.

Urberg, K.A., & M.G. Kaplan. 1989. An observational study of race-, age-, and sex-heterogeneous interaction in preschoolers. *Journal of Applied Developmental Psychology* 10: 299–311.

Reprinted from *Young Children* 50 (6): 18–22. Copyright © 1995 NAEYC.

A World of Difference

Martha M. West

6

Teaching the Third Culture Child

Imagine that a new child, a boy, is enrolling in your class, and the principal has told you that his mother is Japanese. You have not met either the child or his parents. With this limited information, how do you envision this child? What hunches do you have about him?

Now suppose that a different child, another boy whom you have not seen, is enrolling. You know his name is Jason. His father is a professor. How do you see this child? What hunches do you have about him?

Finally, suppose that Jason and the boy whose mother is Japanese are the same child, that both descriptions refer to just one child. Further, Jason's mother is a teacher, and Jason speaks both English and Japanese. Have your presumptions about Jason changed? Are your assumptions about him now different from your earlier hunches?

Jason and his younger sister, Anna, are real children. They are my grandchildren. One year ago their family moved to a new community. In that suburban setting the children,

ages 5 and 7, entered school. My interest in their experiences in their new home probably differs from that of some other grandmothers for two reasons. First, the children's mother is the first non-Caucasian to join my immediate family. Second, I am an early childhood professor who tries daily to model cultural awareness for preservice teachers. For these reasons I have observed, recorded, and reflected upon my bilingual, bicultural grandchildren's lives inside and outside the school community.

I have considered their experiences in the context of child development theory, constructivist philosophy, and my growing understanding of the Japanese social teaching model. As a result, I have drawn conclusions that I hope will inform classroom teachers and those who guide teachers' professional development. The conclusions are case specific. However, they may encourage educators to think about alternatives to the "tourist approach" in multicultural education (Derman-Sparks & the A.B.C. Task Force 1989).

Third culture children

Discussion of the conclusions may also encourage teachers to consider ways to translate children's individual differences into learning opportunities for those whose lives span two cultures—children sometimes referred to as "third culture," so called for the third culture created within them (Tannen 1997). The body of third culture children is growing in size. Global communication, a global economy, the ease of world travel, the continuing influx of immigrants into the United States, diverse groups living together, and marriages across groups may explain the escalation.

This article uses *third culture* to enable conversation within the early childhood community and to encourage educators to become proactive on behalf of third culture children. Third culture children can be those who hold two citizenships and who are more global citizens than citizens of individual countries. Or, third culture children may hold citizenship in only one country but be born of parents representing two different races or ethnic groups. Of course, *race* itself is an artificial term, another label.

Child development theory and constructivism

Wardle (1996) describes the traditional view of multicultural education as one that assumes children's experiences and outlook are predetermined by their cultures. To enhance self-esteem, therefore, teachers should lead children to connect with their group cultures. This approach, of course, assumes that people are all individual products of a single race or cultural group that defines a person's identity. As a result, responding authentically to children whose backgrounds include more than one cultural group exposes the fallacy of a single race or culture approach to diversity. The traditional view may even be associated with shallow, if not limited, expectations for children.

What is more, the traditional view of multicultural education ignores Bronfenbrenner's (1979) contribution to ecological theory. Bronfenbrenner's model assumes that each child exists in his or her own context. The model further suggests that within those individual contexts children's experiences become integrated. Thus race, culture, gender, disability, family, community, and socioeconomic level combine, creating in children unique, integrated contexts rather than a series of distinct, opposing environmental factors (Wardle 1996). Taking this broader perspective enables teachers to move beyond leading children to connect with their group cultures and toward teaching through each child's individual context.

© Jonathan A. Meyers

Making meaning of individual context lies at the heart of constructivist philosophy. Teachers who value constructivism offer learners many opportunities to experiment, discover, reflect, explain, and use their evolving views of the world. In a constructivist classroom, teachers pose relevant problems, honor children's assumptions, respect divergent thinking, encourage initiative, promote cooperative learning, and ground learning in real-life problem solving (Brooks & Brooks 1999).

High-quality multicultural education finds its footing in individual learners' unique, integrated contexts and the understanding learners construct within those contexts. The best teachers have always valued individual contexts. For them, addressing the needs of children like Jason and Anna might begin with simply getting to know children's families better or assessing the degree to which daily experiences at school reflect constructivist philosophy.

The Japanese social teaching model

Teachers can broaden their understanding of constructivist principles and the application of these to multicultural education by studying a variety of teaching models. For example, the Japanese social system, which highly values group contexts, employs a number of teaching practices in the primary grades that seem compatible with constructivist philosophy and well suited for addressing individual contexts. At least three Japanese social practices and

Tips for Teachers of Third Culture Children

• **Refrain from assuming that third culture children speak English as a second language.** They often speak both languages equally well. The whole class will benefit if you give them opportunities to teach their other language to you and their classmates.

• **Recognize that living biculturally does not displace the major milestones of child development.** For example, at age 4 Anna experimented with "bathroom words" just as most other children that age do.

• **Understand that living biculturally poses many opportunities for understanding (and misunderstanding) social norms.**

• **Give children opportunities to teach what they know.**

• **Remember that young children tend to assimilate new information into their already existing mental schema rather than accommodate it.** For example, Jason, having recently attended a concert by a children's choir, described the singers as being 8 years old. His father, who also attended the concert, explained that the choir director said, "Angels they *ain't*," not "These angels, they're *8.*" A*in't* was a foreign word for Jason, so he assimilated it as part of the system he already knew.

• **Be aware that seemingly ordinary experiences may seem extraordinary to the child growing up in more than one culture.**

• **Observe how friendships with other children can be rich opportunities for learning and expanding language.**

• **Talk to third culture children just as you would other children, not sparing vernacular that can help them discover the richness of language.**

• **Model good grammar at all times.** Children tend to imitate what they hear, thereby highlighting the importance of this.

• **Educate every family concerning school culture, because English fluency is different from cultural fluency.**

• **Discover what bicultural families have to offer.** Although family members have jumped the greatest hurdle, acceptance of differences, they sometimes feel conflict about their uniqueness in the context of social practices; support them in their exploration and struggle with their unique experience.

• **Try to see life from the third culture perspective.** For example, instead of saying that Martin Luther King Jr. won the Nobel Peace Prize for teaching that African American people and White people have equal rights, say that he sought equal rights for all people. Capitalize on celebrations that strengthen bonds within families and within the school community rather than on celebrations that become owned by particular groups.

• **Recognize that young children have difficulty decentering and reasoning abstractly.** They tend to focus on their immediate experience and rely upon concrete materials for problem solving. Give children opportunities to share their stories with classmates when they are ready to do so, but provide concrete questions and materials to guide their thinking.

• **Admit that accepting new ideas is seldom easy,** even though you are eager to meet children's needs in a changing world. If your teaching focuses only on superficial cultural differences and similarities, affirm yourself for doing that much and then move on toward recognizing the complexity of human diversity. Begin to energize your teaching and your personal learning by exploring each child's complex individual diversity.

• **Read about other educators' adventures with cultural diversity,** especially Shelley Harwayne's (2000) *Lifetime Guarantees: Toward Ambitious Literacy Teaching.* Harwayne suggests creative ways to highlight children's uniqueness, showcase their common experiences, and support their delightful differences through reading and writing.

• **Get ready to teach more and more third culture children.** These children have the potential for understanding two cultures more deeply. They hold promise for bringing insight to bear upon the problems of pluralistic communities worldwide.

• **Challenge the status quo.** Dare to deconstruct barriers and erect no new ones for children of the third culture.

principles cited by Benjamin (1997) show potential for effectiveness in teaching children of a third culture:

• **Active learning, rather than abstract academic learning,** defines success in the early grades. In other words, academic concepts are by-products of cooperation, individual judgment, and physical and moral strength in the context of active learning. For example, a Japanese teacher might expect young students to learn about the life cycle of plants by planting seeds and nurturing them to maturity rather than simply memorizing and reciting the stages of plant life. Planting seeds with classmates requires cooperation and good judgment. Nurturing the plants requires not only physical ability but also a caring spirit.

• **Expectations of mothers,** such as effort, persistence, commitment, healthy children, and homework supervision, are clearly defined. Therefore, at home as well as at school, a strong focus on experience provides the source of both the unique characteristics of the individual and the qualities that all people have in common. Mothers usually arrange for children to exercise daily, eat nutritious foods, and get plenty of rest. Children hear frequent reminders from mothers and teachers to "do your best" and "keep trying."

• **Opportunities for exercise and relationship building are offered** through long walks home after school and classroom transitions between activities. Children build friendships as they talk, laugh, and play games together. To further strengthen relationships, children frequently benefit from spending two years with the same teacher. During the two-year period, teachers have more time to develop trust with their children, discover their children's strengths and weaknesses, and get to know their children's families.

Conclusions

For a decade or more, educators have read that children of traditionally underrepresented groups, often called minorities, will become the new majority within the United States in the twenty-first century (Spencer 1990). Regrettably, social predictions usually depict all Whites as one group, all African Americans as another, all Asians as one, Native Americans as one, and all Spanish speakers as one. This broad grouping perpetuates the incorrect notion of homogeneity within groups.

Nevertheless, society and classrooms are already becoming significantly more diverse than most of today's majority have ever noted. A multitude of materials and plethora of professional development opportunities promise to prepare educators for teaching in this pluralistic society. Even so, those materials and presentations sometimes lump minorities together, perpetuating the stereotype that all members of a particular minority share the same values and that prejudice does not exist within and between minority groups, which it does.

Most well-meaning efforts ignore one important aspect of the changing demographics. They overlook the fact that if multiple groups within a society function interdependently, then some group members will marry members of groups different from their own. The literature contains few references to this phenomenon. Relative silence about this matter may suggest that educators feel uncomfortable talking about it or that their private lives have not yet been significantly affected by it. Still, members of different ethnic, racial, and cultural groups do produce children whose individual uniquenesses warrant educators' consideration. Telling the stories of bicultural learners is essential for the well-being of these children of the third culture of the twenty-first century.

References

Benjamin, G. 1997. *A year in a Japanese school through the eyes of an American anthropologist and her children.* New York: New York University Press.

Bronfenbrenner, U. 1979. *The ecology of human development: Experiments by design.* Cambridge, MA: Harvard University Press.

Brooks, J.G., & M.G. Brooks. 1999. *In search of understanding: The case for constructivist classrooms.* 2d ed. Alexandria, VA: Association for Supervision and Curriculum Development.

Derman-Sparks, L., & the A.B.C. Task Force. 1989. *Anti-bias curriculum: Tools for empowering young children.* Washington, DC: NAEYC.

Harwayne, S. 2000. *Lifetime guarantees: Toward ambitious literacy teaching.* Portsmouth, NH: Heinemann.

Spencer, M.B. 1990. Development of minority children: An introduction. *Child Development* 61: 267–69.

Tannen, D. 1997. Foreword. In *Different games, different rules: Why Americans and Japanese misunderstand each other,* by H. Yamada. New York: Oxford University Press.

Wardle, F. 1996. Proposal: An anti-bias and ecological model for multicultural education. *Childhood Education* 72: 152–56.

Adapted from *Young Children* 56 (6): 27–32. Copyright © 2001 NAEYC.

Francis Wardle

7

Supporting Multiracial and Multiethnic Children and Their Families

In 1989 NAEYC joined an ever more active movement dedicated to serving children from diverse families by publishing *Anti-Bias Curriculum: Tools for Empowering Young Children* (Derman-Sparks & the A.B.C. Task Force). This movement, known as multicultural or antibias education, developed out of the civil rights movement of the 1960s, the women's movement, and the passage of the revised Individuals with Disabilities Education Act and the Americans with Disabilities Act. As a result, scores of books, training sessions, university classes, multicultural conferences, state diversity standards, and university graduation requirements sprang up throughout the country. And the early childhood community became a leader in helping children previously underserved by our programs—minorities, children with disabilities, those who don't speak English at home, girls, and children of the poor—have increased opportunities to succeed.

But we somehow left out children from multiracial and multiethnic homes. Almost all education books,

lists of children's books, articles, training materials, and diversity resources still use the five traditional racial/ethnic categories—totally omitting multiethnic and multiracial children. A few years ago the editor of the National Head Start Association journal, *Children and Families*, told me they were devoting an issue to diversity. I casually asked her how they would address the needs of multiracial and multiethnic families, particularly since there are many in Head Start. She responded, "Nobody thought about that!" (They did let me add a little piece [Wardle 1999].)

Most of the inquiries I receive from parents of young multiracial and multiethnic children concern the insensitivity of schools and early childhood programs to their family's unique needs and struggles and the lack of information these institutions have regarding their families. These parents ask where they can find materials to assist them in raising their children and to help teachers be more sensitive to their children's needs. These families desperately need programs in which they feel they belong and that support their

sincere efforts to raise healthy children.

NAEYC executive director Mark Ginsberg (2001) points out in a column that this nation is becoming ever more diverse. The 2000 census allowed people to register their identification with more than one heritage and more than 6.8 million did so. Many of these were families with young children. According to the National Center for Health Statistics, the number of multiracial babies born since the 1970s has increased more than 260 percent, compared to a 15 percent increase of single-race babies. More than one million first-generation biracial babies were born since 1989 (Root 1996). Clearly, as Mark Ginsberg states, we must build our organization and our field "to serve *all* children and families" (2001, 53).

To serve *all* children and families, our programs must be places in which:

1. Multiracial and multiethnic children see themselves and their families in books, curricular content, materials, artwork, posters, and doll and people sets. They also need multiracial/multiethnic heroes.

2. Staff assist these children in integrating their diverse and complex heritage into a unified, healthy self-esteem and identity.

3. Activities and curricular approaches never require children to isolate part of their background over another part.

4. These children have a label (multiracial, biracial, mixed) to use to identify themselves and to respond to single-race children and adults.

5. A positive climate supports their parents' choice to cross societal barriers, and no one (staff, parent, child) is allowed to question parental motivation.

6. Staff provide support, accurate information, and resources to help multiracial/multiethnic parents raise their children. (Wardle 1999)

Many people committed to equity and justice believe professionals in our communities need to work harder to change society so that it better fits the needs of individuals, rather than expecting people to adapt to a dysfunctional society (Corey & Corey 1998). This includes changing a society fixated on a single-race approach for categorizing its population, and requires supporting the empowerment of multiethnic and multiracial families to raise their children as they choose.

Professionals committed to principles of equity and justice often follow the ideas, agendas, and leadership of those less empowered (Carter 2001). This makes a lot of sense. We should consult with interracial and interethnic families and seek advice and leadership from people in our field involved in these relationships. We must find ways to enable our field to empower and serve all children and families.

Multiracial and multiethnic children deserve our support in challenging a society that doesn't understand them and in many cases does

---

Ideas for Empowering and Serving All Children and Families

1. Develop and purchase books, classroom materials, curricula, and training programs that address the cultural and ethnic history and unique needs of multiracial/multiethnic children and families.

2. Include a multiracial/multiethnic category in any listing of multicultural resources—books, children's books, classroom materials, training materials, curricula, and so on.

3. View children and people as individuals with characteristics that include racial and ethnic diversity, rather than looking at people as products of single-race/ethnic reference groups.

4. Support the development of a multiracial category on future census forms and immediately implementing the census approach when collecting government statistical data.

5. Address multiracial/multiethnic children and families in all diversity activities and training: college courses, conferences, inservice training, antibias activities, and curriculum content analysis.

6. Include multiracial/multiethnic children and parents in all NAEYC position papers, training standards, accreditation guidelines, and other projects that address culture, diversity, and identity.

---

not accept their parents' relationship. I want my field to be a leader in meeting the needs of these families, just as we have in so many other equity and justice causes.

References

Carter, M. 2001. The journey to becoming a White ally. *Child Care Information Exchange* (140): 71–74.

Corey, M.S., & G. Corey. 1998. *Becoming a helper.* 3d ed. Pacific Grove, CA: Brookes/Cole.

Derman-Sparks, L., & the A.B.C. Task Force. 1989. *Anti-bias curriculum: Tools for empowering young children.* Washington, DC: NAEYC.

Ginsberg, M.R. 2001. Observations and reflections. *Young Children* 56 (4): 53.

Root, M.P.P., ed. 1996. *The multiracial experience: Racial borders as the new frontier.* Thousand Oaks, CA: Sage.

Wardle, F. 1999. Diversity means everybody. *Children and Families* 18 (2): 13.

Books for Children

Adoff, A. 1992. *Black is brown is tan.* New York: HarperCollins Juvenile Books.

Davol, M. 1993. *Black, white, just right.* Morton Grove, IL: Albert Whitman.

Kandel, B., & C. Halebian. 1997. *Trevor's story: Growing up biracial.* Minneapolis, MN: Lerner Publications.

Mandelbaum, P. 1993. *You be me, I'll be you.* La Jolla, CA: Kane/Miller Books.

Pellegrini, N. 1991. *Families are different.* New York: Holiday House.

Janet Gonzalez-Mena and Navaz Peshotan Bhavnagri

8

Diversity and Infant/Toddler Caregiving

Junior, who is new to the center, is excited when he sees a bowl of food. The baby makes happy sounds, kicks his legs, and waves his arms. But when Helen puts Junior in the high chair and places the bowl in front of him, he just sits there and makes no attempt to feed himself. He looks confused and then distressed. Finally he slumps over, a glazed look in his eyes.

His mother explains later that she has taught Junior not to touch his food. In fact, her son has never been in a high chair; he has always been fed on his mother's lap, wrapped up tightly in a blanket to discourage him from interfering with her. Junior obviously doesn't know how to respond to this new arrangement.

ଔ

The scene above provides an example of diversity in caregiving practices. When caregivers come upon a difference like this one, what do they do? If the program policy advocates self-feeding, do caregivers just stick to it and try to convince the mother that she should do at home what they do in the center?

We'd like to suggest that the place to start in this situation is to look for the reasons behind the mother's actions. Why has the mother taught her son not to touch his food? It's easy to assume that she is obsessed with neatness or hygiene. But maybe that's not it at all; maybe her approach to feeding has to do with a particular set of cultural beliefs or traditions.

What if Helen discovers the feeding difference stems from a cultural practice? What should she do? Is it okay if the baby encounters one set of practices at home and another in child care? Every day caregivers are faced with differentiating between negative parenting practices and positive cultural practices. We hope this article will help them do that better.

Exposure to diversity in infancy

Are we perhaps asking too much of some babies to develop a sense of who they are and where they belong *and* relate to caregivers who care for

them differently from the way they are cared for at home? Maybe infants are highly adaptive and can easily adjust to variations of caregiving. Is it possible that variations in caregiving styles and expectations overwhelm and perhaps even harm some infants?

Little specific research has been done on exactly how variations in caregiving impact development. We do not know much about the consequences of differences in caregiving as it is carried out by the parent compared to what the child encounters in child care. We do know that, even when there are no cultural differences, sensitive, responsive caregiving is far more effective than insensitive, unresponsive caregiving (Lamb & Easterbrooks 1981; Ainsworth 1993; Isabella 1993).

Variations in caregiving practices come from many sources, but this article concentrates on those from cultural sources. We're defining culture as "the values, beliefs and traditions of a particular group [from which arise] a set of rules that, to varying degrees, guide the behavior of individuals who are members of that group, whether that group is defined in terms of national origin, racial experience, linguistic experience, religious background, socioeconomic status" (Chang, Muckelroy, & Pulido-Tobiassen 1996, 19). We acknowledge that within any culture exist differences also in age, gender, and sexual orientation.

Cultural sensitivity

When sensitive caregivers meet individual needs, they also may be meeting cultural needs. However, without specific cultural information, caregivers can inadvertently use practices that undermine parents' efforts and tread on their cultural values.

For example, in a videotape (Gonzalez-Mena, Herzog, & Herzog 1995), Akemi, a Japanese American mother, tells a story about her interaction with another mother, a recent immigrant from Asia (she doesn't say what country). She describes how the two are having a little get-together while their babies play on the floor at their feet. Akemi expresses delight when the visiting child gets to his feet and takes a wobbly step. But his mother downplays her son's accomplishment. She tells Akemi how clumsy and stupid her son is. She goes on to point out all the things he cannot do. Akemi is upset that this woman would put down her son right in front of him and tells her so. The immigrant mother is confused by what Akemi says.

Imagine a caregiver observing that scene. Would she realize that what she knows about self-esteem development is not universally accepted? Would she know that in some cultures humility is valued over pride and that negative comments are meant to instill a proper attitude, starting in infancy? Would the caregiver know that attitudes to-

ward pride and humility are directly linked to cultural goals and values (Kitayama, Markus, & Matsumoto 1995)? The mother's negative remarks about her son might upset a caregiver who does not understand the mother's view of what is best for him.

The same kind of linking to culture that is true of self-esteem is also true of self-help skills, independence, dependence, manners, and respect. Values and goals show up as *behaviors* and become organized into *practices*. Any time parents' practices tread on caregivers' values, beliefs, and understandings, some caregivers find it harder to be sensitive and responsive to those parents. Instead of trying to understand the behavior, many just want to change it.

The issue of cultural sensitivity is more urgent now than ever before because today's immigrants represent greater ethnic, racial, and socioeconomic diversity than did earlier European immigrants (Grant 1995), and their caregiving practices are very different from the prevalent European American practices (Lieberman 1995). The new Americans—and even many longtime Americans—have differing customs from those of families firmly rooted in the dominant culture of the United States, although not all the people of the dominant culture are alike either. Diversity is found in every group. Diverse people not only do things differently, but they perceive things differently too. They have distinctive belief systems, perceptions of their children's capabilities, even goals for childrearing, all of which affect their parenting practices.

Although cultural differences demand more attention today, caregivers have little training in diversity. According to a study done by Chang, Muckelroy, and Pulido-Tobiassen (1996), caregivers have neither the skills nor the knowledge

to effectively address issues of race, language, and culture. Caregiver training generally neglects to make the connection between quality care and diversity. "To date, the definitions and measures of quality care are, for the most part, missing an analysis of the implications of racial, cultural, and linguistic diversity in child development and in child care" (20).

A similar study in Canada (Bernhard et al. 1995) came to the same conclusions. Parents' responses showed that "There were cases where teachers had clearly failed to appreciate cultural differences in childrearing practices" (36).

Responding to differences

Suppose that caregivers do have the knowledge they need to understand and appreciate cultural differences. Does knowledge alone guide response? Does sensitivity to diversity mean that caregivers must adopt the parent's way even if it differs from program policy? No. Caregivers must not abdicate their professional responsibility but must make considered decisions with each family and child about what is best to do. And that is not easy when parents and caregivers have conflicting views.

There is no simple rule to follow when caregivers and parents do not see eye-to-eye. Standing firm on all policies and practices is too rigid, and caregivers changing what they do each and every time a parent asks them to is too flexible. Sometimes a family's practices are in conflict with its goals for its children. Sometimes a family practice is risky or actually harmful.

When a caregiver perceives a negative consequence of a particular practice, it is his or her responsibility to help a family sort out and understand the implications. Of course, in a case of obvious harm to the child that fits the legal definition of child abuse, it is the caregiver's responsibility to report to authorities.

When the family and the program do not agree about some practice or policy, the caregiver should ask 10 questions:

1. What is the cultural perspective of the family on this issue?

2. How do the family's child care practices relate to its cultural perspective?

3. What are the family's goals for the child, and how has the family's culture influenced its goals?

4. In view of the goals, is the family's practice in the child's best interest?

5. Are there any sound research data indicating that the family's practice is doing actual harm?

6. Is the program's practice or policy universally applicable, or is it better suited to a particular culture?

7. Did the family choose the program because of the particular philosophy, even if it is based in a different culture from the family's own?

8. Have I attempted to fully understand the family's rationale for its practices, the complexity of the issues, and other factors that contribute to the practices?

9. Have I attempted to fully explain to the family my rationale for my practices and looked at the complexity of the issues and at how my own culture influences my rationale and perspective?

10. What are some creative resolutions that address both the parents' concerns and my own?

Looking for a creative solution that incorporates both the parents' and the caregiver's concerns fits right in with the *both/and* thinking explained in NAEYC's revised *Developmentally Appropriate Practice in Early Childhood Programs* (Bredekamp & Copple 1997). Caregivers can and should avoid the polarization of *either/or* choices and explore

© BmPorter/Don Franklin

more thoroughly how two seemingly opposing views can both be right. It may be hard to explore a situation in which there is a clear conflict of values between what's behind program policy or a caregiver's belief and what's behind parental practices. But even in the case of a value conflict, those devoted to both/and thinking may find a win-win solution. Such solutions usually come from dialogues and often surprise those involved because neither party would have thought of the solution without the other.

Caregivers should be sensitive to differing practices and yet still be professionals and share their expertise. They must recognize that as families outside the dominant culture come in contact with it, they change. But it is equally important to realize and acknowledge that the dominant culture also changes through contact. Cross-cultural contact is a two-way process. Some old values and practices remain intact, some remain but are modified, and

some are shed for newer ones. This process opens up both families and caregivers to operate flexibly in two or more cultures (Patel, Power, & Bhavnagri 1996).

Dialogue and reflective-thinking strategies

Dialogue between caregivers and parents works best when all concerned use what John Dewey (1933) called *reflective thinking*. Individuals should be encouraged to give active, persistent, and careful consideration to any apparent form of knowledge or beliefs in light of the grounds that support it and the conclusions that are drawn from it.

Schön (1987) strongly recommends that practitioners, to be effective professionals, need to systemically reflect on their actions. Lubek (1996) specifically suggests this reflective approach when working with a diverse population. She believes that reflective practitioners who learn to think deeply about the implications of their choices are more likely to tailor their practices to the diverse needs of children in a multicultural society.

How does dialogue using reflective thinking work? Let's go back to the example of Junior, who refuses to touch finger food. When Helen, the caregiver, finds out that in the mother's culture it is highly inappropriate to ever touch food with the hands, she'll want to ask more. She'll want to understand everything she can about this practice and what it's based on.

If the mother does not know about the program's view of self-help skills, Helen can explain. But if Helen does so too soon or too strongly, the effect may be to silence the mother. Helen's goal is to keep communication open, so when she meets with the mother she does more listening than talking.

Let's imagine that as the two continue to talk about their different views, it becomes clear that the mother does not value self-help skills. Helen is surprised. But if she can keep the conversation going, she may uncover the mother's fears about her child becoming too independent. And if they keep talking, Helen may discover that the mother's goal is to keep the family together—and that she believes independence threatens this goal. In many cultures, interdependence and collectivism are valued more than independence and individualism.

Whether Helen agrees or not, she's beginning to see another perspective. The program's goals of independence and individuality are just what the mother is trying to discourage in her child. The parent instead wants to emphasize the interdependence and embeddedness that are valued in her culture. She is in no hurry for her son to feed himself. She doesn't want him to become the in-

dependent individual that is Helen's ideal and a stated program goal.

The reflective-thinking process in this case could result in various outcomes. Perhaps after dialoguing, Helen and the mother agree that the child would benefit from two cultural approaches to feeding. They aim for an early bicultural goal by using one practice in child care (self-feeding) and the other (spoon-feeding) at home.

Conversely, Helen and the mother may concur that early exposure to differences creates identity issues and puts the child at risk for losing his culture. They decide for the present that this child needs to be tied as closely to his roots as possible. They agree that an early focus on independence might separate him from his people and their customs. As a result, the caregiver may consent to go along with the mother's practice of spoon-feeding.

Those are only two possible outcomes; there are others (see Gonzalez-Mena 1992). The results of reflective thinking are unpredictable when both parties are truly committed to dialoguing about their differences in behaviors and practices.

Conclusion

It is time for caregivers to receive additional diversity training so they come to see that concepts of "quality care" must be put in culturally relevant contexts. More minority voices must be heard so that definitions of excellence can be mutually agreed upon.

In the face of diversity, everyone in the early childhood field must become skilled at dialoguing. Only then will infants and toddlers in child care receive what they need, which can be determined only by the trained caregiver and the concerned parent using a reflective-thinking process. It is possible for profession-

als to be both culturally sensitive and professionally responsible.

References

Ainsworth, M.D.S. 1993. Attachment as related to mother-infant interaction. In *Advances in infancy research*, Vol. 8, eds. C. Rovee-Collier & L.P. Lipsett. Norwood, NJ: Ablex.

Bernhard, J., M. Lefebvre, G. Chud, & R. Lange. 1995. *Paths to equity: Cultural, linguistic, and racial diversity in Canadian early childhood education.* Toronto: York Lanes.

Bredekamp, S., & C. Copple, eds. 1997. *Developmentally appropriate practice in early childhood programs.* Rev. ed. Washington, DC: NAEYC.

Chang, H.N.L., A. Muckelroy, & D. Pulido-Tobiassen. 1996. *Looking in, looking out: Redefining child and early education in a diverse society.* San Francisco, CA: California Tomorrow.

Dewey, J. [1933] 1997. *How we think.* Boston: Houghton Mifflin.

Gonzalez-Mena, J. 1992. Taking a culturally sensitive approach in infant-toddler programs. *Young Children* 47 (2): 4–9.

Gonzalez-Mena, J., M. Herzog, & S. Herzog, co-producers. 1995. *Theories of development.* The Developing Child Series. Magna Systems. Videotape.

Grant, R. 1995. Meeting the needs of young second-language learners. In *Meeting the challenge of linguistic and cultural diversity in early childhood education*, eds. E.E. Garcia, B. McLaughlin, B. Spodek, & O.N. Sarachco, 1–17. New York: Teachers College Press.

Isabella, R.A. 1993. Origins of attachment: Maternal interactive behavior across the first year. *Child Development* 64: 605–21.

Kitayama, S., H. Markus, & H. Matsumoto. 1995. Culture, self, and emotion: A cultural perspective on "self-conscious emotions." In *Self-conscious emotions: The psychology of shame, guilt, embarrassment, and pride*, eds. J. Tangry & K. Fisher. New York: Guilford.

Lamb, M.E., & M.A. Easterbrooks. 1981. Individual differences in parental sensitivity: Origins, components, and consequences. In *Infant social cognition*, eds. M.E. Lamb & L.R. Sherrod. Hillsdale, NJ: Erlbaum.

Lieberman, A.F. 1995. Concerns of immigrant families. In *Infant/toddler caregiving: A guide to culturally sensitive care*, ed. P. Mangione, 28–37. Sacramento, CA: Far West Laboratory and California Department of Education.

Lubek, S. 1996. Deconstructing child development knowledge and teacher preparation. *Early Childhood Research Quarterly* 11: 147–67.

Patel, N., T. Power, & N.P. Bhavnagri. 1996. Socialization values and practices of Indian immigrant parents: Correlates of modernity and acculturation. *Child Development* 67: 302–13.

Schön, D.S. 1987. *Educating the reflective practitioner.* San Francisco, CA: Jossey-Bass.

Forging a Caring Classroom Community

For many children, the early childhood setting is the first significant experience with the wider world beyond their own home and extended family. For that reason, the kind of community created in our early childhood classrooms has a big impact. Is it a community where each child feels comfortable and valued, and where all children learn to respect and value others? The readings in this section discuss various aspects of building such a community.

The foundation must be mutual respect and communication (Stone; Vance & Weaver). The physical environment itself conveys, or fails to convey, respect for children and their differences. When children see themselves—people like them and their families—in the images on the walls, the materials, the stories they hear, it contributes to their sense of belonging. Equally important is seeing many other kinds of people who also belong (Derman-Sparks & the A.B.C. Task Force).

In forging a caring community, learning to communicate and resolve conflicts is vital (Kreidler & Whittall; Vance & Weaver). Indeed, learning conflict-resolution skills is a key goal of early childhood education. As we as teachers approach such goals for young children, we need to be knowledgeable about children's development. We need to understand children's cognitive, social, and emotional development at various ages and thus know what to expect of them and how to provide the most effective guidance (Lillard & Curenton).

Jeannette G. Stone

9

Communicating Respect

Excerpted from *Building Classroom Community*

It takes a while. Young children have a long way to go on their journey to becoming compassionate, responsible members of a group. Sharing, turn taking, waiting patiently to have one's say—these are long-term goals we work toward, not behaviors we constantly demand now of young preschoolers (much less toddlers!). To become sharers and turn takers, children need modeling and guidance. They need time to live through childhood egocentricity, immaturity, and inexperience before coming gradually to the point of regarding other people with interest and respect, assuming this is the ideal held by the adults around them.

Children learn to respect themselves and others, as they approach school age, not by our sermonizing or venting frustration with their naturally slow pace but rather by our showing them what respect feels like and sounds like—by our showing respect for them, first of all.

One hears a lot of lip service paid to the concept of respect. Many teachers and parents talk about the necessity for children to show them respect, and they are quite serious about it. However, attitudes and expressions of respect start with grownups and then trickle down.

What conscientious teachers do, how they do it, and how they speak to colleagues, to parents, and to the children themselves all serve as models for ways to talk and listen to people respectfully. At the same time these teachers provide a model within their profession for care of the classroom environment.

Caring for the classroom environment

Respect for young children means that you convey in the daily schedule your understanding and acceptance of children's needs to play, to pretend, and to choose their activities. You accept their need to learn by discovery, by trial and error, and from information at hand. They need to talk, work hard, create, sing, move around, be read to, rest, run, climb, jump, get messy and clean up (with help), and enjoy nutritious food with friends and classmates. Respect for children means that you create safe, appropriate, interesting surround-

ings in which they are comfortable, unhurried, and able to become engaged in a wonderful variety of things to do and to learn.

Modeling respect

By March and April teachers have been communicating their values and information for several months of the school year. Children learn from what adults say and from how they say it. Teachers have enormous influence on children's behavior by speaking directly and honestly to them: modeling with words and manner how people deal with each other with respect, just as they would like to be dealt with. Children should feel good about being in the classroom. They should feel cared for and respected, and feeling that way helps them to behave with care and respect.

Sad to say, all too often one hears disrespectful language directed to children. Grownups bark commands, scoldings, and criticisms. Whether this happens because so many adults are stressed and overwhelmed, careless and insensitive,

Bill Geiger

or holding unrealistic expectations for children's behavior, a tone of combat is set. However, experienced and wise teachers and parents show day after day that it is possible to teach children respectfully even when one feels worn down, if one believes in doing so. Adult courtesy is the only way for children to learn courtesy. Adult consideration for others is the only way for children to learn considerate behavior. It is the same with all behaviors. Honesty begets honesty.

Teachers' consistently lowered voices help kids learn that they don't have to shout. Of course one has to speak loudly on occasion, but not all the time! Grownups who help children put away toys may be subtly teaching how to arrange objects into orderly categories, but they are also modeling ways to extend a helping hand.

Let's say a problem erupts in a classroom of 4-year-olds. Teachers, you're the models for resolving conflict. If you get mad and yell, the children will follow suit. But teachers don't have to scold, shame, threaten. These actions don't cure misbehav-

ior anyway and don't teach children how to behave in the future. Instead, when you model ways that clearly demonstrate your beliefs—taking a firm, calm stand against hurtful behavior, sharing your concerns or wishes with the children, stating your reasons and rules—you are modeling effective ways to solve problems. And I hope you use your hugs, your support, your willingness to listen, your protection, and your respect.

One hears parents and teachers—often overwhelmed by troubles in their lives—speak to children in ways that come across as belittling, hostile, or as put-downs. They use statements such as,

"Stop acting like a baby."

"You did that on purpose."

"Do you want me to bite you to show you how it feels?"

"That's not nice."

"If you keep doing that, I'm never bringing you here again."

"We're not going to have any time on the playground today because you didn't pick up your toys."

Blame, blame, scold, scold. Blaming and scolding fail to accomplish

what adults want to accomplish, which is to persuade children to stop, listen, and redirect their behavior. Blaming and scolding fail to show children how to do that. They merely express adult frustration and anger. There are much more effective, and respectful, ways to speak to children. For example, try,

"No, I won't let you do that. But tell me what the problem is; I promise to listen."

"What else could you do? Let's think about it. I'll help you both figure this out."

"I'm going to stop you. Hitting and knocking people over are *out* in this class. Come, sit here with me for a minute and take a big, deep breath. Then we'll talk about what happened and what you can do next time that will work better—for you and for everyone else."

"Donald! Tell him with your words! Luis, Donald has something to say to you."

"My job is to keep you safe—to keep everybody safe. I want you to help."

"You have five minutes to put away the blocks, and I'll help you start."

This kind of communication models reason and courtesy; it provides kids with an effective model for the times when they will need to work through frustrations and conflicts on their own. It communicates to children the fact that they can trust you. You're on their side, not against them. You may not agree with or permit what they're doing, but you're still on their side. Furthermore, you're not standing over them. You are down face-to-face with them, on their level—serious, sympathetic, supportive. They are learning what it is to be responsible, respectful, and caring.

Adapted from J.G. Stone, *Building Classroom Community: The Early Childhood Teacher's Role* (Washington, DC: NAEYC, 2001), 37–47. Copyright © 2001 NAEYC.

A World of Difference

Emily Vance and Patricia Jiménez Weaver

10

Using Class Meetings to Solve Problems

Excerpted from *Class Meetings*

One October morning Angelina comes to me in tears. Someone has gone into her cubby and eaten the special Halloween cupcake she brought for lunch. She cannot believe anyone would do such a thing. I suggest discussing the problem in class meeting later that morning.

During class meeting I invite Angelina to share her problem. "My mother bought my sisters and me Halloween cupcakes. I saved mine for lunch today. But someone went in my cubby and ate my cupcake. Look, here's all that's left!" She holds up the torn wrapper. The children's faces show deep concern. They appear shocked at the idea of someone going into another's cubby without permission.

"Angelina," I ask, "do you know who was involved in this problem?" She doesn't. Although I have an idea who it might be, it is important for the class to come up with the information themselves.

At this point Jennie raises her hand: "I saw Roberto over by Angelina's cubby." Several children confirm this observation.

I ask Roberto if he knows anything about the problem, and he nods, adding, "Luis was there too." Luis says, "So was Ben." I thank the three boys for their honesty and ask them if they are willing to help find a solution. They all say yes. I acknowledge their cooperation.

"Angelina, do you have any ideas about how to solve this problem?" I ask. Angelina shakes her head. "Roberto, do you?"

"Shake hands," Roberto suggests.

I ask Angelina if this is a reasonable solution. She says, "No, that's not going to solve my problem."

Next I turn to Luis. "Luis, do you have an idea?"

"Say sorry," Luis replies.

Angelina is unequivocal in her response to this suggestion: "That won't solve my problem or bring back my cupcake."

"Ben, how about you? Any idea how to help Angelina with the problem?"

Ben looks down at the floor and shakes his head.

Damien raises his hand: "I think Roberto and Luis and Ben should bring in some money to pay for the cupcake."

Ian adds, "Yeah, if they each give Angelina a quarter she can buy a new one."

I ask Angelina if she feels this is a reasonble solution, and she says yes. I ask Roberto, Luis, and Ben if they are willing to go along with it, and they all agree to.

Angelina goes to lunch with a smile on her face.

ଏଓ

Imagine how you would feel if someone went into your cubby without your permission and ate the special treat your mother had sent you for lunch. How would your anger and disappointment affect your ability to concentrate? If you were given an opportunity to talk to the person who did it—to share your feelings, hear that person's response, and arrive at a solution—consider the difference it would make in your day.

Class meetings have a positive effect on the school day. They offer a forum for group problem solving, with the children solving the problems and the teacher facilitating. They provide an opportunity for everyone to speak out about their feelings in a nonthreatening environ-

Children learn to evaluate ideas and decide on reasonable, respectful solutions.

ment, where thoughts and views can be expressed without fear of ridicule, finger-pointing, or recriminations. They help make school a place that is emotionally safe for children. This feeling of safety enhances children's ability to concentrate and learn.

This is how Gail McClurg explains to her kindergartners the concept of class meeting (which she calls "community meeting"):

> I introduce it very simply as a time when we can talk about our lives together in such a way that everyone can feel safe and have a chance to speak about the things on our minds. When there is a problem, we can help each other look for a solution.
>
> I make it clear as the first meetings proceed that this is a time to problem solve, not to judge. We really need to listen to each other, and everyone is important. (1998, 31)

During class meeting a child who needs help resolving a conflict presents her view of the problem. The other children involved in the incident give their perspectives. With guidance from the teacher and suggestions from the rest of the class, the children involved work out a solution they can all accept. From their

experiences in class meetings, children learn that honesty is valued, feelings are respected, and classmates care about each other.

Creating a sense of community

Respect is key in ensuring a safe, positive environment in class meetings—and in the classroom and school settings. It is the foundation upon which a caring atmosphere is built. The teacher communicates its importance through her words and actions. An adult's first step toward creating a respectful classroom is modeling respect in her own interactions with the children. When the teacher models openness, empathy, and thoughtfulness in helping children resolve their differences, even very young children begin to learn to settle their problems respectfully.

Discussing the value of class meetings, Donna Styles (2001) writes,

> Class meetings unify the class—as conflicts in the class are resolved and feelings are shared, friction is reduced. At this point, the class begins to function as a community, working together toward goals

and showing support for all members. Students feel a sense of belonging to the group, and the tone in the classroom becomes very positive and caring. (9)

The format of class meetings and the sense of community the meetings foster encourage a number of prosocial behaviors. In meetings children learn to take turns and listen respectfully. As they hear and consider others' perspectives, children become more capable of seeing beyond their own egocentric view of situations. They learn to empathize. Recognizing and expressing appreciation for others' constructive actions is another benefit, enhancing each child's social competence while fostering a positive climate in the group. Finally, children learn to evaluate ideas and decide on reasonable, respectful solutions. Learning to solve problems and resolve conflicts in the group, children bring this experience with them and use it in their daily interactions.

References

McClurg, L.G. 1998. Building an ethical community in the classroom: Community meeting. *Young Children* 53 (2): 30–35.
Styles, D. 2001. *Class meetings: Building leadership, problem-solving, and decision-making skills in the respectful classroom.* Markham, Canada: Pembroke.

11

Creating an Antibias Environment through Visual Materials

Excerpted from *Anti-Bias Curriculum*

An environment that is rich in possibilities for exploring gender, race/ethnicity, and different-abledness sets the scene for practicing antibias curriculum.

There should be:

• Images in abundance of *all* the children, families, and staff in your program. Photos and other pictures reflecting the various backgrounds of the children and staff should be attractively displayed.

• If the classroom population is racially/ethnically homogeneous, images of children and adults from the major racial/ethnic groups in your community and in U.S. society.

• Images that accurately reflect people's current daily lives in the United States working and with their families during recreational activities.

• A numerical balance among different groups. Make sure people of color are not represented as "tokens"—only one or two.

• A fair balance of images of women and men, shown doing "jobs in the home" and "jobs outside the home." Show women and men doing blue-collar work (e.g., factory worker, repair person) and pink-collar work (e.g., beautician, salesperson), as well as white-collar work (e.g., teacher, doctor).

• Images of elderly people of various backgrounds doing different activities.

• Images of differently abled people of various backgrounds shown doing work and with their families in recreational activities. Be careful not to use images that depict differently abled people as dependent and passive.

• Images of diversity in family styles: single mothers or fathers, extended families, gay or lesbian families (families with two mothers or fathers), families in which one parent and a grandmother are the parents, interracial and multiethnic families, adopted families, differently abled families (the atypical person may be either a child or a parent).

• Images of important individuals—past and present. They should reflect racial/ethnic, gender, and abledness diversity, and they should include people who participated in important struggles for social justice.

• Artwork—prints, sculpture, textiles by artists of various backgrounds that reflect the aesthetic environment and the culture of the families represented in your classroom, and of groups in your community and in the United States (Neugebauer 1987).

Reference

Neugebauer, B., ed. 1987. *Alike and different: Exploring our humanity with young children.* Redmond, WA: Exchange Press.

Angeline Lillard and Stephanie Curenton

12

Do Young Children Understand What Others Feel, Want, and Know?

Learning to understand the feelings and intentions of other people is a critical part of becoming a functioning member of society. To get along well with others, interact cooperatively, and develop close social relationships, this learning must take place. The development of social understanding is so important to human development and it begins so early that psychologists are beginning to think of it as an innate potential, like the ability to learn language. This view differs from Piaget's theory that young children do not develop the ability to "take the perspective" of others and understand their feelings and intentions until at age 6 or 7 they enter the "concrete operational" period of mental development.

People's understanding that others have mental states is a very interesting feat. When we see someone fall down and cry, we assume the person is *sad*, and *wants* comforting. When we see a child crouched over a piece of paper with a pencil in hand, sounding out letters, we guess that child is *trying* to write letters. An amazing aspect of these understandings is that mental states are usually

not accompanied by any hard evidence of their existence. We have to infer the mental state from what we observe. It appears that even very young children, as early as 18 months of age, also make such inferences, inventing mental states in others (Meltzoff 1995).

Research suggests that humans are unique in this regard, since animals do not appear to invent mental states (Povinelli & Eddy 1996). Animals simply respond to facial expressions, vocalizations, and body postures. People, on the other hand, attribute mental states with gusto, even applying them to cars and ovens and other entities in which they obviously do not belong.

The study of how and when we acquire an understanding of other's minds has taken developmental psychology by storm, with a tenfold increase over the past decade in the number of publications discussing these issues. The reason for this attention is that knowledge about minds has consequences for so many areas of human functioning. Human interactions from the nursery onward are often about what we think others are thinking.

For example, when children learn the meaning of new words, they need to notice the focus of attention of the adult who is supplying the new word. Even by 18 months, children who are busy playing with a new toy will look to an adult's face when she sounds like she is supplying a new word label ("It's a cyclops! Look at the cyclops!"). Further, children will assume the new word refers to whatever the adult is looking at rather than simply assume it refers to their own toy (Baldwin 1991). This suggests that children have some perspective-taking ability even in Piaget's sensorimotor stage.

Another example of how understanding minds is fundamental to human interactions concerns intentions. Dodge and Price (1994) have shown that boys with very aggressive behavior attribute mean intentions to others, while nonaggressive boys who are in the same situation do not. Other research has shown that children with delinquency problems have trouble taking others' perspectives, and that training them in role taking by discussing how others view the world is associated with reductions in their aggressive behavior (Chandler 1975). Children with autism also show marked deficits on many tasks requiring an understanding of minds. Some researchers have even claimed that "mindblindness," the inability to understand others' mental states, is the fundamental deficit of autism (Baron-Cohen 1995).

Talking about others' intentions and mental states helps very young children, even those who are not abnormally aggressive or delinquent, to understand mental states. For example, when parents talk more with their children at age 2 about others' emotions, the children by age 4 have a better understanding of others' minds.

What do young children know about minds, and when do they know it?

Studies of young children's developing understanding of mental states have focused on four areas: children's understanding of (1) the relationship between information from the senses (perception) and what people know, (2) the emotions of others, (3) others' desires, and (4) others' beliefs.

Perception

Three-year-olds have some rudimentary understandings of how sensory experience is related to what people know. Even before 3 years of age, a child knows to behave differently toward his mother if she is out of the room when a coveted item is hidden (and therefore needs some clues about where to find it) than if she is in the room when the item is hidden (O'Neill 1996). By 4 or 5 years of age, children realize how they learned something.

In one study, two objects identical except for their color were shown to children. One of the objects was placed in a tunnel, and the children felt it but did not see it. When asked what color it was, children under 5 tended to positively assert that the object was one of the colors ("It's blue!"). When asked how they knew, children often responded with the impossible: "It felt blue!" (O'Neill, Astington, & Flavell 1992). By age 5, most children realized they could not know an object's color by feeling it.

Emotions

Simple emotions are understood very early. Happiness is usually the first emotion children master, followed by anger and sadness (Borke 1971) and fear (Michalson & Lewis 1985). Repacholi and Gopnik (1997) had 18-month-olds observe a woman looking at broccoli, smiling at it, and saying, "Mmm! Broccoli!" Next she made an ugly face and said, "Yuck!" while looking at the children's preferred food, Goldfish crackers. When asked to give the experimenter some food, most toddlers chose to give her broccoli instead of the crackers. Fourteen-month-olds, in contrast, tried to give her the Goldfish crackers.

This study suggests that by 18 months of age children realize that others' desires might differ from their own and they can use emotional expressions to interpret those desires. Children also learn early how situations relate to emotions. For example, by age 3 most children assume that people are happy at birthday parties and sad when a dog bites them (Harris 1989).

Although young children can understand emotions based on desires, they have difficulty understanding emotions, such as surprise, that are based on beliefs. Understanding surprise is difficult because the emotion is a mismatch between a person's beliefs and reality. Most children do not understand surprise until they have mastered belief, which occurs usually at age 5 (Hadwin & Perner 1991). They also find it hard to understand the notion that emotional expressions might not represent true feelings. For example, until age 5 or 6, children do not seem to realize that one might smile upon receiving a gift even if one does not like the gift (Saarni 1984). Preschoolers also have difficulty understanding ambivalent feelings, such as being happy about getting a new bicycle but disappointed because it is the wrong color (Kestenbaum & Gelman 1995).

Desires

Children's earliest understanding of the mental states of others has been described as *desire psychology* (Wellman 1990), because they interpret someone's actions in terms of what that person might want. By age 3 children understand that desires are positive attitudes toward something outside of themselves. They can also understand the differences between what is wanted and what is reality. For example, when talking about ice cream, one young child said, "I don't want it cold. I wanted it warm" (Bartsch & Wellman 1995, 71).

Similarly, children realize that although one person might like something, another might not. They also have a grasp of how desires relate to actions. Three-year-olds predict that if someone wants something and does not succeed in finding it, the person will keep looking. Furthermore, they understand the link between desires and emotions: that if someone gets what she wants, she will be happy, and if someone does not get what she wants, she will be sad (Wellman & Woolley 1990).

Beliefs

A major development of the preschool years is an understanding that others have beliefs about the world that affect what they do. Until about age 4, children have a tendency to act as if everyone knows and believes what they themselves know to be true. If a child falls down at school, she expects her mother to know about the event because she herself knows about it. If a child knows that the ladder on the slide has a broken rung, he believes that his friend knows it too (and will be careful without being told).

One way psychologists have studied children's understanding of belief has been by using *false-belief tasks*. In one such task, children are shown a doll and told that the doll has left a treasured candy bar in a drawer and gone out to play. Children see the doll's mother move the candy to a cupboard. The doll returns, and children are asked where the doll will look for his candy. Until they are 4 or 5 years old, children usually predict that the doll will go straight to the cupboard to retrieve the candy bar (Wimmer & Perner 1983). Older children usually understand that the doll would falsely believe the candy was in the drawer.

This error holds even in greatly simplified circumstances and even when the child herself is the actor. For example, in another type of false-belief task, children first are shown a cracker box and asked what is inside. Most respond, "Crackers!" Then the children are shown that the box actually contains leaves, not crackers, and they now are asked what they had thought was inside. Although the task is very simple and the children are asked about their own mental states rather than someone else's, until age 4 or 5 a child will usually respond, "Leaves!" (Gopnik & Astington 1988).

This outcome is not due to a problem with the word *think*, because the same error applies when the word *say* is used. It is not due to embarrassment, because the error holds if children are asked what a friend or parent would think. It is not due to

misunderstanding the temporal aspect of the question, because when asked what someone else would think was inside if they were seeing the closed-up box for the first time, 3-year-olds still usually say, "Leaves!"

It seems that until children are about 4 years old (perhaps a year later in children from families with low incomes [Holmes, Black, & Miller 1996]), they have difficulty with the notion that our beliefs about the world are sometimes false. What appears to underlie this error is a failure to understand that our minds represent a version of the world, like a photograph represents some state of affairs at the time it was taken. Perhaps children view minds more like photographs that are updated to match reality.

Most young children act as if there is only one way to represent the world, an object, or a situation, and other lines of research support this. In *appearance-reality tasks*, for example, children are shown fake objects, like a candle that looks just like an apple. After discussing its appearance and reality, children are asked both what it is (really and truly) and what it looks like "to your eyes right now." Children older than 4 will give two answers: it is really a candle, but it looks like an apple. Younger children, however, give just one answer, usually claiming that the object looks like what it really is: a candle (Flavell, Green, & Flavell 1986).

Children do not understand that one reality can be represented in two different ways. This misconception about minds presumably has important effects. For example, children's lies before age 4 may be told only to influence behavior rather than with full understanding of the consequences for belief.

Psychologists' studies have suggested ages at which most children acquire certain understandings about minds. The fact is that even a

2-year-old might make a comment that reflects a grasp of false belief. At age 2, after answering the phone, one author's elder daughter announced, "I thought it was going to be Dad, but it was Sally!" What this suggests is that under highly supportive conditions children might occasionally evidence early insight about some concept, like mental representation, but mastery of that concept might be years off. Development is rarely all or none (Siegler 1998). Most children appear to have a pretty solid understanding of mental representation around age 4 or 5.

How we can support the development of children's understanding of others

When children have developed a *theory of mind*—an understanding that others have feelings and desires and beliefs—they are likely to engage in more positive interactions with others (Leekam 1993; Lalonde & Chandler 1995; Happe & Frith 1996). Since an ability to understand other minds is related to positive social relations, a major goal in both home and school settings becomes supporting this development. Researchers believe that to some degree the capacity for understanding other minds comes with biological maturation and accompanying increases in cognitive ability. In addition, studies suggest that engaging in pretend play (Youngblade & Dunn 1995) and having conversations about mental states (Dunn, Brown, & Beardsall 1991) may support the development of children's social understanding.

Encouraging pretend play

One reason that pretending may help children understand the mental states of others is that in social pretense the child must negotiate the pretend world and come face-to-face with others' representations of it. Piaget would endorse such a view, in which intense peer interaction promotes social understanding. Another aspect is that, in pretending to be other people, the child takes on others' views of the world. Regardless of why pretend play appears to help, it does seem that facilitating social pretense in children close to age 4 could helpfully boost them over the edge to understanding that people mentally represent their worlds.

Talking to children about minds

A second way of helping young children understand others' minds is by talking to them about minds and mental states. Dunn has found that talking more about emotional states in natural contexts to children at 33 months is associated with better performance on false-belief tasks at 40 months (Dunn, Brown, & Beardsall 1991).

Many children's books center on changes in feelings, and reading such books and discussing the feelings may also assist children's understanding that minds represent the world. Additionally, reading such books and discussing the feelings may also aid children's understanding of how other people think and feel.

Researchers have also found that younger siblings understand false beliefs earlier than do older siblings (Lewis et al. 1996). Perhaps this is because the more siblings a child has, the more feelings there are to talk about, and younger siblings might be particularly influenced by such talk.

There is evidence that children who are deaf whose parents do not use sign language are delayed in passing false-belief tasks, whereas those children whose parents do sign pass such tasks at the usual age. This finding further supports the

© Subjects & Predicates

role of conversation in developing social understanding.

Finally, although we may balk at the idea of organized lessons around mental states, some researchers have found that both explaining thoughts by using cartoon-type "thought bubbles" and discussing false beliefs with children after watching carefully constructed false-belief videotapes assist them in understanding false beliefs. Such methods are now being used to help children with autism.

The role of culture

Another powerful influence on children's growing understanding of others' minds is most likely culture, but research on this topic is relatively scarce. Most psychologists who have studied children's theories of mind have been guided by mainstream cognitive development approaches that pay little attention to the impact of culture. It has been generally assumed that certain basic understandings occur in children at about the same age everywhere in the world with only minor variations due to cultural practices. One study did find that children of Baka pygmies of Cameroon passed false-belief tasks at about the same age as did most of their European and American peers (Avis & Harris 1991).

Yet different cultures do have different ways of understanding minds (Lillard 1998), and cultural understandings may well influence children. One prominent difference is how much attention is paid to minds. Although Northern Europeans and Americans (at least middle-class, more highly educated families) tend to focus a lot of attention on how minds and mental states cause behaviors, people from Asian cultures pay more attention to how the situations people are in dictate behavior.

Perhaps a subtle difference in the concept of the person underlies this distinction, some viewing the person as an autonomous unit seeking to fill her own desires and others considering the person as part of a larger social whole whose actions are dictated by the needs of the group, not the self. Such concept differences appear within the United States as well, with rural American children (whose parents most likely have no more than a high school education and a working-class income) resembling Asian children in that they refer more to context-based reasons for behaviors than to mental-state reasons (Lillard, Zeljo, & Harlan 1998; Lillard 1999).

Cultures also differ in their attention to certain types of mental states. One study suggests that African American children engage in more emotion talk than do European American children (Blake 1994). Japanese families also talk more to their children about emotions, engaging in what could be seen as intensive empathy training (Azuma 1994). As one example, instead of telling children to eat their dinner so they will grow or because they are lucky not to be starving like children in some other part of the world, Japanese parents are apt to emphasize that a poor farmer worked hard to grow the food and that the children will hurt his feelings if they do not eat it. When a single sock was found in a classroom during a visit one author made to a Japanese preschool, the teacher said to the class, "This poor sock has no partner. Poor sock. Can we help the sock?"

Such cultural practices train children to respond with feeling to those around them as behooves one in Japanese society. Indeed, Japanese adults are not supposed to talk about mental states. References to mental state are taboo, because a truly sensitive person should know others' mental states without being told

about them. These adult conventions may necessitate a great deal of talk about mental state with children, so they learn to be very good at making inferences about mental states before they become taboo topics.

Another apparent cultural difference related to how we understand minds is the extent to which children are allowed to live in mentally constructed worlds as opposed to a single-objective world. Middle-class European American parents appear to socialize children to see the priority of personal views over reality. One recent study reports that middle-class European American parents even accept their children's false statements, apparently to protect their children's self-esteem (Wiley et al. 1998). For example, when a child asserted that Santa Claus comes at Easter, her mother yielded, "Oh, I'm confused," rather than correcting her. Working-class European American parents, in contrast, tended to correct their children, expecting them to get the story right.

Such cultural differences probably lead children to think differently about minds and behaviors. Indeed, researchers have found that children from working-class rural homes tend to explain behaviors as being mandated by circumstances, while children from middle-class urban homes tend to explain them as arising from desires and emotions (Lillard, Zeljo, & Harlan 1998). If reality can be any way that you imagine it, minds become more important. Such views have implications for classroom behavior. In Mexican culture the teacher is revered, and children are expected to learn the teacher's way as the one right way (Delgado-Gaitan 1994); Asian culture is purportedly similar. In contrast, European American children are expected to learn to think critically and challenge the teacher, imposing their own reality on the topic.

Summary

Generally, research suggests that children who understand others' minds at an early age may be more able to get along well with others and that parents and teachers can support the development of this understanding by encouraging pretend play and discussing mental states with them from storybooks or real-life encounters. It is probably not worth discussing the concept of thoughts with toddlers because it may be beyond their understanding. However, some research suggests that by age 3, discussions of what other people are thinking may be helpful.

The fact that discussion leads to understanding aspects of the mind, coupled with different approaches to minds across cultures, suggests that we need to be sensitive about minds and behavior. Every child develops ideas about minds and behaviors, but the ideas individual children have may be different depending on their cultural milieu.

References

Avis, J., & P.L. Harris. 1991. Belief-desire reasoning among Baka children: Evidence for a universal conception of mind. *Child Development* 62: 460–67.

Azuma, H. 1994. Two modes of cognitive socialization in Japan and the United States. In *Cross-cultural roots of minority child development*, eds. P.M. Greenfield & R.R. Cocking, 275–84. Hillsdale, NJ: Erlbaum.

Baldwin, D.A. 1991. Infants' contribution to the achievement of joint reference. *Child Development* 62: 875–90.

Baron-Cohen, S. 1995. *Mindblindness: An essay on autism and theory of mind.* London: MIT Press.

Bartsch, K., & H.M. Wellman. 1995. *Children talk about the mind.* Oxford, England: Oxford University Press.

Blake, I.K. 1994. Language development and socialization in young African-American children. In *Cross-cultural roots of minority child development*, eds. P.M. Greenfield & R.R. Cocking, 147–66. Hillsdale, NJ: Erlbaum.

Borke, H. 1971. Interpersonal perception of young children: Egocentrism or empathy? *Developmental Psychology* 5: 263–69.

Chandler, M.J. 1975. Egocentrism and antisocial behavior: The assessment and training of social perspective-taking skills. *Developmental Psychology* 9: 326–32.

Delgado-Gaitan, C. 1994. Socializing young children in Mexican-American families: An intergenerational perspective. In *Cross-cultural roots of minority child development*, eds. P.M. Greenfield & R.R. Cocking, 55–86. Hillsdale, NJ: Erlbaum.

Dodge, K.A., & J.M. Price. 1994. On the relation between social information processing and socially competent behavior in early school-aged children. *Child Development* 65: 1385–97.

Dunn, J., J. Brown, & L. Beardsall. 1991. Family talk about feeling states and children's later understanding of others' emotions. *Developmental Psychology* 27: 448–55.

Flavell, J.H., F.L. Green, & E.R. Flavell. 1986. *Development of knowledge about the appearance-reality distinction*. Monographs of the Society for Research in Child Development, vol. 51, no. 1, serial no. 212.

Gopnik, A., & J.W. Astington. 1988. Children's understanding of representational change and its relation to the understanding of false belief and the appearance-reality distinction. *Child Development* 59: 26–37.

Hadwin, J., & J. Perner. 1991. Pleased and surprised: Children's cognitive theory of emotion. *British Journal of Developmental Psychology* 9: 215–34.

Happe, F., & U. Frith. 1996. Theory of mind and social impairment in children with conduct disorder. *British Journal of Developmental Psychology* 14: 385–98.

Harris, P.L. 1989. *Children and emotion*. Oxford, England: Basil Blackwell.

Holmes, H., C. Black, & S. Miller. 1996. A cross-task comparison of false belief understanding in a Head Start population. *Journal of Experimental Child Psychology* 63: 263–85.

Kestenbaum, R., & S.A. Gelman. 1995. Preschool children's identification and understanding of mixed emotions. *Cognitive Development* 10: 443–58.

Lalonde, C.E., & M.J. Chandler. 1995. False belief understanding goes to school: On the social-emotional consequences of coming early or late to a first theory of mind. *Cognition and Emotion* 9: 167–85.

Leekam, S. 1993. Children's understanding of mind. In *The development of social cognition: The child as psychologist*, ed. M. Bennett, 26–61. New York: Guilford.

Lewis, C., N. Freeman, C. Kyriakidou, K. Maridaki-Kassotaki, & D. Berridge. 1996. Social influences on false belief access: Specific sibling influences or general apprenticeship? *Child Development* 67: 2930–47.

Lillard, A.S. 1998. Ethnopsychologies: Cultural variations in theory of mind. *Psychological Bulletin* 123: 3–33.

Lillard, A.S. 1999. Developing a cultural theory of mind: The CIAO approach. *Current Directions in Psychological Science* 8 (2): 1–5.

Lillard, A.S., A. Zeljo, & D. Harlan. 1998. Developing cultural schemas: Behavior explanation in Taipei, the rural U.S., and the urban U.S. University of Virginia. Typescript paper.

Meltzoff, A. 1995. Understanding the intentions of others: Re-enactment of intended acts by 18-month-old children. *Child Development* 31: 838–50.

Michalson, L., & M. Lewis. 1985. What do children know about emotions and when do they know it? In *The socialization of emotions*, eds. M. Lewis & C. Saarni, 117–39. New York: Plenum.

O'Neill, D.K. 1996. Two-year-old children's sensitivity to a parent's knowledge state when making requests. *Child Development* 67: 659–77.

O'Neill, D.K., J. Astington, & J.H. Flavell. 1992. Young children's understanding of the role that sensory experiences play in knowledge acquisition. *Child Development* 63: 474–90.

Povinelli, D.J., & T.J. Eddy. 1996. *What young chimpanzees know about seeing*. Monographs of the Society for Research in Child Development, vol. 61, no. 3, serial no. 247.

Repacholi, B.M., & A. Gopnik. 1997. Early reasoning about desires: Evidence from 14- and 18-month-olds. *Developmental Psychology* 33: 12–21.

Saarni, C. 1984. An observational study of children's attempts to monitor their expressive behavior. *Child Development* 55: 1504–13.

Siegler, R.S. 1998. *Children's thinking*. Upper Saddle River, NJ: Prentice Hall.

Wellman, H.M. 1990. *The child's theory of mind*. Cambridge, MA: Bradford Books/MIT Press.

Wellman, H.M., & J.D. Woolley. 1990. From simple desires to ordinary beliefs: The early development of everyday psychology. *Cognition* 35: 245–75.

Wiley, A.R., A.J. Rose, L.K. Burger, & P.J. Miller. 1998. Constructing autonomous selves through narrative practices: A comparative study of working-class and middle-class families. *Child Development* 69: 833–47.

Wimmer, H., & J. Perner. 1983. Beliefs about beliefs: Representation and constraining function of wrong beliefs in young children's understanding of deception. *Cognition* 13: 103–28.

Youngblade, L.M., & J. Dunn. 1995. Individual differences in young children's pretend play with mother and sibling: Links to relationships and understanding of other people's feelings and beliefs. *Child Development* 66: 1472–92.

© Robbie Borine

William J. Kreidler and Sandy Tsubokawa Whittall

13

Resolving Conflict

Excerpted from *Early Childhood Adventures in Peacemaking*

Children learn to solve conflicts in many ways. The principal way they learn is by watching how adults, family members, peers, and media characters handle conflicts. Not all of this modeling is good. Adults, for instance, do not always have all the tools they need to resolve conflicts; and cartoon characters are notably poor role models. Children often need additional help to understand what conflict is and how to resolve it without violence or disrespect.

Conflict resolution builds on other skills: communication, cooperation, expressing and managing feelings, and appreciating diversity. These are the essential ingredients needed to resolve conflicts. While young children rarely engage in negotiating or conflict solving spontaneously, they can be guided through the process so that they not only do well, they enjoy it. The pride and self-confidence they develop allows the whole group to function more smoothly, releasing the teacher from constant pressure to intervene.

Teaching conflict resolution from a developmental perspective

Each child develops in his own way and according to his own timetable. The role of the caregiver or teacher is to help guide the child from one level to the next. Children need adult help to master the social skills associated with resolving conflict. Remember that children who are the same age may be at different developmental levels. Also, at moments of stress or anxiety, a child may slip back into old patterns or forget new skills and need your assistance to get back on track. Make sure every child knows you appreciate his special gifts, regardless of the level he is starting from. This helps him feel confident that he can contribute to the group and become a valued member.

Start at each child's level

• **3- and 4-year-olds** are apt to see things from only one point of view—their own. The 3-year-old who hits, for instance, may not fully understand that the hitting hurts the other child. For the same reason, children this age often do not want to share toys and other materials and are likely to get into conflicts over them. They need active intervention and guidance to begin to appreciate other children's needs and feelings.

• **5- and 6-year-olds** are experiencing competition for the first time. If they lose, their feelings are easily hurt. When conflicts arise, they will need help finding the words to express those feelings before they can move on to resolve the conflict. This is also a good reason to introduce cooperative games and activities, which reinforce the message that every member of the group is important.

• **7- and 8-year-olds** need to feel that they are in control of a situation in order to "save face" in front of peers. The best solution to conflicts for children this age is one that both parties negotiate so that both can feel like winners. The teacher can help children begin to develop the skills they need to understand and respect each other's point of view and to work out a peaceful solution.

Choose goals and skills

The goal of conflict resolution is to help children who are engaged in conflict to find solutions that work for everyone. Some of the discrete skills that help children reach these goals are:

• Distinguishing between Thumbs Up and Thumbs Down solutions (what will work and what won't work)

• Following a sequence of problem-solving steps, such as the Talk It Out Together method

• Suggesting their own solutions to conflicts

• Cooperating to put solutions into practice

• Calming down and getting control

In responding to conflicts that arise in the classroom, remember that there is a difference between teaching and preaching. Preaching is unlikely to give children new skills or understandings. Instead, use the conflict situation to help children acquire a new skill or reinforce ones they have already been taught. Look at the conflict as an opportunity for learning rather than an "I told you so" moment.

Thumbs Up/Thumbs Down

This simple process is used to evaluate solutions. Children decide whether all the parties in a conflict would give a particular solution a thumbs-up sign or a thumbs-down sign. Using stories or puppets to portray different scenarios, ask children to suggest solutions and have the whole group practice using the signs.

Talk It Out Together

This method is a problem-solving process that's easy for children as young as 4 to remember. (1) Get together. (2) Take turns talking and listening. (3) What will help? (4) Choose a plan. (5) Do it!

This is a good example of a time you will want to focus on readiness more than mastery. Few preschoolers will master this process initially, and most will need help remembering and implementing it. By introducing it and practicing it, children will begin to acquire some of these skills, but even older children may still need help in using them or rely on adults to get the process started.

Stop

Teach the stop sign (hand up). Discuss how it is important for children to say stop or make the sign for stop so they can walk away and gain control of their feelings. Remind them that it's okay to stop unsafe behavior by walking away from it; they don't have to resolve a conflict right away.

Tips for daily practice

Practice

One way to help children become familiar with some basic conflict resolution techniques is to practice them when there isn't a conflict. Allow some time for role playing or games when children aren't involved in a problem and can focus on how some of the techniques work.

Give starters

Try giving starters to help children talk about conflicts as they arise. For example, "I saw that you were in the housekeeping area. You were playing. . . . " This provides children with a few thoughts and words to help them begin to talk about what happened.

Paraphrase

Paraphrasing is an important tool to help children hear what they are telling you reflected back to them. This will help them retell their story of the conflict. This technique also allows you to include feelings in the conversation. For example, "So you were trying to tell Justin to stop hitting and he wouldn't stop. That must have been hard. What happened next?"

Connect cause and effect

Young children tend to see conflicts in very concrete terms. When asked what the problem is, they typically remember what just happened or what is right in front of them ("He hit me!"). It is important to use techniques to help them talk back through the chain of events that led to the conflict. For example, "He was playing with the truck, you wanted it and tried to take it from him, and then he hit you. Is that right?" Become the bridge between cause and effect by helping children see the events leading to the conflict. This will allow you to better understand

---

what really occurred as well as help children begin to understand cause and effect.

Promote creativity

Help the children find creative solutions. Ask questions like "What could you do if this happened again?" or "What could you do now to make this situation better?" Focus children's attention on inventing something new. One way to do this is by holding a one-to-one brainstorm where they can think of a few different ideas for resolving the conflict.

When it's appropriate, give children responsibility for solving the problem. You will often need to supervise this, of course, but try as much as possible to let them solve it. For example, set a kitchen timer for seven minutes and ask the children to see what solutions they can create in that time. If they can't come up with anything, you will be available to help them.

Use scripts

Young children may need scripts to help them through parts of the problem-solving process. For example, suggest to a child: "You could say, 'I want to try taking turns.'" Sometimes children will come up with the idea of sharing or taking turns but won't know how to explain it. By helping them present their ideas, you can help them become better communicators in conflict situations.

Help with implementation

The most difficult part of problem solving for young children is implementing the solutions they develop. They will most likely need help. For example, if children choose sharing as a solution, ask, "How will you share the blocks?" First try guiding

them by asking questions that will encourage them to create their own solution. Allow them to try the solution even if you think it will fail. Use this as an opportunity to promote more problem solving. In the end you may need to tell them how to implement the solution.

Developing Emotional Vocabulary

Make a feelings chart: Post the feelings chart at the front of the room. To start a feelings chart, write the word *happy* at the top of a sheet of newsprint. Draw a happy face to provide a visual cue for nonreaders. You can also take pictures of your children demonstrating the emotion. Ask children to suggest other words they know that mean "happy." List these words under the happy face. Extend the chart to include lists of words for other emotions, such as *sad* or *mad*. Students can add new words as they learn them. You can define other words for them by giving examples. For instance, you might say, *"Frustrated* is the way you feel when you are trying really hard to do something and it won't work, like when you can't find a piece for a puzzle." If you give a concrete example, you can draw a symbol, such as a puzzle piece, to remind children of the association between the word and the feeling.

Use role plays: Role plays are a good way to demonstrate feelings and then match words to them. Remember, children under 5 or 6 need help to participate in role-playing. Use puppets, dolls, or another adult to do role plays with this age group. Gradually include one or two children in pantomimes and role plays as they become familiar with the format.

You may want to give guidelines for audience behavior during these activities. For example, you might say, "I want you to use good listening skills. Keep your eyes on the speakers; no talking; save your applause for the end." You can also take this opportunity to model giving feedback: "I like the way you said your part. I could really tell you were feeling sad."

Use stories: Use stories and books to help children learn new words for feelings. When reading stories or books, look for new words that describe feelings children are already familiar with (*thrilled, petrified, miserable,* etc.). After reading the book, provide the sentence starter, "A time I felt _____ was _____." Children can use this as the launching place for a discussion or a journal entry. Writing or drawing in a journal is a good outlet for emotional expression. (Children too young to write can dictate as they draw.) The activity can also lay the groundwork for developing empathy, as children realize that other people sometimes feel the same way they do.

Source: *Early Childhood Adventures in Peacemaking* by W.J. Kreidler & S.T. Whittall with N. Doty, R. Johns, C. Logan, L.P. Roerden, C. Raner, & C. Wintle, pp. 5-4–5-5. Copyright © 1999 by Educators for Social Responsibility & Work/Family Directions. Reprinted with permission.

Five Styles of Handling Conflicts

	Uses	Limitations
Direction		
When you say, in effect, "Do this," you are directing. Direction is a nonnegotiating approach. An adult authority decides what needs to be done and gives the direction that it be done. It's important to recognize that directing need not be unkind or authoritarian. Children can be told nicely, but clearly, what they need to do.	When safety is at stake; when children are out of control and need help getting back into control; when there is no time to discuss or negotiate; when the problem is not important enough to spend much time or energy.	Doesn't build children's independence in problem solving; may cause resentment on the part of children; may not really solve problems.
Mediation		
A third party—either a staff person or any trained person—sits with children and helps them work out their conflict by creating an environment where problem solving can take place. This is done by strictly enforcing ground rules: be honest, no interrupting, and no name calling or put-downs. The mediator helps the disputants define their problem, develop solutions, and choose a workable solution.	Because the disputants are solving the problem themselves, they are invested in the solution. Also, it helps get to the root of some persistent problems.	Takes time! The conflict may not be worth the time and effort compared to the learning that comes from it.
Arbitration		
Also involves a third party who hears both (or all) sides, then tells the disputants how they should handle the conflict. This may be done with some input from the disputants, or by simply saying, "This is what you're going to do."	Efficient. Gives the disputants a chance to state their point of view, but doesn't spend a lot of time on problem solving.	May not get to the root of the problem. The disputants may not learn anything about solving conflicts.
Judgment		
Sometimes the emphasis needs to be not on problem solving but on determining who was right and who was wrong. Children depend on the adult to act as a judge, to listen and weigh the evidence, and then to pass a fair judgment.	When there has been clear wrongdoing and the parties involved want justice; when there is a need for consequences to be decided upon for actions.	Doesn't build independent problem-solving skills; keeps children dependent upon adults; is by nature a win-lose solution rather than a win-win solution.
Listening Sympathetically		
Just listening, not asking a lot of questions or giving advice or solutions, is lending a sympathetic ear. Children have a great need to be listened to regarding their conflicts. It is not uncommon for them to be able to figure out their own solutions once they have expressed their feelings and feel they have been heard.	Respects children and lets them express their feelings and opinions; helps them clarify their positions and feelings; gives them attention and support; can be combined with other methods of resolving conflict.	Takes time; may not lead to problem solving; disputants may feel problem is unresolved.

When it's not working

Validate their feelings

Children need some validation of their feelings before they can solve a problem in a safe and structured way. When a conflict is beginning to get out of hand, you can intervene by giving them a chance to tell you how they feel. You may need to help by providing possible descriptions and words.

Take time to cool off

Don't try to solve problems with children when emotions are still running high. Give them a chance to cool off. Make it clear that you are not punishing them, just giving them a chance to collect themselves. A kitchen timer is handy for this purpose. When the bell rings, ask children if they are ready to talk about the conflict.

Bring the conflict to closure

Many conflicts are over before an adult has the chance to intervene. Children may still need to learn from the experience, however. To bring a conflict to closure, bring the participants together and ask the following questions: What happened? How do you feel? What could you do if this happened again? What could you do now to make things better? Then look for opportunities to help children do what they said they would do when similar situations arise.

Choosing your course of action

While many conflicts occur among young children, not all of them are suitable as teachable moments. You will need to consider a number of factors, including how much time you have, how much you think the children will learn from this situation, and how important the problem seems to be to the children involved. In addition, some problems cannot be handled on the spot, either because of the time or situation or because the children need to cool off before they can discuss their differences.

In deciding what to do, consider the following questions:

• Which children are involved? How upset or angry are they? What do they need from you and each other to work out the problem?

• Is there enough time to devote to the problem? Can the children deal with the problem right away or do they need some time to calm down? Is everyone in an appropriate place to hold the discussion? If problems cannot be addressed right away, it is important for children to hear the reason and to be told that the discussion will take place at a specific time (e.g., after snack, when we get back inside).

• What is the conflict about? Is it a difference over resources or a difference in opinions? Is it a problem with a clear, immediate solution or is it more complex? Is the problem one that recurs frequently or is it unique to the children involved?

• Should the discussion be private or public? Some discussions are best handled with only the children involved, especially when the conflict affects only them or is related to an immediate situation. For some children, airing a dispute in public may be too difficult. However, some problems, particularly those that involve experiences that are common to most children, provide an opportunity for group problem solving. Some problems can also be handled privately and then discussed at a later date in more general terms.

Adapted from W.J. Kreidler & S.T. Whittall with N. Doty, R. Johns, C. Logan, L.P. Roerden, C. Raner, & C. Wintle, *Early Childhood Adventures in Peacemaking* (Cambridge, MA: Educators for Social Responsibility; and Boston, MA: Work/Family Directions, 1999), 8-1–8-11. Copyright © 1999 Educators for Social Responsibility (800-370-2515) and Work/Family Directions. Reprinted with permission.

Building Relationships with All Families

Relating to families is a vital and increasingly complex aspect of our early childhood educator role. New challenges and opportunities stem from the growing cultural and linguistic diversity in our communities (Sturm). To add complexity, families themselves take varied forms. Teachers encounter children being raised by single parents; couples, married or unmarried; blended families; grandparents; two mothers or two fathers, in lesbian- and gay-headed families; and adoptive and foster parents (Clay; Greenberg). The extent to which individual family units connect to the extended family and community also varies (Jones & Moomaw). Families differ significantly in their perspectives and practices as well as in the circumstances that shape their daily lives (Pelo & Davidson; Kaufman). [Note that Section IV also looks at the implications of families' circumstances, including socioeconomic status and the stresses that often accompany poverty.]

Diversity in families affects our early childhood programs in several ways. First, in viewing families as partners in children's education, we are committed to respect families' different perspectives and practices and work with them to resolve conflicts about what is best for the child (Bredekamp). Second, our early childhood programs and schools need to respond to the realities in families' lives today. For example, in the majority of households all the adults work outside the home, and many of them have multiple jobs or varying shifts. In considering how to involve and support families, we need to take such differences into account. Finally, as contributors to this section point out, it is important for children to experience in the curriculum and learning environment not a narrow, stereotyped view of families but a wide array of images and stories that reflects the diversity of children's lives.

Sue Bredekamp

14

Resolving Contradictions between Cultural Practices

Excerpted from *Developmentally Appropriate Practice in Early Childhood Programs*

What if parents want you to spank their child? This is inevitably the first question, it seems, when we introduce the issue of cultural context for consideration by early childhood professionals. The spanking issue is among the easiest to resolve because most states prohibit corporal punishment in child care or school; in those that do not, early childhood educators can turn for guidance to their profession's code of ethical conduct, which clearly considers the practice unethical (NAEYC 1992).

But more important than finding a simple answer to the dilemma, which might actually cut off communication with the parents, a professional could see the apparent contradiction as the opening for a dialogue.

If parents want their child spanked, they probably have concerns about the child's behavior, perhaps his social skills or emotional control. They may be worried that the child will be a problem in school and will not acquire the important skills needed for the future. Without continuing a dialogue with the family, the teacher may make incorrect

assumptions about the family's concerns and priorities or about the child's needs. The first step, then, in resolving what appears to be a conflict between the family and the teacher is to open communication with families, not close it (Delpit 1988).

The ensuing dialogue will be more productive if the professional has thought through the rationale for her decisions about practice. Equally important, the teacher should be aware of her own perspective and values and how these influence her practice, be open to learning new information, and be respectful of others whose perspective or values may differ from her own. With such a basis for communication, the potential conflict may be more easily negotiated and resolved (Phillips 1994; Neuman et al. 1995).

A successful negotiation is one in which both parties change as a result of the interaction, not a situation in which one party loses and the other wins. For instance, one outcome of the conflict over spanking could be the teacher gaining respect for the family's deep concern for their child's well-being and information

about his behavior and experiences at home (i.e., he is the youngest of a large family and frequently must defend himself from older siblings). As a result, the teacher may modify her own tendency to ignore the child's disruptive behavior in favor of more direct coaching of impulse control. For their part, the parents may learn some more effective strategies for disciplining their son.

Many dilemmas faced by early childhood professionals are far less clear-cut than the unacceptability of spanking by teachers. Individuals preparing to become early childhood professionals must learn that one aim of their work is to deal with these kinds of tensions, which inevitably arise in the real world of practice. Because teachers must mediate between the knowledge base in the discipline and the children and their parents, contradictions are bound to emerge. Rather than striving to remember the "right answer," teachers must see themselves as thinkers and problem solvers who construct new understanding from discussing questions with parents and colleagues and who stay open to transformations in children, in parents,

Make a commitment to resolve contradictions without choosing between the values of the families and the school.

and in themselves as teachers. When contradictions arise, the early childhood educator begins a process of information gathering, decision making, reflection, and communication.

A strategy for making decisions and negotiating conflicts

Antonia Lopez (1994), former education director for the Foundation Center programs in California, uses a wonderful, true story to help people understand how the process described above becomes possible when they remain open to it. She illustrates how two views that initially sound like irreconcilable opposites can, with thought, be resolved.

The Foundation Center operated a child care program in a Mexican American community where the program's goal was to be an extension of values in the community. Staff were hired from among the families, and the school worked hard to build a sense of collaboration between the school culture and community culture. However, one behavior rooted in the Mexican American culture—the giving of gifts to teachers as expressions of parents' esteem—seemed to be causing problems. The gift giving was generating feelings of pressure and competition between families that school personnel feared would work against the spirit of community they wanted to build. In short, the cul-

tural practice (giving gifts to teachers) appeared to contradict or undermine other values the school sought to promote (cooperative rather than competitive relationships). Yet teachers feared that to simply ban the gift giving would be perceived by the parents as personal rejection.

Recognizing what was at stake in choosing either extreme of the dilemma, Antonia and the teachers made two rules:

Rule 1: You cannot accept the gifts.
Rule 2: You cannot reject the gifts.
Their challenge was to reconcile these seemingly contradictory rules. They worked out a strategy to accept gifts on behalf of the entire center and to work them into the operation of the program for the general benefit of the entire community. Once they made a commitment to resolve the contradiction without choosing between the values of the families and the school, the question became, "How can we receive the gifts in the spirit in which they are offered?"

When teachers confront situations in which parents' cultural expectations, values, or traditions appear to contradict the values or knowledge base of early childhood educators, the two rules generated from the teachers at the Foundation Center should prove to be useful: you cannot accept *and* you cannot reject. This exercise forces the professionals to reflect on their cherished beliefs and negotiate a compromise acceptable to them and the families they serve.

Antonia Lopez describes a four-step process that her staff uses to approach such apparent contradictions. Four questions are asked:

1. Are the concepts clear?

2. Can you restate the concepts? (When the concepts are restated, they may appear less contradictory.)

3. So what? (Upon analysis, does the issue really matter to children's well-being?)

4. What are the cultural implications or incongruities? (Is the issue really a matter of culture, a difference of opinion, or a difference in information?)

These questions and the process they provoke can provide an excellent framework for resolving many types of conflicts or contradictions.

References

Delpit, L. 1988. The silenced dialogue: Power and pedagogy in educating other people's children. *Harvard Educational Review* 58: 280–98.

Lopez, A. 1994. Personal communication.

NAEYC. 1992. *Code of ethical conduct and statement of commitment.* Washington, DC: Author.

Neuman, S., T. Hagedorn, D. Celano, & P. Daly. 1995. Toward a collaborative approach to parent involvement in early education: A study of teenage mothers in an African-American community. *American Educational Research Journal* 32 (4): 801–927.

Phillips, C.B. 1994. The movement of African-American children through sociocultural contexts: A case of conflict resolution. In *Diversity and developmentally appropriate practices: Challenges for early childhood education,* eds. B. Mallory and R. New, 137–54. New York: Teachers College Press.

Adapted from S. Bredekamp, "Developmentally Appropriate Practice: The Early Childhood Teacher as Decisionmaker," in *Developmentally Appropriate Practice in Early Childhood Programs,* Rev. ed., eds. S. Bredekamp & C. Copple (Washington, DC: NAEYC, 1997), 45–47. Copyright © 1997 NAEYC.

A World of Difference

15

Skills for Working with All Families

When early childhood educators work with families whose backgrounds are different from our own, we gain new perspectives with which to examine our backgrounds and develop a better understanding of both ourselves and others. But working with families whose characteristics and circumstances differ significantly from ours sometimes can be intimidating and discouraging. The financial challenges faced by families with low incomes, coupled with cultural differences, can overwhelm educators. We may not know how to provide support.

Our program serves families from all around the world. Almost half of them speak a language other than English at home. Their incomes range from transitional assistance to a two-parent computer executive team. Working with such a diverse population has required me to fine-tune my skills and to help my staff improve theirs. This article shares stories of real families and gives ideas on how to become better educators and communicators.

What are the challenges?

Early in my career, a young parent of a child enrolled at our center shared her excitement about the coming weekend. Her younger sister was to be the first in her family to graduate from high school. This incredible accomplishment made me view my graduate degree and certificates in an entirely different way. In my family the question was not whether I was going to finish high school but which graduate program I would pursue. But graduating from high school in spite of an abusive and, fortunately, absent father, a 19-year-old sister with two children, and an immigrant mother working a part-time minimum wage job was an extremely good reason for this family to cheer.

My experiences working with families at low income levels have taught me much about how values are affected by culture and economic status. Like their more financially solvent counterparts, families with low incomes put the best interest of the child first. They are more willing to miss work for a sick child, a field trip, or a class party than I expected.

Very few complain when their sick child is sent home; they come quickly and keep their child home until he or she is completely well. One-third of the center's families attend monthly parent meetings. When we schedule a field trip, I have to limit the number of parents who can join us so that we don't need another bus. It does not matter if the trips are on Friday mornings. Parents make arrangements with their employers to miss work so they can join their children.

The families are truly interested and active in their children's lives. Children's health and safety are not neglected even if they require parents to make personal sacrifices. When dollars are very tight, I am sure the parents skip a meal or two so they can give their children a special book or outfit. These families depend on their extended families and each other in times of need. In this close-knit community, when someone needs help, help is given—be it financial, physical, or emotional.

Over the years, my respect has grown for the parents of the children at our center. Very few adults I know have the self-confidence to acknowl-

looking more frazzled than usual and eager to talk. I knew from previous conversations that she was enrolled in an evening GED course and did not have a steady job. Now, in addition, her boyfriend, who lives with the family and is the father of the second child, was not working due to a back injury. Her mother, who is mentally ill and HIV positive, had moved out, and two younger siblings were taking the GED class with her. However, her boyfriend had been acting strangely for several weeks, and she was concerned that he was using cocaine.

We discussed what behaviors she had witnessed and what interventions she had tried. She said that even if she asked her boyfriend to leave, he would not go. And, because she received housing assistance, moving herself and the children was not feasible.

After further exploring the situation, I provided phone numbers for drug abuse hotlines and rehabilitation centers. She left feeling slightly better since her concerns had been validated and now she had a plan. A few days later, she called with an update. Each of the contacts had said that since the boyfriend was an adult, she could not force him to address his substance abuse. Instead, this bright young parent decided to continue talking with her boyfriend, and she left the phone numbers in one of his drawers. Over the next couple of weeks, she noticed that he was going out in the evenings. Never worried about his faithfulness, she began to feel optimistic. After two weeks of being clean and attending drug abuse meetings, he proposed.

With great excitement she announced to me one day that they would be getting married. I was most impressed, however, with her understanding that the situation was not completely resolved. She had shared her needs with her boyfriend:

edge their limited knowledge in a situation and to ask for help. But this is not the case with the families at our center. When I recommend a therapist or an outside resource, I know the family will make the contact. They show respect for my suggestions by encouraging their friends to bring their children to the center. I have never felt so appreciated as an educator or caregiver. The parents whom I serve are very giving and genuinely thankful for the hard work of teachers and other staff.

My greatest challenge in working with families is communicating effectively. Most of the adults have little formal education and, for the most part, English is not their home language. I need to choose words carefully and speak at a moderate pace. In notes and in conversations, I strive to explain things very clearly. Most articles and print resources are written at a higher literacy level than our families can handle right now,

so I often read them with a family and ask questions to make sure they understand.

Clear communication is especially important when helping parents learn behavior management and discipline techniques that encourage their children to exercise self-control. There is never a reason to hit a child, and yelling rarely produces the desired results. Yet these are often the most common forms of discipline. To minimize the possibility of physical abuse and neglect, I encourage parents to enroll in child discipline workshops, and I share articles and clippings about appropriate guidance strategies. Many workshops are delivered at high literacy levels, so some parents may feel uncomfortable and leave. I recommend workshops selectively so that the delicate balance between learning and comfort can be met.

A few months ago, a 19-year-old mother of two came into my office he must stay sober and either get a job or apply for disability.

This parent has a valuable skill—she knows when to seek help and where to find it. As head of her extended family, she must overcome incredible odds, but I have no doubt she will succeed. And with her success, her children have a much better chance of succeeding in school and life.

My responding to that young parent and family was not necessarily difficult, nor was their situation unique. Many of the skills I used are appropriate for working with any family, not just the ones whose lives seem to crumble around them.

What can we do?

At our center we use the following strategies for supporting and involving families. They can be adapted to fit the needs and circumstances of other settings.

Establish strong relationships between the center and the home. Use empathy and patience to forge relationships with families. Let families know they are respected, as are their decisions, ideas, and values. Make time for their concerns, encourage their questions, and address each one with the consideration it deserves. Try to stay organized, so supporting parents can be a top priority.

Validate without judging. Listen while families share the details of any serious problems with which they are coping. Acknowledge their concerns without judging their actions, responses, or values. Discuss and help them evaluate the appropriateness of possible actions and sources of assistance.

Link families with needed resources. Maintain an up-to-date list of responsive community agencies with their addresses and phone numbers. When parents are in crisis, give them a few contacts to help ease their stress. When serving families with limited English skills, provide information in their home language, if possible. Locate community volunteers who can translate important information. Hire teachers who are bilingual.

Use varied communication techniques. Adults have different learning styles and reading abilities, so it is best to use a combination of communication strategies. Since some parents are embarrassed by their limited reading abilities, they may not ask for help or may sign documents without understanding them. Use simple language and translations whenever possible. Provide a monthly parent newsletter and notes as needed. Schedule monthly parent meetings so families can ask questions of their child's teacher or other staff. In addition, keep an open-door policy so parents can call or visit whenever they wish. To enhance regular communication, encourage teachers to make themselves available during drop-off and pickup times. When appropriate, refer families to free or low-cost English as a Second Language (ESL) classes.

Support community collaboration. In communities with large numbers of families with low incomes, there usually are public and private agencies that offer needed resources and services. By working together with other early childhood programs, including public schools and Head Start, we can access resources to enhance child care affordability and quality. Some agencies provide free parent groups and training sessions, including ESL classes, with meals and child care. Literacy fairs and domestic violence task forces provide information to families in need. GED programs and posted agency newsletters alert parents to job opportunities. Legislative advocacy workshops empower parents by showing how they can make a difference.

Summary

The advantages of working with our families are dramatic. I gain valuable friends and a greater understanding of different cultures and values not to mention my own belief system. The knowledge that I definitely make a positive difference in children's lives is what brings me to work every day.

Clearly, the skills outlined above are not just for early childhood professionals who work with families considered at-risk because of low incomes. They have been used by early childhood educators for many years across a broad spectrum of society. Families without solid financial resources are no less skilled or intelligent than middle- or upper-income families. In many cases, they are merely unaware of their options. By developing strong relationships, validating parent questions and concerns, offering resources, providing various types of communication, and collaborating with other community agencies, early childhood educators can make a positive difference in the lives of all families, including those with low incomes.

Reprinted from *Young Children* 56 (4): 81–83. Copyright © 2001 NAEYC.

James W. Clay

16

Working with Lesbian and Gay Parents and Their Children

A center had enrolled the children of four lesbian couples. The teachers were relating very well to the children. However, they felt uncomfortable when the mothers requested that the children refer to both women in the family as "mother." "A child can only have one mother," the teachers argued, forgetting about the children being raised by a mother and grandmother who call both "Mama." The director suspected that this issue was just the tip of the iceberg of what was really bothering these teachers. Among other things, their religious beliefs and ethnic values were strongly condemnatory of homosexuality. It is a credit to their professionalism that they did not let these values get in the way of the care they gave children.

The center director engaged my services to conduct a workshop to provide sensitivity training for these teachers. In preparation, I did some research on gay and lesbian parents. The results are not really so startling. The desire to have children is a basic human desire—it has nothing to do with sexual orientation. Some lesbians and gay men want to love and care for a child. In this way they are just like other parents and like the staff in child care centers.

If staff members understand the differences and similarities between gay and lesbian parents and other parents, they can offer quality care. Staff may be uncomfortable discussing the subject of homosexuality or being around gay people. That is all right. The goal is for staff to respond to these parents with the same respect they show other parents. With some additional information, staff can use the skills they already have to provide excellent care for these families.

Definition of terms

Lesbian mothers and gay fathers are not a homogeneous group. Many lesbian mothers and gay fathers became parents during a previous heterosexual relationship. While in the relationship they were probably not openly gay, nor did they identify themselves as gay. They may not even have yet known they were gay. In most cases, after the divorce or separation, the mothers retain custody of the children. Whereas a lesbian mother separated from her former spouse is usually the primary caregiver for her children, a gay father is not. In many ways gay fathers are like other separated fathers without custody.

In recent years, many lesbian couples have become parents through means of artificial insemination. Some gay men enter into a relationship with a woman with an agreement to have a child and share the parenting. Sometimes this agreement is with a lesbian. Adoption is an option for single men and women in states that permit individuals to adopt, although it is very difficult for a man to adopt a child on his own.

While investigating this subject, I attended a meeting of the local Gay Fathers Coalition. Similar organizations exist in most large cities in the country. The evening I attended, 40 or so fathers were present for a potluck dinner. They allowed me to interview them using a survey (modified for men) designed by Virginia Gregory (1986) to gather information from lesbian mothers. Gregory, a lesbian mother and former center director, had attended several regional women's gatherings and interviewed lesbian mothers. Some of the information that follows is based on

A World of Difference

those interviews and surveys with both men and women. The rest is based on formal research already completed on the population (e.g., Schulenburg 1985).

Lesbian and gay parents

How do lesbian and gay parents compare to other parents in their ability to parent? The answer is quite simple: There is no appreciable difference in their ability to parent compared to heterosexual parents. Similarities far exceed differences. Apparently, the ability to nurture is not related to sexual orientation (Bozett 1985). In fact, the gay fathers I spoke to prefer to see themselves as *fathers* who happen to be gay, rather than as *gay* fathers. Lesbian couples who adopt or have children by means of artificial insemination go through great difficulties to become parents and really *want* children. Research does not demonstrate that being gay is a liability to parenting.

Most gay fathers see themselves as similar to single or divorced fathers. Many lesbian mothers are similar to single mothers, particularly in one important aspect: Many believe strongly in providing a male role model for their male children (Hitchens & Thomas 1983).

Is there anything about being gay that makes these parents unique and therefore affects their parenting style? Research shows that there are three distinctive qualities of lesbian mothers. First, lesbian mothers exhibit higher self-reliance than other mothers. Second, *some* lesbian mothers (and gay fathers) feel guilty about their sexual orientation. This guilt, like guilt from any source, can have a negative impact upon their children (Hitchens & Thomas 1983). Generally, as time goes by, these parents learn to manage their guilt, and the effect on the children is decreased. (Guilt by no means afflicts all gay and lesbian parents.)

Third, lesbian mothers (and gay fathers) have to deal with their children's problems about their family being different. These problems come in the form of the prejudices of school personnel and neighbors against the sexual orientation of the children's parents. As a result, lesbian mothers and gay fathers try to make things as "normal" for their children as possible. They realize that their family situation is *potentially* stressful for their children.

In addition, Gregory (1986) found a few other unique aspects of lesbian parenting. Lesbians who had been open about their sexual orientation within their community before becoming a parent felt they lived in a fishbowl. They perceived themselves as being constantly under scrutiny. This added stress to their parenting. They also found they had more than the ordinary adjustment and integration problems if they found a new partner. The new stepparent had even less support than a new partner in a heterosexual relationship because there was little social validation for the relationship itself.

One question all these couples faced was how much adult-adult affection to express in front of their children. For instance, teachers might accept the fact that a child's parents are lesbians. Nonetheless, they might not be ready to hear that "my mommies kiss each other." Lesbian mothers usually determined the level of affection to display based upon their children's age and their general openness with their children.

The children

What is the effect on a child of being raised by a lesbian or gay parent? More specifically, does a parent's being gay have any effect on the sexual identity of the child? This question is the one most commonly asked by teachers of young children who live in lesbian and gay households. Studies show that the incidence of being gay among children of gay and lesbian parents is approximately the same as in the rest of the population. There is no apparent relationship between a parent's sexual orientation and the sexual identity of the child. Gay and lesbian parents note that second-generation homosexuality is rare, and that the parents of most homosexual adults are heterosexual.

Is there evidence of confusion in gender or sexual identity for the child? There is no confusion as a result of the parent being gay. Studies also show that the overall level of emotional adjustment of children of lesbians is the same as that of children of heterosexual mothers.

What is the effect on the children of society's disapproving attitudes and prejudices toward gay men and lesbians? Gay parents are very sensitive to this issue. The fathers I spoke to expressed concern about protecting their children from harmful public opinion. Society's prejudices do have negative effects on the children. Parents have to select carefully the terminology they give their children to describe their family unit to others. Many children learn early on they have to be secretive about their parents' sexual orientation as a matter of self-preservation. Some of their teachers, peers, or peers' parents react unfavorably to the information that their parents are homosexual.

Some children also feel different and isolated from their peers, and as a result they become lonely. They seek friends with whom they can be honest and open. As lesbian and gay adults increasingly "come out," it becomes ever more customary for homosexual families to form a sense of community: Thus the children are *not* one of a kind.

In general, if the child's parents are well-adjusted and open about their homosexuality, there is a good chance that the child is well-adjusted too.

Classroom education about family diversity is important for the healthy self-identity of all children.

There are several positive effects a child raised by a lesbian or gay parent may experience. First, the family situation can increase the child's appreciation of diversity by providing a nontraditional adult role model (Riddle 1978). That is, having a parent who is different makes it easier for a child to be different and independent. That child is also being prepared to be more tolerant, accepting, and nonjudgmental. Lesbian mothers feel their children are more sensitive to issues of social justice. They also feel their family situation gives their children strength, sensitivity, compassion, and maturity beyond their years. In any case, the parents' disclosure of their homosexuality to their children is found to deepen the parent-child relationship. The parents and children need each other for mutual support. The result is a very close family unit.

How educators can address the needs of parents and their children

Special staff education is necessary to support these families. Administrators must realize that gay and lesbian parents exist and that they need to be treated with the same respect shown other parents. In fact, like single parents, they may require a little extra support. "Gay and lesbian parents are faced with child care program brochures showing only mothers and fathers together with their children [and] applications asking for 'Mother's Name/Father's Name' instead of 'Parent's Name/Parent's Name'" (Shuman 1988). A simple change in the application form and a rewrite of the brochure will show sensitivity to these parents.

Staff members may need help in examining their fear of homosexuality (homophobia). Resources are available (e.g., Robinson & Barrett 1986; Bozett 1987; Derman-Sparks and the A.B.C. Task Force 1989; and the other references in this article). One simple form of support is greatly appreciated by gay and lesbian parents: Staff should use contemporary terminology (in this case, "gay" and "lesbian") just as they would with other minority groups.

Classroom education about family diversity is important for the healthy self-identity of all children. Pictures, puzzles, and children's books should present a broad range of family structures. Even if families with gay and lesbian parents are not presented, the fact that diversity is noted is supportive for these children. It affirms that a family can be many different things. If gay and lesbian parent family groups are mentioned, they should be presented in a positive light.

Teachers must also alert gay and lesbian parents to any harassment of their children resulting from their family being different. Teachers can help parents develop strategies for preparing children to deal with harassment. On the positive side, staff can let parents know who their child's friends are. This is particularly important if their friendships have been limited by their being different.

Parents need support. In many cases, however, gay and lesbian parents want to maintain secrecy about their homosexuality. This choice of secrecy should be respected. These parents might need extra encouragement to attend school and classroom social events. Through these events they can build contacts and break down their isolation from the school community. If these families need additional support, inform them that gay and lesbian parent organizations exist in most large cities. Post the phone numbers of these organizations along with the numbers of other local parent support groups you make available to the parents. These organizations are listed in local gay newspapers and in the national Gay Yellow Pages.

As I assured the director and teachers in my workshop, I am not advocating exposing parents who wish to remain invisible. I am advocating expanding the range of family structures that teachers recognize and can learn to support. It is enough to let all parents know you offer services to all families and respect them as individuals.

References

Bozett, F.W., ed. 1987. *Gay and lesbian parents.* New York: Praeger.
Bozett, F.W. 1985. Gay men as fathers. In *Dimensions of fatherhood,* eds. S.M.H. Hanson & F.W. Bozett, 327–52. Beverly Hills, CA: Sage.
Derman-Sparks, L., & the A.B.C. Task Force. 1989. *Anti-bias curriculum: Tools for empowering young children.* Washington, DC: NAEYC.
Gregory, V. 1986. *Lesbian/gay family survey.* Unpublished manuscript.
Hitchens, D.J., & A.G. Thomas, eds. 1983. *Lesbian mothers and their children: An annotated bibliography of legal and psychological materials,* 2d ed. San Francisco, CA: San Francisco Lesbian Rights Project.
Riddle, D.I. 1978. Relating to children: Gays as role models. *Journal of Social Issues* 34 (3): 38–58.
Robinson, B.E., & R.L. Barrett. 1986. *The developing father: Emerging roles in contemporary society.* New York: Guilford.
Schulenburg, J. 1985. *Gay parenting: A complete guide for gay men and lesbians with children.* Garden City, NY: Anchor.
Shuman, S. 1988. Including everyone: Children of gay and lesbian parents. *Massachusetts Child Care News* 14 (10): 4–5.

Adapted from *Young Children* 45 (3): 31–35. Copyright © 1990 NAEYC.

"She Is So My Real Mom!"
Helping Children Understand Adoption as One Form of Family Diversity

Adoption as a method of family building is becoming more and more common and is more noticeable as international and transracial adoptions increase. In two independent schools in Philadelphia, 50 percent of the girls in first grade were born in China and adopted by American families. Thinkers and leaders in the field of adoption teach that the more openness and education there is about adoption issues, the better off everyone will be.

Early childhood teachers, the first contacts outside the immediate family for many children, are in a key position to convey knowledge about adoption and model acceptance of it. A normalizing attitude can make a huge difference for children who came into their families by adoption, for their siblings and other family members, and for the children who create the social climate that adopted children have to navigate.

As early childhood educators educate themselves about adoption issues, they can proclaim inclusive messages that make all children feel good about their stories. We can refrain from colluding in secrecy, shame, and ignorance about adoption. Each one of us has our own interesting life story; each family is unique; there are many right ways to live a life—these are the important messages to convey.

From the point of view of the young adoptee, the most pressing issue is coping with the sense of being different. We all know that little children don't like to be different: if Diego has Pokemon shoes, Sammy wants them too. If the dominant culture proclaims a norm of family consisting of mother and father raising biological children, then any child in a family with two mothers, or different skin colors, or just one single parent, or with an adoption story is different. The earliest pain about adoption for young children comes from being different.

The early childhood program's job is to normalize these diverse stories. "We are a nursery school with many different kinds of families," or "We are all part of the United States, and the United States has many different kinds of families." If you don't have diversity in your particular classroom or school in the ways families come together or in family structure or race, you can present a diversified reality through pictures, stories (even if you have to make them up), and children's literature. Through our language we instill a sense of belonging and that we are all in this together; no one is being singled out or isolated as an example of diversity for the rest of the class.

Another source of pain for adopted children is the ignorance and thus insensitivity of well-meaning and sometimes not-so-well-meaning peers. Children who came into their families by adoption frequently hear questions such as "Why didn't your real mom want you?" "Why is your skin a different color from your mom's?" "Your mom isn't your real mom." These questions create pathways of doubt about self and identity for adopted children.

Early childhood educators can play a powerful role in creating a climate of awareness about adoption issues so that each adopted child does not have to be the point person for all ignorance and curiosity. Teachers can teach in general, without singling out the adopted members of the class, that some people

© Cleo Photography

while disqualifying taunting and persistent, insensitive questioning. One teacher of 4-year-olds responded to taunts of "You don't have a daddy!" and "You are adopted, na na na na na na!" by saying to the taunted child, "I don't think Jordan has learned how to be respectful yet. Tasha, you and I will have to explain about all the different, good ways families work. When Jordan's a little older, he'll understand."

One situation in which teachers can advocate for diversity in family life is in the inevitable family tree activity. Don't assume that all family trees are going to look the same! A good way to accommodate variety is to put the child's name in the center of the page and to connect all important people to the child, instead of using the traditional genogram format that assumes there will be one father and one mother for each child in each generation. Putting the child in the center allows room for birth parents and other diverse family formats.

Finally, because adopted children are usually very wanted children, teachers are likely to find motivated, committed parents who will welcome the teacher as an ally. Adoptive parents are usually glad to respond to a teacher's interested query, "I'd love to hear how you've been telling Annie her adoption story." The more information you have about the particular adoption stories of your children, the more you'll be able to foster relevant awareness and respond appropriately to issues that arise.

As we enlighten ourselves about the full diversity of children's lives, we make the world a safer and healthier place for all our children.

Reprinted from *Young Children* 56 (2): 90–91. Copyright © 2001 NAEYC.

have birth parents who gave them life and "forever parents" who raise them. They have two sets of "real" parents, each as real as the other.

Sometimes birth parents are unable to take care of a baby, so they make a loving plan to give the baby a family that can take care of him or her. The grownups make that plan because it is their best decision, not because of anything about the way the baby looks or acts. Teachers can

become comfortable talking, when the issue arises, about how children usually have the same color skin as their birth parents. Often when a teacher speaks acceptingly in a general way about these issues, an adopted child will pipe up, "I'm adopted."

Teachers can turn potentially harmful peer interactions around so that they empower adopted children as experts on their own situation,

Connie Sturm

Creating Parent-Teacher Dialogue
Intercultural Communication in Child Care

Arlena, age 2, enters the toddler room wearing new glasses. Ida, her mom, tells the teacher that the glasses must stay on, whether Arlena wants them on or not. If the glasses don't correct a vision problem, the child will require eye surgery. The teacher tells Arlena that her glasses are darling, but the toddler is already heading for the playdough table, unimpressed.

As soon as her mom leaves, Arlena yanks off the glasses and throws them down on the floor. The teacher rushes over.

"Oh dear, Arlena, let's put your glasses back on."

"No!"

"Arlena, these glasses look so pretty and they're so good for your eyes!"

But Arlena slips out of reach, while the teacher hesitates, wondering what to do. Throughout the day Arlena rejects the glasses despite gentle, sympathetic coaxing. The teacher does not force them on her, fearing that coercion will only increase the child's aversion.

When Ida returns, the teacher explains that it might be unrealistic to

expect a 2-year-old to wear glasses all day.

"No, no, no," Ida responds. "She has no choice. I don't have health insurance to pay for an operation, and she's going to wear those glasses! She wore them all weekend at home."

Suddenly the teacher realizes that this parent, whose cultural background differs from her own, might use a different approach in talking with her child about the glasses.

"Tell me exactly what you say when you tell her to put on the glasses. How do you say it?" asks the teacher.

"I tell her, 'Put your glasses on right now!' She just does it. She knows that if she doesn't, *I will*. She understands that I *mean* it!"

The next morning, Arlena throws the glasses down as soon as her mom walks out the door.

Imitating Ida's firm tone, the teacher says, "Arlena, put your glasses on."

"No!"

"Yes! Right now, and I mean it!" The teacher is not yelling, not unkind, just strong and confident. She prevents Arlena's escape and waits.

After a thoughtful pause, Arlena matter-of-factly puts on her glasses and bounces off happily to find a book. For the rest of the day, despite a few tests, the glasses, amazingly, stay on.

The importance of culture in communication

The teacher in this story felt uncomfortable speaking in such firm tones. I know because I am that teacher. Until then, I thought I knew all the "right" child guidance methods. But Arlena and Ida taught me that not all children can experience success with the methods that are most comfortable for me.

I began to think about culture and communication in child care. I knew that culture means more than holidays and food; it includes all the subtle patterns of communication—verbal and nonverbal—that people use every day. I noticed how easily I valued cultural diversity in the abstract or in the form of occasional holidays, yet how readily I rejected cultural differences when they appeared in the form of parents' differ-

Our Parent-Teacher Dialogue Project

Our group launched an intercultural dialogue project. The 10 teachers who participated in this project work in culturally diverse, nonprofit child care centers. We conducted 23 dialogues among ourselves and 19 parents of infants, toddlers, and preschoolers in child care. Teachers conducted the first 10 dialogues between themselves, one-on-one, to practice intercultural skills. Then five teachers dialogued with parents on 13 occasions. These groups varied from two to four people, including one or two teachers. Each person shared his or her own child-rearing values, beliefs, and practices.

We used the word *dialogue* to represent two-way communication that attempts to illuminate all perspectives as fully as possible. We assumed that knowledge about one another's unique life experiences fosters shared meaning and mutual understanding between parents and teachers. Therefore our goal was to identify patterns of communication that reduce or increase expression of unique cultural, familial, and emotional meanings.

The most successful dialogues captured the most specific information about individuals' family cultures, daily lives, family histories, and honest feelings. We placed special importance on personal stories as a particularly self-revealing form of discourse. We also valued parents' emotional expressions. Of course we realized that while some people value emotional expression, others value quieter, more subtle communication. Some people prefer privacy. We knew that each dialogue would have its own rhythm and style.

Methods to encourage open dialogue

We began with a list of questions about family routines, relationships, values, and goals based loosely on recommendations in the current literature (Gonzalez-Mena 1993; California Department of Education 1995). We selected and phrased questions to fit the emergent characteristics of each dialogue. A flexible approach to the questions allowed parents and teachers to focus on the topics in which they were most interested and with which they were comfortable. The purpose of the questions was not to elicit specific answers as much as to encourage open, free-flowing conversation.

Giving parents control of the discussion. We found that an open exchange of information occurred more often when teachers used certain conversational methods. One method was to give the parent as much control as possible over the content of the discussion, striving for an equal balance of power in dialogue. For example, when a parent answered a question, rather than moving to the next question on the list, the teacher pursued that answer with a follow-up question. In this way the conversation evolved from the parent's answers rather than primarily from the list of questions. Here is an excerpt from a taped dialogue:

Teacher: Tell me a little about the other people in your family. What role do grandparents and other relatives play?

Parent: The kids just love seeing their grandparents. When they see their grandpa, they feel so excited, and they feel so close to him. It's really nice.

Teacher: How do the grandparents interact with the children?

Parent: My mom is a very hands-on person. She bathes the kids, she does everything. Sometimes it's a vacation for us to go over to my mom's house. She's doing it less and less because she's getting more and more grandchildren. But especially with my oldest son, it's such a treat: "I'll give them a bath!" She feeds them dinner—she's the one, not the mom. She's very hands-on.

My dad is, also. When I'd have to go to work an extra day, my dad would take care of my two boys and he'd change diapers—he did everything, took them out to the park. He's a very capable caretaker for my kids. So they've been lucky. We are a tight family. We socialize with family a lot. I think that's probably part of my culture.

Teachers sharing personal experiences with parents. Another approach that seemed to encourage more personal storytelling was a teacher's own self-revelation. The more teachers shared personal experiences, the more some parents shared their own cultural perspectives. For example,

Teacher: I used to be a single mom on public assistance. I felt that some people made a lot of generalizations about single mothers. It's like, if you don't have a father in the family, you don't have a real family.

Parent: Of course that's not true. My mother raised us, but with the help of everybody—everybody contributed to our upbringing. My grandfather is known as Daddy; I call him Daddy. It means everything. My children refer to him as Grandfather-Daddy. You have your grandmother; you respect her the same way you respect your mom. You pick up everything from your uncles, your aunts; everybody has a say in the way that you are brought up.

The older I get the more I appreciate that, and that's exactly how it is with my children. I am the parent, but the other family members have just as much to say as I do. I like that. I know that what I tell my children, my brother's going to support that as well. It's just totally different. My uncle was my mentor and my best friend. Each person has several different roles to play; it's a whole network of family, not just one mother and one father.

I haven't had to be a single parent like a lot of other people I know. When I became single, I didn't notice a real big change. I didn't lose a lot of support. I had all the support I always had, less one. With 10 other people, it didn't really matter.

Parents sharing childhood experiences. Questions about parents' childhood experiences also established a more familiar, intimate base of information as a context for understanding parents' child-rearing methods:

Teacher: Tell me about your parents' approach to discipline. How did they discipline you?

Parent: Even if I thought something wasn't right, if they said that's the way it's going to be, that's the way it's going to be.

I was the one that mostly got in trouble. To give you a perfect example, my mom was having a tea party at the house. She was having a lot of church members over, her friends. She went to the bakery, and she bought all these different pastries. We were supposed to stay next door at the neighbor's house. And while she went back to the store again, I snuck in through the kitchen window with my friend. I was in about the fourth grade. I snuck in because I wanted some of the treats she bought.

When my mom came back, we had already left and there were all these fingerprints of chocolate. So she called next door. She knew it was me. I was the tomboy in the house. Stupid me, I didn't rub the chocolate off my hands or face.

I heard her calling me. "What, Mom?" "Were you in my party stuff?" I shook my head. She said, "Don't you want to tell me the truth?" She was angry with me.

Back then they were more apt to spank you. So she sent me to my room, and she told me I was going to get a spanking. But for some reason she did not believe in spanking on a Sunday. She said, "I'm not going to spank you today because today is Sunday, but I am going to spank you tomorrow." That was torture!

Later, when the same parent shared her own philosophy on guidance, her words took on much greater meaning:

Parent: My husband totally disagrees with spanking. That's one reason why he wanted communication instead, because that's something neither one of us had. His parents believed in spanking, too. He always said that he did not want to raise his kids like his parents did, and I felt the same way.

Asking direct but sensitive questions. Bicultural parents often shared more about their cultural perspectives when the teacher asked direct but sensitive questions about culture or ethnicity:

Teacher: How do you think your ethnic background influenced your experience growing up?

Parent: We went back and forth [between the United States and Mexico] because my father was working in the fields. I was born here after my parents came and I was raised up to 6 here, then we moved to Mexico. Then we came back. Even though I spent more time here, I think I'm more Hispanic than I am American. We were going back and forth, and it was kind of hard because my father was working in the fields and the canneries, so we didn't finish anything here or there.

When I was in kindergarten, other children used to hit me and call me names. It was awful. They just looked for me, and this one girl used to hit me. I was a quiet girl. I was so afraid that I carried a jump rope; I had that to protect me. The principal—nobody—paid attention. They didn't help me—not in kindergarten, not in sixth grade. My mother went to the school many times. But they didn't do anything until one day my mother smacked a girl who was hurting me. She couldn't believe she did it. But then they left me alone. I don't want my daughter to go through what I did. Oh, no! I would stand there—I don't know what I would do. It starts making me think angry things that I don't want to feel. I am going to counseling right now about this.

Respecting parents' "comfort zones"

Some teachers viewed direct questions about culture as inappropriate without first establishing a high level of trust with parents. Even sensitive questions might jeopardize some parent-teacher relationships. We found that people have different rules and values about discussing culture and ethnicity. Respect for each person's "comfort zone" is essential. Clearly, intercultural competence requires that we adapt to different values and different rules for communication.

We also found that self-revealing dialogue occurred more often when teachers

• asked for parents' opinions,

• asked for clarification,

• expressed a desire to learn from the parent,

• discussed ways to support a family's values,

• created an informal, nonjudgmental climate, and

• acknowledged that there are many points of view on a topic.

ent approaches to child rearing. Many colleagues shared similar concerns. Michelle, a teacher of 3-year-olds, told me this story:

Imagine Yanli—shy, timid Yanli—marching into my classroom with her mom this morning. She walked right up to me and said, "Michelle, move please!" I was sitting in front of the blocks she needed. I thought to myself, "Yes! Exactly the assertiveness girls need!" But as I silently cheered Yanli's new spirit, I glanced at her mom's face. It revealed horror and embarrassment.

Her facial expression bothered me all day. My first impulse was to criticize the mother: she should not teach Yanli to be meek and submissive! Then I decided to ask the mother how *she* felt. When I talked to her, she said she felt terribly worried about her daughter. Relatives and friends disapproved of Yanli's new outspoken behavior. She might become an outcast in her own community.

I realized then that I did not understand the complexity of this family's life at all. I was making judgments based on *my* experience, without taking the time to learn about *theirs*. We had just celebrated Chinese New Year. Suddenly I saw how phony it was to celebrate a family's holiday and then totally reject the way they live their everyday lives!

Teachers compare their experiences

A small group of teachers decided to explore these issues together. We noticed that cultural differences take many forms. Ursula had insisted that one set of parents stop allowing their daughter to share their bed because she assumed that sleeping in a bed of one's own fosters greater independence. Ursula imposed her own beliefs and values without considering the possibility that the parents also have valid reasons for their actions.

When a parent asked Jill not to pick up her baby every time he cried, Jill disapproved. She based her beliefs on her own emotional response to the baby's cry without reflecting on the source of those feelings or the origins of that mother's powerful emotions.

Emma felt annoyed when a parent requested that her child's clothes be changed every time he got slightly messy. Spotlessness wasn't an important value for Emma, so she simply assumed the parent was unreasonable, never imagining that both ways might be valid.

Francisco disagreed with a mother about the way she dressed her 10-month-old. "He's got so many layers of clothing, he can't bend enough to sit down, much less move around and explore!" Francisco described. "I took some clothes off when the mom left. When she came back, she wouldn't talk to me."

As our discussion group talked about these issues, we realized that unexamined values, beliefs, and patterns of interaction—learned when *we* were children—exert a powerful influence on our communication and caregiving routines. Our sincere intentions did not prevent us from rejecting parents' diverse values when they challenged our own cherished beliefs. We were often unable to set aside our own cultural values long enough to listen to parents.

Cultural diversity challenges old beliefs about child rearing

Increasingly, trends toward demographic diversity challenge us to communicate with parents whose cultural backgrounds differ from our own. What happens when we fail to communicate effectively? When we fail to create a supportive, collaborative relationship with a parent, what

effect do we have on that child? How do we affect children's attachments to parents? How do we affect their embryonic sense of identity? Surely children cannot thrive in the shadow of a teacher's belief that the ways of their parents are inferior or wrong.

As our discussion group revisited our personal beliefs about culture, child development, and parent communication, we understood more clearly that children's development takes place through participation in social and cultural activities. Development is a social and cultural process as well as an individual one (Vygotsky 1978; Rogoff 1990; Phillips 1994). In other words, children learn a great deal about who they are, where they fit, and how the world works from a web of relationships and interactions with teachers, peers, and especially parents.

When the skills and values learned at home are very similar to those promoted at school, self-confidence builds and children thrive. But when the skills and values learned in relationships at home are subtly devalued by the relationships in child care, children experience insecurity and confusion about what kind of people they are, where they came from, and how to succeed (Schoem 1991). To avoid confusion and to promote optimal development, we must find ways to validate the skills and values learned at home as well as those learned in school and child care (Au & Kawakami 1994). We demonstrate that both ways are valid by creating warm, supportive relationships with parents from many cultural backgrounds. For our discussion group, the question remained, How?

What we seemed to need most were intercultural communication skills. This goal became the focus of our discussions. By *intercultural communication skills*, I mean awareness of the individual, class, and cultural assumptions that influence our own communication with others who are culturally dissimilar; the ability to suspend ethnocentric evaluation in order to understand what others mean; and the flexibility to respond and adapt to a variety of cultural styles and perspectives to achieve mutually satisfying communication.

Communication scientists tell us that intercultural competence can be learned only in intercultural relationships—in risk-taking, anxiety-provoking, confusing, and sometimes embarrassing intercultural encounters (Gudykunst 1991). Researchers also tell us that people can and do develop a broad intercultural perspective with the emotional and behavioral openness and flexibility to adapt to new situations and communicate effectively with many different people.

Not only do we possess this potential, but early childhood professionals have an obligation to reach for it. Why? Because children need to know that their teachers respect and value their parents' opinions; and because children, too, can learn intercultural competence, just as they do ethnocentrism and racism, from the words—and especially the nonverbal behavior—of the important adults in their lives. We can teach nothing more important than this, for without intercultural competence, peace and unity are not possible in a diverse society.

What we learned from our project

We concluded our group project with optimism, although we discovered no simple, universal answers to our questions. The teachers found that the shift from miscommunication to intercultural competence can

© BmPorter/Don Franklin

not be made with ease and grace; we were obliged to learn by making mistakes. However, we learned to notice when our own behavior opened or closed dialogue. We learned to set aside judgment and listen with the intent to understand. We expanded our repertoire of dialogue skills. We learned a great deal about parents and families. Both parents and teachers said they felt more trust and connection with one another after the dialogues.

Most important, we no longer feel paralyzed by the overwhelming challenge of diversity issues. Two broad goals emerged from our project:

• The early childhood profession has an ethical responsibility to understand the role of culture and ethnicity in child development.

• Early childhood professionals must develop effective skills to meet the cultural and linguistic needs of families from all cultures.

Where to begin? With a nod to Alcoholics Anonymous, I offer this answer: "One dialogue at a time."

References

Au, K., & A. Kawakami. 1994. Cultural congruence in instruction. In *Teaching diverse populations: Formulating a knowledge base*, eds. E. Hollings, J. King, & W. Hayman. Albany, NY: SUNY Press.

California Department of Education & Far West Laboratory for Educational Research and Development. 1995. *Infant/toddler caregiving: Guide to culturally sensitive care*. Sacramento: Bureau of Publications.

Gonzalez-Mena, J. 1993. *Multicultural issues in child care*. Mountain View, CA: Mayfield.

Gudykunst, W. 1991. *Building bridges: Effective intergroup communication*. Newbury Park, CA: Sage.

Phillips, C. 1994. Growth and development in a diverse society. Lecture given at Pacific Oaks College, Pasadena, California, 20 April.

Rogoff, B. 1990. *Apprenticeship in thinking*. New York: Oxford University Press.

Schoem, D. 1991. *Inside separate worlds: Life stories of young Blacks, Jews, and Latinos*. Ann Arbor, MI: University of Michigan Press.

Vygotsky, L. 1978. *Mind in society: Development of higher psychological processes*. Cambridge, MA: Harvard University Press.

Reprinted from *Young Children* 52 (5): 34–38. Copyright © 1997 NAEYC.

Who's in the Family?

Excerpted from *Lessons from Turtle Island*

Family structures in many traditional Native American cultures differ from the nuclear family organization in many American homes. Grandparents, aunts, and uncles are all integral parts of the family. In my Lakota upbringing, the main responsibility of parents was to love and provide sustenance for their children. Grandparents, aunts, and uncles took the important roles of teachers and disciplinarians. This does not mean that parents did not also teach and provide discipline, but primarily they gave unconditional love and support while grandparents, aunts, and uncles concerned themselves with teaching and guidance. In the Lakota culture, aunties are also considered to be a child's mothers, and uncles are their fathers.

Sometimes high school students ask me how many wives I have. They have trouble understanding the differences in family structures. In terms of mainstream culture, I am married and have a wife. In Lakota society, on the other hand, I have a partner who completes me and is called my "half-side." We have children together. Her sisters are considered to be my wives because my responsibility is to teach and discipline her sisters' children. I am called "grandfather" by the children of my nieces and nephews. This closely aligned family structure does not mean, though, that Lakota men have more than one partner, or half-side.

When schools call the family of a Native American child to come to school for a conference, they should not be surprised if an uncle, aunt, or grandparent also comes. That is their role. If the school tries to exclude this important family member, it can create a barrier between the school and the family. Schools should let families decide who needs to be at the conference and thus foster cooperation and support between home and school.

Educators should also realize that not all Native American families are part of traditional, extended families. Many have assimilated into mainstream society and have family structures and roles that are similar to the dominant culture. Schools cannot make assumptions about any child's family structure. That is why it is so important for teachers to get to know the families of the children they teach.

CB

Talking about families gives us many opportunities to focus on our commonalities as people. As we share multicultural books about families in our classrooms, children quickly perceive that children from other races and cultures also have families that love and nurture them.

Unfortunately, in many cases the only images children see of Native peoples are violent ones. The stories they hear are of marauding Indians attacking peaceful pioneers. At an educator's conference on the Oneida reservation in Wisconsin, conference organizer Brian Doxtater commented, "Why are warrior images the only ones people ever have of us? Why don't they ever see us as fathers and husbands and teachers and doctors?" This is a question all educators must take to heart, including those of us working with the youngest children.

Adapted from G.W. Jones & S. Moomaw, *Lessons from Turtle Island: Native Curriculum in Early Childhood Classrooms* (St. Paul, MN: Redleaf, 2002), 65–67. Copyright © 2002 G.W. Jones & S. Moomaw. (www.redleafpress.org) Reprinted with permission.

Ann Pelo and Fran Davidson

20

Partnership-Building Strategies

Excerpted from *That's Not Fair!*

Activism projects naturally grow out of an antibias, multicultural curriculum. Keeping parents and families involved in and informed about classroom activities, including activism, is key to building an open and honest connection between home and school.

Create a program that is relevant to family cultures

Teachers have the responsibility to learn about the cultures of children's families and to reflect those in the classroom. The values and goals of children's families and the communities in which they live significantly shape their approaches to activism projects. For example, they affect what children have experienced and understand about social injustice and social change.

When teachers truly collaborate with parents, rather than seeing themselves as experts who relay information, families participate actively in the classroom rather than passively receiving teachers' services. And when families are actively

involved in their children's classrooms, then activism projects can't help but be grounded in the children's cultures and community.

Teachers may find that they share many values with children's families and that it is easy for them to build their classroom around those values. Sometimes, though, teachers discover that the dispositions that families want their children to develop are quite different than the dispositions that they seek to foster. Conflicts of values and goals, whether small or large, are bound to come up when a teacher begins to work with children to identify and address issues of unfairness. At times like these, it's the teacher's job to understand the reasons behind these different wishes and to find or create common ground with parents.

Fran: In my classroom, I valued long stretches of play, interspersed with meetings to debrief and plan more play. However, many of the families at Madrona valued direct teaching as a way to pass on cultural values and strategies: they viewed preschool as a preparation for life. And they liked the idea of sharing what they were teach-

ing their children at home with others in the preschool. This was a way to bring their culture into the classroom and to provide enrichment for other children and adults. They took great pride in assembling materials and setting up a learning station for a lesson in origami, for example, or preparing latkes, working on a quilt, or learning the basics of carpentry.

I respected families' goals for their children and wanted to be responsive to their requests, so I worked with parents to build a daily flow that allowed for both play and direct teaching. This balance was negotiated at parent meetings, where the importance of play was a regular topic of conversation, as was cultural relevancy. In the course of processing these values and priorities, the parents and I decided to set aside space in the art room in which parents could instruct children.

We agreed that participation in these activities would be a choice for children, never a requirement. I coached parents about ways to make the activities feasible for young children. As structured activities led by parents became part of every day, children began to stop by, first to observe and then to participate. I noticed that

© BmPorter/Don Franklin

these supervised and structured activities were more attractive to children who had particularly low energy than to children whose play energy was abundant and focused. I learned to welcome these activities not only as a source of cultural enrichment but also as a haven for wandering, scattered energy.

Because parents were learning to value and respect the children's play, and because Fran was learning the value of cultural sharing and enrichment, everyone was open to negotiating a way for both to happen in the classroom.

Ask parents directly about their values and goals

When teachers set the tone for open, honest discussion about values and beliefs, they create an atmosphere in which a range of ideas and feelings are honored. Begin seeking out parents' values, beliefs, and ideas when a family first enrolls in a program.

On the enrollment form itself, parents can be asked to share their goals and hopes for their children, as well as to describe their cultural heroes and important family days. Home visits by the teacher continue this sort of sharing.

Some teachers devise ways for families to tell their cultural stories, knowing that their values are often embedded in them. For example, once some level of trust has developed amongst families, and between families and teachers, an entire parent meeting can be built around sharing cultural stories. Teachers can ask families to think about questions like, "What are some important beliefs and traditions that your family life is built around?" and "What are the ways in which you pass those traditions from one generation to the next?" Or teachers can ask families to describe their family sense of humor, or primary celebrations, or the origins of a name. Teachers can ask family members to bring a photo or memento to share during the meeting; this can spark rich conversations

among parents and teachers, sometimes revealing the interplay of past and present and hopes for the future.

Or, in a less public way, parents can be invited to respond to a questionnaire that will give teachers a cultural profile of the children and their families. Questions may range from "Who lives in your home? Include family pets!" to asking for specific ways a family's home culture (including beliefs and values) can be supported and reflected in the classroom.

Fran: At Madrona, there were monthly antibias meetings where big issues like cultural values and the impact of bias on family cultures were discussed. These were important meetings, but not everyone could attend. So I developed the Family Story as a strategy to include a greater number of voices in our discussions and planning.

Knowing that families have different strengths and skills when it comes to communicating, I suggested several ways in which they could offer up their cultural stories: They could write their stories, they could record their stories on audiotape, or they could share their stories with me during our home visit. Or they could even share them with me as we chatted before or after school. Regardless of the mode, I invited each of them to "describe your family's history, what you like to celebrate, your values and priorities, and your cultural identity." Once done, these stories informed much of what happened in the co-op throughout the year. And although I was the custodian of the stories, and the spokesperson on behalf of each family, I brought this rich data to board meetings, to curriculum planning meetings (both parents and teachers), and to event planning meetings to ensure that the multiple perspectives of the co-op members were represented. And I often asked for clarification of the values and beliefs embedded in these cultural stories as

A World of Difference

we navigated the often bumpy terrain of a social activism project. What I learned helped me understand what sorts of activism projects they would be likely to support, as well as helping me make bridges between home and school in other ways.

Be honest, clear, and forthcoming about your own values and goals

Conversations about values and beliefs call on teachers to open their hearts, to share personal experiences, to be known by families in a more intimate way, and to acknowledge the possibility that they may hold values different from those held by the families in their programs. Even teachers who easily discuss such difficult developmental topics as biting or toilet learning generally steer away from these more vulnerable and risky conversations about values and beliefs. However, teachers' work grows from their values and beliefs; this is particularly true of activism projects.

It is disingenuous for teachers to pretend that their values and beliefs do not play a significant part in their work with young children, particularly when it comes to activism issues. Activism projects are not simply about supporting the children's social, emotional, and cognitive development; they are not simply about children's awareness of unfairness, but also—and significantly—about teachers' deeply held beliefs about injustice and inequity in the classroom, in the community, and in the larger world.

When teachers are honest and straightforward with parents about what they value as social activists and about their intentions to support activism with the children, they can build deep and authentic relationships with parents—not necessarily always based on complete agree-

ment, but definitely based on trust. Parents know that the teacher has no hidden agenda that they must ferret out or guard against; they can talk openly about the values and beliefs that undergird the life of the classroom.

Whenever teachers meet with families, whether informally in hallways, classrooms, or playgrounds or more formally during home visits, open houses, parent meetings, or conferences, they can make clear what they value about children's growth and learning and the ways that activism feeds that growth and learning.

Ann: I seek to build a foundation of honesty and openness with families, beginning with easy topics like what I really appreciate about their children, why I do this work, why I stay at Hilltop. I try to focus our early conversations on what my goals are for children—not just the "academic" learning that I hope they experience (and on which parents place high value) but also the social and emotional learning that I prize. These sorts of conversations build relationships that can carry the weight of the heavy stuff, the feelings and experiences that give rise to activism projects. I continue to feel shy with families, especially talking about myself, yet every year I am rewarded by the response. Parents seem to deeply appreciate knowing who I am—which really isn't surprising, since I'm with their children for many hours each week. And they typically respond by sharing their hopes and values with me, often relaying their struggles, hopes, concerns, and dreams for their children.

During these conversations, teachers can begin educating parents about the ways in which activism grows from children's developmental tasks even when children are very young. For example, 2-year-old children respond to unfairness in unmis-

takable ways. Claudia fiercely takes back the teddy bear that Lucy snatched out of her stroller. Ian screams to let everyone know that he is outraged that Deirdre knocked him to the ground. LaVonna growls as she yanks on Willie's hair after he pushes her aside at the water table. Snatching, screaming, growling, and pulling hair are a few of the many ways that very young children let one another and adults know that they object to unfairness.

Teachers can point this out to parents, communicating ways that they support young children's response to unfairness: "When LaVonna pulled Willie's hair, I saw that she was mad that he forced her out of the way at the water table. I told her, 'That really made you mad when Willie took your place at the water table. You pulled his hair to let him know. But pulling hair really hurts people, so next time say no in your biggest voice. I'll come help you and Willie solve your problem.' I wanted to help LaVonna learn a new way to stand up for herself when something unfair happens. I gave her a name for her feelings, validated her thinking, and then offered a better solution—an action plan—for her. This is how even very young children learn to work together to address unfairness."

Four-year-olds seem to be on "unfairness watch" full time. The refrain, "It's not fair!" echoes through preschool classrooms as children notice inequity, bias, and injustice. This is a critical time for families and teachers to acknowledge children's feelings, extend their thinking, and help shape thoughtful actions instead of impulsive reactions. Teachers can help parents understand that 4- and 5-year-olds are developmentally eager to take on issues of unfairness. Teachers can point out that adults nurture children to care about other people and the environment when they encourage them to be ac-

© Subjects & Predicates

tive rather than passive or indifferent in the face of unfairness. They can remind parents that 4- and 5-year-old children are stepping into a solid sense of their power, competence, and goodness, and that adults can support that developmental work by supporting children's observations of and responses to injustice.

Encourage dialogue among parents

Some parents may come to an understanding of and involvement in activism projects through their conversations with other parents rather than with teachers. It may be the insights of other parents that bring credibility to the idea of young children's being activists. Or it may be that as parents talk together, they come to a shared understanding of the role that activism plays in their children's growth and learning.

During parent meetings, parents can share feelings and insights about emerging activism projects with one another; this can happen both spontaneously, as families and teachers talk together about children's experiences in the classroom, and intentionally, as teachers plan for parent discussion. If a family misses a parent meeting, teachers can ask another family to fill them in on the discussion and decisions; this provides an opportunity for parents to exchange ideas and to stretch one another's thinking.

Teachers can encourage dialogue among parents in other ways. They can create a regular space in the school's newsletter for parents' views. They can plan activities for parents at school open houses and other gatherings in which parents talk in small groups about specific issues.

Fran: During the Persian Gulf war of the early 1990s, I became acutely aware of how difficult it is to honor families' values when those values are different from mine. In the classroom I emphasized peaceful resolutions to conflicts and talked often with the children about elements of peace. Most families felt comfortable with these classroom conversations and with our language about "peaceful solutions to problems." But when our conversations about peace expanded to include

discussion of the Persian Gulf war, some families became uneasy.

Many of the children came to school wanting to talk about weapons and destruction and their own feelings of vulnerability. They wanted to figure out how the war could be ended so that "people wouldn't get hurt." Yet there were others for whom war seemed exciting. Their families talked about the necessity of war to overthrow oppressors and to protect and free people. War-related issues showed up frequently at outdoor time, in dramatic play, and in the block area.

This was a really uncomfortable time for me and for many of the parents. Passions flowed strongly in both directions. The fierce differences among families grew from their experiences and feelings about war and freedom and oppression. Because our school was built around diversity, we could not sidestep differences of beliefs. Parents were talking about the war and their beliefs about it all the time— in the hallways, in the front yard, in the classrooms. There seemed no way for us adults to come together on how to approach conversations about the war with the children, other than emphasizing that we all hoped it would end soon. Despite the tension, I was glad we were having conversations about our conflicting values rather than avoiding one another.

Maintain communication with parents throughout an activism project

When an activism project begins to grow, it is important that teachers maintain close communication with families about the children's thinking. Certainly, some children keep their families posted about what happens at school, and some parents are able to hang out in the classroom regularly enough that they are aware of the ways in which projects are unfolding. However, teachers need

A World of Difference

to be intentional about keeping parents informed about the course of activism projects, so that parents are aware of what their children are exploring and how they can be involved.

Nurture adult dispositions for activism

Some parents already see themselves as seasoned activists, while others do not identify themselves as activists at all. Teachers can nurture parents' dispositions to act in the face of unfairness at the same time that they nurture those dispositions in the children. When parents come to see themselves as activists, they are often eager to build partnerships with teachers in support of children's activism.

An important aspect of teachers' work involves educating parents about child development and children's learning and about issues in the community that impact families. Teachers have important information to share, and they are often eager to educate parents.

But parents also have knowledge in some of the same areas. They, too, are preparing their children to be successful in the world beyond home and preschool. Just as teachers are eager to share their expertise, so are parents eager to advocate on behalf of their children.

It certainly is not teachers' intent to silence parents. However, teachers may unwittingly promote one-way communication and education by talking at parents or taking every opportunity to fill parents with ideas and advice. Parents soon learn to show up and listen rather than show up and contribute. To genuinely include parents in classroom projects and activities, teachers need to create a more equitable balance between talking and listening.

When teachers deliberately shift from the role of educating parents to the role of collaborating with parents, opportunities for teachers and families to work together will naturally grow.

As soon as an activism project begins to bubble up—when children first notice and express strong feelings about unfairness—teachers can begin to comment to parents about what they observe in the children's behavior. They can invite parents to pay attention to children's feelings and to think about how their children understand unfairness. Teachers can ask parents what they observe about their children at home and at school in connection with the burgeoning issue.

Fran: At a parent cooperative preschool, parents expect to be "in the know." That's a great thing, because it keeps parents attuned to what's happening in the classroom, but it also has its drawbacks.

I experienced some of those drawbacks when I tried to build curriculum around children's play, experimenting with the ideas of emergent curriculum. This was hard for parents. They wanted to know, from the beginning of the year, what was in store not only for the children but also for themselves. They had contributed to the monthly curriculum planning, they were there as assistants in the classroom, and they were invested in seeing their curriculum plans come to life.

I began to coach parents to notice what the children were doing, asking them to think about why the children were doing it. I invited them to document the children's play. I put a notebook in every room of our school and asked parents to record what they saw the children doing and saying.

As parents stepped into the practice of recording what they saw and heard, they began to pay more attention to what the children were really doing. They began to understand the ideas I

had been trying to communicate about emergent curriculum and could identify the ways in which children worked on issues of unfairness on their own, outside the activities we planned. At parent meetings and during classroom time, parents began to share with one another their hypotheses and conjectures about the meaning of children's play. They took on the challenge of noticing and communicating what seemed to be important to the children.

At the co-op, asking parents to document children's play was a way to educate parents and to enrich the dialogue we had with one another. Parents became more active members of the teaching team, more willing to identify issues and offer their skills and resources.

As they become aware of children's feelings, parents may become more aware of their own feelings and ideas about injustice. Recognizing that parents, like their children, need opportunities to reflect on their feelings and ideas and to collaborate with others, teachers can ask parents about their experiences with activism. Some parents may have forgotten passions and commitments from an earlier time; other parents may not see their work with churches, schools, and community organizations as activism. When parents reconnect with their histories of activism, they more deeply understand their children's work for fairness.

As an unfairness issue gives rise to an activism project, teachers can ask parents questions like, "How does your family talk about this issue?" and "Do you think that this is an important problem to solve?" These sorts of questions can encourage parents to think about unfairness issues in new ways. Once parents begin identifying themselves as active participants in a project rather than passive observers of it, they become increasingly eager to support their children's work as change-makers.

When teachers authentically involve families in activism projects, there is a good chance that projects will grow in ways that teachers don't expect. For example, during a project about homelessness in Ann's class one year, one family offered to organize a toy and clothing collection for children at a homeless shelter. This was not part of Ann's original thinking about the project, but grew out of that family's deep support for the children's passionate efforts to help people who were homeless. Ann initially resisted the idea of a toy and clothing collection, mostly because it wasn't in her plans. After realizing that her resistance was based on her reluctance to share her position at the hub of the project, Ann was (sheepishly) able to welcome the family's offer to coordinate a toy and clothing collection, appreciating the family's involvement.

When teachers are willing to change their minds in response to parents' ideas and misgivings, they enhance the trust that families feel in their partnerships. Parents experience teachers' taking their ideas seriously and teachers' willingness to learn about and accommodate values and ideas different from their own. This willingness is at the heart of cultivating authentic partnerships with parents.

Barriers to partnerships

Although many teachers say that they value working closely with families and complain when it doesn't happen, many factors discourage parents from becoming involved. What keeps teachers from being able to achieve full partnership with parents? What prevents this open sharing and discussion of different perspectives that can support flourishing activism projects in early childhood programs? The barriers to authentic partnership with parents

can be circumstantial or attitudinal. Here are some of the ones we've observed:

• **Teachers have limited time and energy.**

• **Teachers may have set expectations about parent involvement.** The expectation that parent involvement ought to take only certain forms gets in the way of true collaboration by applying a one-size-fits-all mentality to an issue that cries out for inclusive, flexible, and creative thinking.

• **Teachers have developed habits and routines.**

• **Partnerships require that teachers share their authority.** Teachers need to make room for parents; include them in decision making; share their thoughts with parents; listen openly to parents' ideas; and invite parents to contribute ideas, resources, and honest feedback.

• **Teachers and parents may experience language, culture, and class differences.** Teachers have the responsibility to investigate these differences and understand how they affect their relationships with parents.

Fran: I really thought a lot about cultural differences when I thought about how to involve families in the classroom. Teachers are gatekeepers of sorts, deciding what will and what will not happen in the classroom. As a White woman of European descent, I was concerned about occupying the gatekeeper role, especially in a classroom with children from a range of cultures. Some of the questions I found it useful to ask myself were, How might my membership in the dominant culture impede the flow of other people's cultural agendas into the classroom? What behaviors and expectations of mine might get in the way of building trust, stifling the urge in parents to share with me their dreams

and visions for their children? What could I do to be an ally for parents of color? What about me would invite them to share the hard issues and how they would impact their children's futures?

• **Working parents are typically not available during the school day.** Without deliberate attention to the particular challenges of involving working parents, chasms can open that separate parents from their children's daily life.

• **Some parents may be consumed by day-to-day survival issues.** Some parents are legitimately focused on survival—feeding their children, maintaining or finding a place to sleep each night, getting medical care when someone in the family is sick.

• **Parents and teachers fear being judged.** These worries cause an undercurrent of tension that promotes distance rather than partnership between teachers and parents.

• **Parents pay teachers in child care programs.** This conflict can be exacerbated when parents, struggling themselves, nonetheless are substantially better compensated than teachers.

Parents and teachers both want what's best for children, and for the most part these dreams are much the same. This is revealed when parents and teachers figure out ways to come together to share beliefs and hopes, values and goals. When authentic partnerships are forged as an outcome of this sharing, very little can stand in the way of parents and teachers collaborating to support flourishing activism projects.

Adapted from A. Pelo & F. Davidson, *That's Not Fair! A Teacher's Guide to Activism with Young Children* (St. Paul, MN: Redleaf, 2000), 108–24. Copyright © 2000 Ann Pelo & Fran Davidson. (www.redleafpress.org) Reprinted with permission.

IV

Regarding Social Class and Family Circumstances

Not only does an antibias learning environment include nonstereo-typed images of many races, cultures, or types of families; it also sends the message that all kinds of work are valuable. In stories, pictures, play materials, and other aspects of the curriculum, young children's experiences should extend beyond professional, white-collar jobs and familiar "community helper" roles such as police officer and firefighter. Children should have opportunities to develop knowledge of and respect for a wide range of occupations and work (Ramsey; Taus). Likewise, as teachers we should ensure that children encounter images and information about all kinds of places to live—homes that are familiar to them as well as those that differ from the kind they know best (Wellhousen).

At the same time, we need to consider the varying needs and abilities that children may have as a result of their socioeconomic background and family circumstances. Readings in this section consider how we can meet the needs of children living in poverty (Helm & Lang), mi-grant children and families (Duarte & Rafanello), families with an issue such as alcohol or drug abuse (Rice & Kaplan-Sanoff), and children who are experiencing loss and disruption because of divorce (Sammons & Lewis).

Be It Ever So Humble
Developing a Study of Homes for Today's Diverse Society

A unit on homes, appropriate in light of how important home can be to young children, is common in many early childhood curriculums. Unfortunately, teachers often present concepts and implement activities related to this theme that are outdated or biased. Seefeldt (1993) has found that teachers overlook the importance of planning experiences specifically for and with the children in their classroom. Rather than altering lessons and activities to reflect the constant societal changes that impact children's lives, many teachers repeat the same preplanned, packaged units year after year. This results in developmentally inappropriate practices as well as the perpetuation of biases.

Concepts introduced about homes to children that may be incorrect, outdated, or biased include the following:

1. All children have homes.

2. A home is a house in a neighborhood.

3. The immediate members of the child's family all live together.

4. Children have only one place they call home.

5. Home is a safe, loving, good place to be.

These assumptions are based on stereotyped concepts and ideas about what constitutes a home. While some people may believe that these assumptions reflect the way the world should be and that they serve as a standard for which one should strive, the fact remains that these stereotypes do not hold true for a large percentage of the population. Perpetuating any stereotype is not in the best interest of children.

The antibias approach is very effective in teaching teachers and children to challenge stereotypes associated with characteristics of groups of people, such as gender, ethnicity, culture, age, or disability. A true antibias approach includes confronting all stereotypes; therefore, an approach to studying the diversity of children's homes is needed.

To plan a unit on homes without bias, teachers first must familiarize themselves with the homes and home lives of the children they teach. They must be especially sensitive to those children who come from homes that are unfamiliar and different from their own. After obtaining this background information, teachers can initiate the unit on homes with the help of the children. Learning centers can be established and reorganized to reflect the theme. Children's understanding of homes can be broadened through visual displays and children's literature. When teachers take the time and effort to plan and implement themes without bias, everyone benefits.

Places children call home

Children today have a wide variety of places that may be home to them. Sometimes home is a temporary place to stay, such as a shelter for homeless families or a shelter for women and children who are victims of family violence. The National Coalition for the Homeless (Stronge 1992) estimates the number of homeless children between 500,000 and 750,000 annually. McCormick and Holden (1992) interviewed families and teachers of homeless children. When parents were asked what early childhood teachers need to know about families living in shelters, they responded that:

1. Children are embarrassed about their situation

2. Parents in shelters care about their children the same as parents in permanent housing

3. Teacher requests to donate or bring items from home create a great hardship for the homeless family

Teachers who worked with homeless children and their families reported:

1. Play is particularly important for homeless children because they usually have no designated places to play outside of school

2. Children need choices and challenges in a supportive environment

3. Teachers should offer parents patience and sensitivity

Another population of children without a place to consistently call home is transient children. This includes children who move from place to place within the same community, often due to economic hard-ship, as well as those who move seasonally, such as children of migrant-worker families. These children and their homes should be recognized—without bias—in the curriculum. Of course, many children whose parents are divorced have *two* homes.

Initiating a unit on homes

Once a teacher is thoroughly familiar with what constitutes the concept of home for each of her students, she can begin the homes unit. A web is an excellent way to initiate themes (Krogh 1990; Wortham 1994). It reveals what children already know about a subject and what they would like to learn (see "A Sample Web on Homes").

After developing the web, teachers and children can take a walk around the school and community. They can discuss and take notes on types of houses, colors, structures, roof lines, names of various parts of homes, and so on. Upon return to the classroom, they can add new ideas or concepts to the web.

As the unit continues, develop other related webs, such as "Work people do at home," "Sounds at home," "Rooms and their uses," and "Animal homes." Remember, all webs should be approached from an antibias rather than stereotyped perspective.

Visual displays

The focal point for this approach is visual displays in the classroom. As teachers assemble homes for a display, they should make sure the concepts of homes presented are authentic, not stereotypical. Pictures may come from a file of illustrations/pictures collected, from photographs of children's homes taken during home visits, or from children's drawings. Visual displays introduce children to geographical, regional, and cultural differences in

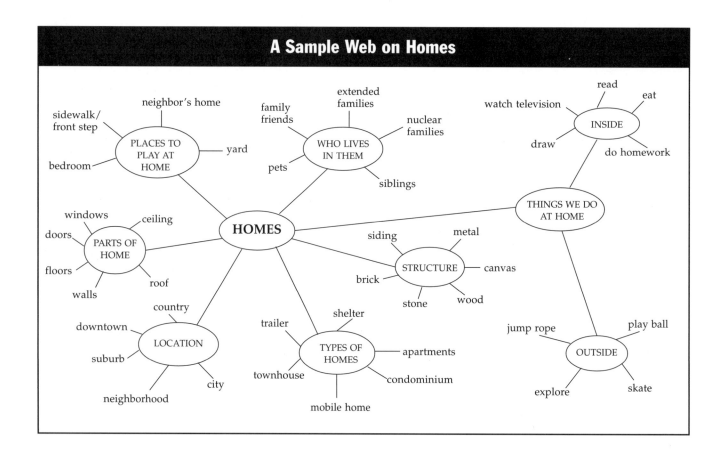

A Sample Web on Homes

homes. Remember, displays also should be created without introducing or reinforcing stereotypes about groups of people and the way they live in the present or past.

Learning centers

Many learning centers can be created or adapted to reflect the home theme. As children play, teachers have the opportunity to observe and listen to their interactions. These observations provide additional insight into children's ideas about home. Teachers should allow children to take the lead in making decisions, requesting additional, related materials, or suggesting activities. Once teachers begin collecting and organizing materials and children begin interacting with them, the possibilities are endless.

Children's literature

Books are a powerful means for presenting messages to children. Through books children learn about the variety of homes and the diverse activities that go on within them. They see families and homes that look familiar as well as those that may be very different. Introducing homes through literature teaches children there is no one right place to live and provides a lesson in understanding and tolerance of others. Teachers can choose appropriate titles from a large collection of books on homes and related topics.

Conclusion

Children have strong emotional attachments to the places they call home. Compared to previous generations, fewer children are raised today in single-family dwellings.

Obtaining Background Information

The first step in planning an antibias unit on homes is teacher preparation. Teachers can familiarize themselves with the homes, families, and community of the children through home visits. Home visits are beneficial for reasons other than obtaining background information. According to Hildebrand, "A home visit is the single most effective act that can be performed for developing harmonious relationships between parents and teachers and between the child and teacher" (1993, 338).

Through home visits, teachers can learn

• about the child (interests, fears, attitude toward school, eating and sleeping habits, sources of cognitive stimulation);

• about the parent (attitudes about school, discipline techniques, educational background, perception of parent and teacher roles); and

• about the family (lifestyle, roles of family members, sibling relationships, preferred leisure activities).

Home visits also provide parents with information about the early childhood setting and what is expected of their child. Visits should make parents feel comfortable and welcome at school and should encourage their involvement in their child's education.

Kostelnik, Soderman, and Whiren (1993) offer helpful suggestions for making home visits successful. First, clearly identify the purpose of the visit and share this information with the family. Next, plan how time during the home visit will be spent. While parents are completing forms and interest surveys, you can get to know the child. Take along playdough and crayons and paper to involve the child during the visit. Also take a camera to snap pictures of the child and the family in their home. Finally, follow up appointments with a letter home, a thank-you note, or a phone call.

Sensitive teachers can better meet the needs of children by becoming familiar with their homes and by addressing the similarities and differences among homes. Appropriate activities and resources help teachers model acceptance of all children and their homes.

References

Hildebrand, V. 1993. *Management of child development centers.* New York: Macmillan.
Kostelnik, M., A. Soderman, & A. Whiren. 1993. *Developmentally appropriate programs in early childhood education.* New York: Merrill.

Krogh, S. 1990. *The integrated early childhood curriculum.* New York: McGraw-Hill.
McCormick, K., & R. Holden. 1992. Homeless children: A special challenge. *Young Children* 47 (6): 61–67.
Seefeldt, C. 1993. *Social studies for the preschool-primary child.* New York: Merrill.
Stronge, J.H., ed. 1992. *Educating homeless children and adolescents: Evaluating policy and practice.* Newbury Park, CA: Sage.
Wortham, S. 1994. *Early childhood curriculum: Developmental bases for learning and teaching.* New York: Merrill.

The Stress of Poverty

Excerpted from *Teaching and Learning in a Diverse World*

People who have at least some financial security are often unaware of the role affluence plays in our lives. A number of years ago I worked for a federally funded child care center in a low-income neighborhood. At first I was impatient with families and fellow teachers who always seemed to have "a crisis a minute." After a while, however, I realized how much my crisis-free life was dependent on my relative affluence. If my car broke down, I could get it repaired right away and did not experience weeks of relying on friends or public transportation. When I needed to go to a doctor, I made an appointment, went, and was back in an hour or so. I did not have to spend a day waiting in a county hospital emergency room to get the same service. Many requests from schools reflect this same blind spot. Money for field trips, requests for supplies, help with typing and photocopying a newsletter all require money or some equipment that may seem trivial to middle-class parents but may be a real burden to poor or working-class parents.

To clarify our assumptions about different social-class groups and the causes of unequal income distribution, we can also ask ourselves the following questions: What images come to my mind when I hear that someone is a sanitation worker? a doctor? an assembly-line worker? an executive? a maid? a manager? What do I assume about the race, gender, education, and character of people in different jobs? Which people do I assume are more like me? Whom do I want to get to know? What are my assumptions about why some people are affluent and others are poor? Do I think it is fair? inevitable? Whom or what do I blame for the disparities in wealth and opportunity? poor people? wealthy people? the system?

Despite its egalitarian principles, the United States has been moving *away from,* not toward, more equitable distribution of wealth, especially during the last two decades (Huston 1991; Thompson & Hupp 1992). During the 1980s the numbers of children growing up in very poor (deprived) households and in very affluent (luxurious) households increased, whereas the number of children growing up in "frugal" (i.e., working-class) or "comfortable" (i.e., middle-class) households declined.

One quarter of all children under the age of 6 are living below the national poverty level (National Center for Children in Poverty 1996). Most analysts attribute this trend to the reduced numbers of well-paid semi-skilled and low-skilled jobs, cutbacks in federal programs that supported poor families before the 1980s, and the changes in family configuration that have resulted in higher numbers of female-headed households. This last *cause* may also be an *effect,* because the lack of well-paying jobs has reduced the number of men who are gainfully employed and can provide for their families (Wilson 1987), meaning that more women are raising children on their own.

In a series of interviews (Cook & Fine 1995) poor African American mothers talked about some of their dilemmas. One mother described the impossible task of working and providing adequate supervision for her children, one of whom had already been in jail on a drug-related charge:

I think I'm a good parent. I don't take drugs. . . . I don't have drugs in the house so it's not something he's seen me [do] . . . then society says, well, you're supposed to know what your children are doing at all times. It's not so. . . . I take two hours to travel to work, two hours to travel back, and I'm on my feet 10 hours a day. So that's like 14 hours a day that I'm out of the house. (127)

The mothers also described their anger and frustration at the disregard and scorn that they encounter at institutions such as the schools. "Oh . . . they're uppity. They're uppity. . . . I feel if I didn't [finish school] you shouldn't sneer at me. . . . And I believe if they come as beings as one, no one higher than the other, you can find more parents coming in, coming in helping" (128). What is striking about this quote is that despite her frustrations, the mother was still expressing some optimism—if the school personnel would treat parents as equal partners, then the parents would participate in the school.

These mothers also have to constantly monitor their children and fight the forces of peer pressure. Cook and Fine (1995) point out that the usual advice—"Just say no" and "Don't fight"—is "wholly inadequate to the context. These women cannot, on a daily basis, narrate the lessons of remote liberalism so many of us try to preach from afar" (132). Mothers described how they have to help their children learn how to live in a world filled with temptation and how to "associate with the 'less than desirable' individuals in their community without offending them, yet also know how to escape them at appropriate times" (134).

These mothers are caught in a terrible bind. Their children need enormous support, monitoring, and advice in order to negotiate the unrelenting hardships of growing up poor—situations that would terrify and paralyze most White middle-class families. Yet the jobs that they can find usually pay little, have long and inflexible hours, and often require several hours of commuting.

So these mothers are less available than their middle-class counterparts for supervising and supporting their children. Cook and Fine challenge parents and teachers who are protected by racial and economic privilege:

Imagine. . . a context in which you can no longer lie to your child [about being safe] because she hears shots out the window; where public institutions, your only hope, evince a strong ambivalence, sometimes antipathy, toward you and your kin; where the most enduring public institutions are the prison and the juvenile justice system, and the most reliable economic system involves underground drug trafficking. Imagine further that despite your best attempts to get your children to believe in "what could be," your children see little hope for themselves. . . . What kind of childrearing practices would you invent? (137)

Against this horrific backdrop of every imaginable frustration and indignity, these women fight bravely on.

References

Cook, D.A., & M. Fine. 1995. "Motherwit": Childrearing lessons from African American mothers of low income. In *Children and families "at promise": Deconstructing the discourse of risk*, eds. B.B. Swadener and S. Lubeck, 118–142. Albany, NY: SUNY Press.

Huston, A.C. 1991. Children in poverty: Developmental and policy issues. In *Children in poverty: Child development and public policy*, ed. A.C. Huston, 1–22. Cambridge, England: Cambridge University Press.

National Center for Children in Poverty. 1996. *One in four: America's youngest poor* (Abridged). New York: Columbia School of Public Health.

Thompson, T., & S.C. Hupp, eds. 1992. *Saving children at risk: Poverty and disabilities*. Newbury Park, CA: Sage.

Wilson, W. 1987. *The truly disadvantaged: The inner city, the underclass, and public policy*. Chicago: University of Chicago Press.

Kay Taus

Valuing Different Kinds of Work

I grew up, like most of us, with the idea that so-called "intellectual work" was much more valuable than physical labor. Everything in this society teaches us to devalue certain kinds of work and to devalue the people who do it as well. Since my father was a carpenter at one time and a TV repairman at another, I grew up with ambivalence. I saw his skilled hands at work yet sensed the prevailing attitudes of the society that negated his skill. I also went to a high school where the majority of other kids were wealthy. I deeply resented the class biases that existed.

Now, as a teacher, I have children of very many different class backgrounds. I want to develop a respect for different kids of work and an understanding that families have a great variation in the style of life they can afford. Even very young children have already begun to make judgments about their classmates based on clothing or the number of trips to nearby Disneyland.

Georgianna Duarte and Donna Rafanello

23

The Migrant Child

Maria and Sergio yawn loudly as their mother Rosa kisses them lightly on the cheek and tells them it's time to get up. It's 4:30 A.M. and the Rodriguez family of eight begins their day. Rosa prepares breakfast and prods the four older boys to rise and get washed up. The boys will join their parents picking chilies in the fields. Although Maria and Sergio, the youngest of the six children, are too young to work in the fields, they must rise early to travel the hour's bus ride to their Head Start program. Maria and Sergio watch their brothers dress in the heavy clothing that protects from the insects and pesticides in the field. The temperature today will reach 100 degrees, and the boys cry in frustration about all the clothing they must wear. Finally their father turns on the lights and the conversation turns to the weather.

Who is the migrant child?

Rafael Guerra, a migrant educator and former migrant worker, describes the invisibility of migrant children's lives. "I think of the migrant child as a handicapped child. He's somebody else's problem. They let him go from place to place and then he moves down the road and becomes somebody else's problem. Out of sight, out of mind" (Buirski 1994, 142). The children of migrant farmworkers—"invisible children"—number over 2.8 million (Velasquez 1994). Numbers are approximate because no system exists to provide a reliable count or profile of migrant children (Martin 1996). Each year more than two million seasonal farmworkers, in nearly every region of the country, provide the manual labor necessary to grow and harvest the fruits and vegetables we eat. Of this group, an estimated 900,000 are migrants—workers who travel from one place to another following the harvest (Rothenberg 1998).

The majority of migrant workers in the United States are Hispanic men with families (Leon 1996) who move at least once a year. The economic demands of the work often require that families uproot their routines several times during an annual crop cycle (U.S. Department of Health and Human Services [DHHS] 1994). This trend has increased in recent years due to weather instability.

One of migrant families' greatest strengths is the extended family. Cousins, aunts, uncles, and grandparents often travel together for work. This extended family provides a strong foundation through recounted stories, songs, and family traditions. Stories from their homelands are told over and over again, and family recipes are passed down. Traveling together serves to further strengthen the bond. "The fact of their movement—like nomads they follow the crop—intensifies their bond. The constant dislocation precludes any real connection to the society around them. This moving family has only itself as an anchor, creating a tightly knit but otherwise vulnerable community" (Buirski 1994, 7).

Home is where the work is

The quality and availability of migrant housing vary greatly. Nationwide, the housing for many of these families is expensive and poor in quality. Growers often provide substandard housing, an array of trailers, or small farmhouses. If the grower provides housing, it frequently has many restrictions. For example, in many areas housing is available only to men, or cooking is prohibited. Regional communities are frequently reluctant to lease or rent to migrant families because of prejudice, misinformation, or reluctance to offer short-term leases. Consequently, many families double up or live in cars or low-cost hotels.

The mobility of the migrant family takes its toll on the children. When children's homes keep moving and are determined by changing employment, their development can suffer. And constant moving may contribute to feelings of mistrust and isolation in young children. They may have difficulty forming attachments with other children and adults.

We know that children thrive in safe, secure educational environments. However, few programs are available to the migrant child and family in which the needs of the entire family are addressed. In many regions child care programs are reluctant to enroll migrant children because of their transience and unpredictable attendance. Other programs report that they are unsure how to meet the needs of the migrant child.

© José M. Duarte

Migrant Head Start

This article focuses on Migrant Head Start. Today, a total of 25 grantees and 41 delegate agencies provide services in 33 states to more than 30,000 migrant children (DHHS 1999). Migrant Head Start programs are challenged to meet the needs of families in which everyone works and inadequate wages and deplorable living conditions are the norm. Designed to respond to the unique needs of this population, Migrant Head Start programs have helped counter the effects of migrant life on

children and families since 1969. As with many federal programs, however, there are not enough funds to provide care for all eligible children.

Children of migrant workers are a special concern of Head Start because the families are often isolated from community resources and existing networks of services (Zigler & Valentine 1979). By definition, Migrant Head Start families earn more than half of their annual income from agricultural work and move at least once within each two-year period in search of farm work (DHHS

1999). Those who move more often are given priority. Families also must meet Head Start income eligibility guidelines.

Two types of Migrant Head Start grantees serve this population—Home-Based Grantees in the southern part of the United States provide services to families from October through May, while Upstream Grantees provide services as families move northward in search of agricultural work during the spring, summer, and fall months. Families in the Upstream locations rarely have family members who can provide child care outside traditional center hours. Therefore, migrant centers provide extended day services, usually up to 12 hours a day and up to seven days a week during the height of the harvest season. Some grantees open and operate centers for as few as six weeks. There are a number of program options in all areas. Each grantee can select or blend center- and home-based care.

There are several notable differences between migrant and regional Head Start programs. First, more of the children served in Migrant Head Start are infants and toddlers (over 40 percent). Second, regional Head Start programs usually follow the traditional September-to-June school year and run half a day. Migrant Head Start programs open when the families arrive in an area, and they operate as long as there is a need. Local Migrant Head Start programs begin enrolling children as early as March and continue as children arrive in the region.

Hours of operation are based on the needs of families served rather than on a traditional school model. Programs sometimes operate from 4:00 A.M. until midnight and may serve children ages 6 weeks to 5 years. Programs are bilingual and bicultural, to fit the needs of the Spanish-speaking and non-White migrant population. In many areas, increasing numbers of Central American children are present.

Health, education, and nutrition specialists follow children as their parents follow the crops, establishing centers wherever families stop to work, and records of children follow them via mail or electronically wherever the families go. These specialists perform an important and useful function for children and families who are isolated from existing programs for many reasons. They provide health care intervention services

Threats to Families' Health

Each year 24,000 children are injured and 300 die as a result of farmwork-related accidents (Rothenberg 1998). In addition to the long hours toiling in the fields, migrant farmworkers and their families are exposed to pesticides and other hazardous materials, motorized machinery, and dangerous tools and vehicles. These frequently surround the living and play spaces of migrant children. Packing sheds and processing plants are often accessible to children as they play.

Children are more likely than adults to be harmed by pesticide exposure. Trini Gomez, a social worker and former migrant worker, reports, "Farmers spray on weekends, families start working again Monday. Kids develop rashes, red eyes, sore throat—blame it on the heat. Upset stomach also. High rate of cancer, and kidney problems" (Buirski 1994, 36). Further, farmworker children, like their parents, are not fully covered by workers' compensation benefits.

The poor physical and mental health of migrant children is often the result of lack of prenatal care and families' existing environmental conditions (Ruducha 1994). Migrant farmworkers and their families are more likely to experience significant maternal and newborn health problems, such as high-risk pregnancy, hypertension, and skin disorders. Infant mortality among California's migrant farmworkers is 30 per 1,000 births, more than double the infant mortality rate for the overall U.S. population (Gaston 1992). In addition, the mortality rate among migrant children is more than 50 percent higher than the already high rate among infants.

The U.S. Department of Health and Human Services found, "The disease patterns of the migrant farmworker population today are similar to those found in the general population of the U.S. well over 60 years ago" (Gaston 1992, 240). Poor nutrition causes dental problems and anemia. Lack of dental care, inaccessibility to mental health care, and lack of substance abuse programs systematically keep migrant families in high-risk health categories. Families have high rates of infectious disease as well as chronic illnesses. The rate of diabetes is as much as 300 percent higher than that of the general population. The life expectancy of migrant farmworkers is estimated to be 49 years, compared to the U.S. national average of 73 years.

Most migrant families do not have health insurance and are frequently ineligible for Medicaid because the time required to process applications may exceed the time the family stays in one location. Further, growers or employers may refuse to document earnings, negatively affecting the family's ability to qualify for programs and assistance.

and accessibility to continued educational services, and they maintain a tracking system between programs.

Staffing poses a major challenge to Migrant Head Start programs. The short and unpredictable seasons and operating hours make recruiting and retaining staff a unique challenge. Equally challenging is the critical need for training and mentoring of

Making a Living

Migrant farmworker families comprise a large population living in extreme poverty. According to Buirski (1994), "Migrant farmworkers have the lowest earning power of all occupational groups in the United States, disease is rampant, and living conditions are squalid" (7). A 1993 study reported that migrant farmworker life still consists mainly of "poverty, hard manual labor, unsanitary living conditions, lack of medical insurance or access to care facilities, high rates of illness, early death, economic uncertainty, and personal humiliation" (DHHS 1993, 25).

Migrant farmworkers remain among the most neglected groups of our nation's poor, and their children grow up facing a constant cycle of poverty. The typical migrant family of five earns less than $5,000 per year (Rothenberg 1998), compared to the typical median household income of $40,816 in the United States (U.S. Bureau of the Census 1999).

Economic necessity is the cause behind most child labor. Despite child labor laws, children as young as 4 work beside their parents, as their hands are more nimble for picking and their backs more supple for bending (Buirski 1994). The educational impact of migrant child labor on children includes school entry at an older age, high dropout rates, disrupted attendance, and inability to concentrate due to fatigue or illness (Davis 1997).

new staff. Unfortunately, more stable programs have more appeal to teachers seeking new positions than do Migrant Head Start programs.

The educational program

Migrant children's needs for high-quality child care are the same as those of other children, except that continuity of care may be even more critical (National Head Start Directors Association 1995). Constant, unpredictable change characterizes migrant children's daily lives. Predictability in their daily school activities—familiar routines, toys, and caregivers—can help stabilize their world and help them make sense of their experiences. The specialization required for these programs poses a challenge. There are few bilingual staff with expertise in infant and toddler development and a CDA credential who are willing to work for a short season.

There are six major challenges of migrant education: interrupted schooling, limited English-language proficiency, poor health and nutrition, social isolation, economic marginality, and lack of self-esteem (Leon 1996). Linda Jacobs Altman's comments about Amelia illustrate the migrant child's search for belonging: "Amelia wanted to go someplace where people didn't have to work so hard, or move around so much, or live in labor camps . . . Amelia wanted to settle down, to belong" (1993, 3, 5).

Best practices recommend that environment and instructional practices reflect the language and culture of the children they serve. Head Start has played a pioneering role in embedding multicultural sensitivity in early childhood programs (Slaughter et al. 1988). Indeed, Head Start performance standards require a multicultural approach, and a great

deal of work has been done in the context of Head Start to develop and implement multicultural curricula, most recently through the National Head Start Multicultural Task Force.

Challenges to teachers

Teachers who work with young children must carefully and thoughtfully respond to the linguistic and cultural needs of these children (Kagan & Garcia 1991; Bowman 1994; NAEYC 1996; Romo 1996). Program staff should support bilingualism by encouraging children to develop and maintain their first language and, later in their development, helping children to read and write in English (Garcia 1983; Cardenas 1986; Zigler & Lang 1991; Leon 1996). Specifically for migrant children, labels in Spanish help them to learn the written language of their culture.

Sorting bins of vegetables and fruits is a familiar activity from their home lives. Photographs, pictures, and materials that depict their cultures and farm life can help them to feel accepted in a new place and also validate the importance of work to the family. In addition, children of migrant families need to find themselves in children's literature; books should include stories from migrant families.

Lesson plans should emerge from the interests of the children and families and be based on their understanding of the world. Migrant children understand a great deal about travel, climate, and the environment. Their life experiences build a strong foundation of important conceptual experiences that they bring to the classroom. Units on agriculture, weather, traveling, forms of transportation, the preparation of foods, oral storytelling, and family are good places to start planning curriculum.

Teachers can build on children's understanding of the world by curriculum webbing based on what the child brings to the classroom. In Texas, for example, many workers harvest tomatoes. Easel painting pictures of tomatoes, serving tomato snacks, and comparing tomato crops all build on what the child knows.

A full-service program of developmentally appropriate activities for children (Bredekamp & Copple 1997) that also provides services for the entire family can help families make a smoother transition to their new (temporary) home. Although Migrant Head Start is available to children across the nation in thousands of rural areas, all early childhood programs can benefit from exploring how they can meet the needs of migrant children as they move across our country. Local child care programs could benefit from partnering with their local migrant programs to better understand the challenges and needs of these children.

Interestingly, many communities are unaware of the existence of migrant programs and the fluctuations in their community population. Early childhood coalitions and community projects exist in many programs, particularly in Texas. In high migrancy states like New Mexico, Washington, Florida, and Texas, many staff are former migrant children.

The Importance of Migrant Farmworkers

Migrant workers' contribution to the U.S. economy is little understood or appreciated. In large part the vitality of the agricultural industry and the eating habits of Americans depend on them. Despite national mechanization in the farming industry, a large percentage of farms continue to depend—some totally—on the strenuous labor of the migrant worker for crop harvesting and food processing. Emphasis on healthy foods and nutrition has increased the need for hand labor. Roman Cruz, an outreach worker and former migrant worker, exclaims, "You know, people, they sit down and have a great salad and they don't know where it comes from. Somebody has to pick that asparagus, somebody has to pick all the fruits and vegetables" (Buirski 1994, 62).

Family members go to the fields to perform a variety of tasks. Each fruit or vegetable requires different skills for harvest and planting, as well as a keen sense of time. Each day's work depends upon the weather. While many consider this unskilled labor, it actually requires an enormous amount of understanding of crops. As the weather changes, the entire family moves according to the needs of the work and the development and progress of the crops. Given the instability of weather, drought or severe rains can have an impact on thousands of families and their homes and employment.

Children's Books

Ashabranner, B. 1997. *Dark harvest*. North Haven, CT: Linnet.
Brimner, L.D. 1992. *A migrant family*. Minneapolis, MN: Lerner.
Bunting, E. 1998. *Going home*. New York: HarperCollins.
Gates, D. 1976. *Blue willow*. New York: Viking.
Jimenez, F. 1999. *The circuit: Stories from the life of a migrant child*. Topeka, KS: Econo-Clad.
Jimenez, F. 2000. *The Christmas gift*. Boston: Houghton Mifflin.
Williams, S.A. 1997. *Working cotton*. Orlando, FL: Voyager Picture Books.

Family involvement

Migrant families value education for their children as a way out of the farmworker's life, but they struggle with supporting education in the face of economic pressures (Fuentes, Cantu, & Stechuk 1996). Often migrant workers visit their children's classrooms in the early evening, after long hours working in the field, or attend parent meetings as late as 9 P.M. to learn of their children's experience in the program.

Because most migrant parents are foreign born, and 80 percent do not speak English, children often help their parents make sense of life in the United States by acting as translators, reading instructions, paying bills, and sometimes negotiating with growers (Rothenberg 1998). This dynamic can make developing effective parent involvement programs challenging. Since most Migrant Head Start staff do not speak the families' languages, primarily Spanish, communication can be difficult. Velasquez (1994) recommends that Migrant Head Start staff be bilingual to effectively communicate with migrant parents about their children's needs and the services the program offers.

Migrant Head Start programs, like many Head Start programs, enroll children of parents with limited education. According to one source, an estimated 70 percent of adult migrants have less than a high school education (Velasquez 1994). The importance of involving parents in the program is extended when those same parents become staff. Parent involvement is also parent education.

The extended families of migrant children can be brought into the curriculum through family sharing and classroom responsibilities. Classroom activities focused on problem solving and collaboration build on the lessons taught in migrant homes. This could easily be articulated through helper charts and learning centers.

Conclusion

Maria and Sergio are lucky because they are younger and get to sleep a bit longer. Their school bus doesn't come until 5:30 A.M., and when they arrive at school, breakfast is waiting. Most of their classmates speak Spanish. While not all of their teachers speak Spanish, most understand the language and continue to learn new words in Spanish every day. Maria loves going to school.

Early childhood programs are challenged by children like Maria and Sergio every day. Many programs are responding to diversity, and they address the unique challenges of the migrant child and family. Just as there is a prevalent cycle of hardship and struggle in the lives of migrant children and families, there is a positive strength and cycle of goodness that can be reflected in program quality. The educational environment in an early childhood program must continue to nurture and focus on the emotional and social needs of the children, since bonding is difficult with this very mobile family system. There are many children like Maria and Sergio who wake to kisses, ride a bus, and wave to their parents in the field.

Poet Trish Hinojosa writes, "About our life—about our land; talkers talk and dreamers dream; We must find a place between" (Buirski 1994, 10). Perhaps this "place between" is Migrant Head Start. Building on the strengths of families, Migrant Head Start provides a refuge, a haven of support and encouragement.

These hardworking families have the strength of each other to see them through the struggles of their daily lives, and they deserve our respect, not our pity. The children "work beside their parents, defining themselves in the context of their work and their place in the home. Even those who do not physically labor in the fields, but travel nonetheless with the harvest, obtain their identity through the family migration and enterprise. They are moved by the love and hope of family working together to create a future" (Buirski 1994, 7).

References

Altman, L.J. 1993. *Amelia's road.* New York: Lee & Low.

Bowman, B. 1994. The challenge of diversity. *Phi Delta Kappan* 76 (3): 218–25.

Bredekamp, S., & C. Copple, eds. 1997. *Developmentally appropriate practice in early childhood programs.* Rev. ed. Washington, DC: NAEYC.

Buirski, N. 1994. *Earth angels: Migrant children in America.* San Francisco, CA: Pomegranate Artbooks.

Cardenas, J. 1986. The role of native-language instruction in bilingual education. *Phi Delta Kappan* 67: 359–63.

Davis, S. 1997. *Child labor in agriculture.* ERIC, ED 405 159.

Fuentes, F., V. Cantu, & R. Stechuk. 1996. Migrant Head Start: What does it mean to involve parents in program services? *Children Today* 24 (1): 16–18.

Garcia, E. 1983. *Bilingualism in early childhood.* Albuquerque, NM: University of New Mexico Press.

Gaston, M. 1992. *Implementation of the Helsinki Accords: Migrant farmworkers in the United States.* Washington, DC: Bureau of Primary Health Care, Health Resources and Services Administration, U.S. Department of Health and Human Services.

Kagan, S., & E. Garcia. 1991. Educating culturally and linguistically diverse preschoolers: Moving the agenda. *Early Childhood Research Quarterly* 6: 427–43.

Leon, E. 1996. *Challenges and solutions for educating migrant students.* ERIC, ED 393 615.

Martin, P. 1996. Migrant farmworkers and their children: What recent labor department data show. In *Children of La Frontera: Binational efforts to serve Mexican migrant and immigrant students,* ed. J.L. Flores. Charleston, WV: ERIC Clearinghouse on Rural Education and Small Schools.

NAEYC. 1996. *Position Statement. Responding to linguistic and cultural diversity: Recommendations for effective early childhood education.* Washington, DC: Author.

National Head Start Directors Association. 1995. *The uniqueness of Head Start.* Washington, DC: U.S. Department of Health and Human Services.

Romo, H.D. 1996. *The newest outsiders: Educating Mexican migrant and immigrant youth.* In *Children of La Frontera: Binational efforts to serve Mexican migrant and immigrant students,* ed. J.L. Flores. Charleston, WV: ERIC Clearinghouse on Rural Education and Small Schools.

Rothenberg, D. 1998. *With these hands: The hidden world of migrant farmworkers today.* Berkeley, CA: University of California Press.

Ruducha, J. 1994. *Migrant child health: A curriculum on the role of social, cultural, and economic factors.* ERIC, ED 382 436.

Slaughter, D.T., V. Washington, U.J. Oyemade, & R.W. Lindsey. 1988. Head Start: A backward and forward look. *Social Policy Report, Vol. 3, No. 2.* Washington, DC: Society for Research in Child Development.

U.S. Bureau of the Census. 1999. U.S. Census Bureau: Frequently asked questions about income statistics. Online. Available: www.census.gov/hhes/income/incfaq.html.

U.S. Department of Health and Human Services, Administration for Children, Youth and Families. 1994. *Description of Migrant Head Start programs.* Washington, DC: Author.

U.S. Department of Health and Human Services, Administration for Children, Youth and Families. 1999. *Head Start fact sheet.* Washington, DC: Author.

U.S. Department of Health and Human Services, National Advisory Council on Migrant Health, Bureau of Primary Health Care. 1993. *Recommendations of the National Advisory Council on Migrant Health.* Washington, DC: Author.

Velasquez, L.C. 1994. *Migrant and seasonal farmworkers: An invisible population.* ERIC, ED 386355.

Zigler, E.F., & M.E. Lang. 1991. *Child care choices: Balancing the needs of children, families, and society.* New York: Free Press.

Zigler, E., & J. Valentine, eds. 1979. *Project Head Start: A legacy of the war on poverty.* New York: Free Press.

Judy Harris Helm and Jean Lang

24

Overcoming the Ill Effects of Poverty

Excerpted from *The Power of Projects*

The effects of poverty on children's development and education include decreased verbal ability and achievement (Duncan & Brooks-Gunn 1997). Children from families with lower socioeconomic status are more prone to reading difficulties and lower overall academic achievement than children from families with higher socioeconomic status (Snow, Burns, & Griffin 1998). Patterns of interaction, especially verbal interaction, between children and parents are significantly different in lower-income families (Hart & Risley 1995).

It is important to remember, however, that despite these concerns, educators should not assume that a child from an economically disadvantaged environment is automatically going to have difficulty in school.

—J.H. Helm

Practical strategies

Throughout our years of working with children, we have seen the doors to the world of school open for many poor children during the process of doing a project. One of the greatest advantages of project work for children in poverty is the motivation for learning academic skills and the opportunity for meaningful practice and perfection of these skills. As they eagerly search through books to find answers to questions, label their drawings, make literacy materials for play environments, and struggle to write their questions and thoughts, they discover that literacy is a valuable tool. We have seen the same development with mathematical skills. Children learn that counting, measuring, and solving problems using math are useful skills to learn. Project work is the closest a child can come to the world of work, and it is often while doing a project that a child first sees the relevance of learning these skills to adult jobs. This is especially important for children who do not live in optimal environments.

Children's self-images change during project work. They begin to see themselves as learners and problem solvers; they build self-confidence in their ability to find answers to their own questions; and they learn that adults can be resources of information and assistance. These experiences increase their ability to cope and find solutions to problems within their home environments.

We have observed that projects become a vehicle for the development of strong relationships between teachers and families. A project can provide a common focus for parents, children, school personnel, and even members of the larger community. All of these people come together for the purpose of helping children in their investigations and supporting the growth of children's knowledge, skills, and dispositions toward learning. Projects also widen families' awareness of resources available in their communities.

Not all project work will automatically provide these benefits for children living in poverty. In our work with classrooms and teachers, we have realized eight practical strategies that teachers can use to maximize the effectiveness of project work for children living in poverty.

Practical strategy 1: Maximize opportunities for self-initiated learning

Self-initiated learning occurs in project work as children choose and explore materials and artifacts, select activities, and create structures or play environments. Children can learn how to take independent action and solve problems with minimum adult help. Grotberg (1995) identifies these skills as building blocks of resiliency. By maximizing the opportunities for self-initiated learning that occur in project work, teachers are providing opportunities for children to develop the inner strengths of self-confidence and self-esteem.

One way teachers can maximize self-initiation is to consider children's interests when selecting the topic for a project. After a topic is chosen, teachers can also involve children in determining what they want to know about that topic and what they want to investigate within the project. For example, self-initiated learning occurred when the study of an author turned into a museum project. The teacher introduced children to books by Eric Carle and showed how his pictures were different from those in other books. The children became interested in collages, so the teacher read books about art to them, including a book that mentioned an art museum. Most of the children had never been to a museum and had many questions about the museum in the book. The teacher followed the children's interest and arranged a visit to an art museum.

Teachers can maximize self-initiated learning in projects by allocating enough time for it to occur. The class that participated in the Airplane Project stayed focused on the topic for 10 weeks even though there were two major interruptions in their school schedule. We have observed that children's attention spans during project-related activities are longer than during other classroom activities. Deep engagement in project work enables the development of more complex questions for investigation. Extended study encourages children to continue to think about the project away from school, discuss it with parents, and take independent action as they bring relevant materials into the classroom.

Maximizing self-initiation in project work does not require that topics emerge totally from the children. Teachers can initiate topics for study. In working with children who have had few experiences outside the home or beyond the block where they live, we have found it helpful to introduce children to a variety of topics. The teacher often initiates a topic and then observes children's interests as they develop background knowledge about it before a decision is made to proceed with a project (Helm & Katz 2001; Katz & Chard 1989).

Practical strategy 2: Support children's emotional involvement in learning

Teachers can help children develop resiliency by providing opportunities for them to identify their feelings and talk about them (Grotberg 1995). During project work, teachers can maximize emotional involvement by encouraging and supporting discussions about how the children feel about what they are doing. In a classroom with second-language learners, the teacher told the children that arrangements had been made for them to visit a flower shop. The children responded positively but not with great enthusiasm until one of the children said, "You mean this is a trip? We get to ask questions and take our clipboards and draw stuff? Cool!" Immediately the children became excited and eager for the visit. This story illustrates the difference between the emotional involvement generated by typical classroom activities, such as a traditional field trip, compared with project activities, such as a field-site visit.

The documentation that occurs during project work also provides an opportunity for children to talk about the events and experiences of a project. Even very young children are able to see the differences between first, second, or third attempts at drawing, painting, or writing. They often express pride in their work or talk about working hard, being frustrated, or mastering a skill. As one child commented to a teacher after he had worked through a particularly challenging problem, "I must be a genius to have thought of that!" (Helm, Beneke, & Steinheimer 1998, 102). Viewing documentation at culminating events such as open houses or project parties is an excellent way to celebrate the accomplishments of the project and to focus parent-child conversations on the developing knowledge, skills, and dispositions of the children.

Practical strategy 3: Focus on the environment and culture of the child

In classrooms where children have had limited experiences outside the home, it is especially important to support topics of study that are based on the child's environment. Projects that focus on the child's neighborhood and immediate community are not only more likely to engage children's interest and lead to in-depth investigation, but they are also more likely to engage the interest and involvement of parents. Encouraging parental involvement is especially beneficial to children living in poverty. When a project relates to children's surroundings, they usually have some familiarity with the topic and can more easily express curiosity and develop their own questions.

Again, the teacher does not have to wait for children's interest in these local sites to emerge. We have found that children who have not had many opportunities for self-initiated learning are unlikely to spontaneously generate questions and show intense curiosity. Interest and curiosity emerge, however, if the teacher provides an introduction to the topic. A teacher will often survey the neighborhood around a school by taking a walk with the children. It is helpful to document signs of interest or comments that the children make during this walk. They may become interested in a local construction site, the donut shop on the corner, or a passing fire truck. If the children express interest, a project may develop. If not, at least the teacher has introduced them to new components of their community and broadened their knowledge.

Introducing children to topics of study within their own neighborhood also makes it more likely that the experience will be culturally relevant to children and families. A neighborhood store where the families shop is more likely to have foods that are part of the child's life and literacy materials, such as labels and signs in the language used by the children's families. A local restaurant might be where the children eat or a parent works. A bus stop or a subway station may be an important place in the life of the family.

Topics that grow from explorations of the community and neighborhood are often easily related to curriculum goals. For example, a project about a local fire station is likely to involve learning about how people help each other through their jobs—a common social studies goal. Projects about neighborhood birds, animals, or the weather are related to science curriculum goals.

Practical strategy 4: Encourage the strengthening of intellectual dispositions

It is important that children growing up in poverty develop dispositions to use academic skills, to read and write, and to think reflectively.

When guiding projects with children, it is important to provide ample opportunities for children to

- Make sense of their experience
- Theorize, analyze, hypothesize, and synthesize
- Make and check predictions
- Find information on their own
- Strive for accuracy
- Be empirical
- Grasp the consequences of actions
- Persist in seeking solutions to problems
- Speculate about cause-effect relationships
- Predict others' wishes and feelings (Helm & Katz 2001)

Children in middle- and upper-income families are often encouraged to discuss their ideas, answer questions, and explain their thinking. For example, one of the questions that the children had during the Airplane Project was "What button makes the plane go up?" This created much discussion. When thinking about the "up button" on the airplane, the children developed their own hypotheses and then were able to determine the accuracy of their ideas during the field-site visit to the airport.

Practical strategy 5: Encourage children to solve their own problems and practice social skills

Children have many opportunities in project work to learn to work with others. When learners take responsibility for their work, are self-regulated, and are able to define their goals and evaluate their accomplishments, they are energized by their work; their dispositions to solve problems, to seek deeper understanding, can be developed and strengthened (Jones et al. 1994).

Teachers can also engender social development as children learn to share the work of the project. Chil-

dren are encouraged to sign up for various jobs based on their interests and questions, and they work in teams and learn to rely on others to get information they need. For example, during the field-site visit to the airport during the Airplane Project, the children signed up to sketch one part of the airplane. The same subdivision of labor was used in constructing the airplane, and the children used their sketches as a plan for construction.

Project work also provides a context for leadership skills to emerge. Teachers can increase the value of project work by standing back and giving children opportunities to develop leadership skills. The more experienced children tend to lead discussions, formulate questions, and serve as models to the younger, less experienced children, who then learn by observing the student leaders. The following year these younger children become the leaders of the group. Children also mentor each other. We have observed that children appear to attend more to the theories and conclusions of their peers than to adults who simply tell them the right answer.

Practical strategy 6: Maximize opportunities for parent involvement

Parents become very interested and involved in projects, and the project becomes something that children and parents talk about at home. Parents serve as visiting experts and answer children's questions; assist in the teaching of relevant skills, such as how to assemble something out of wood; and become colearners as they explore the topic alongside their children. Project work also provides opportunities for parents to observe teachers interacting with children. For example, a parent accompanying a class on a field-site visit may see how the teacher draws the children's attention to an object or process. A parent's expectations for his or her own children may rise. We have observed that parents are often surprised at how well their young children can draw, write, count, and photograph.

Practical strategy 7: Emphasize the role of literacy

Learning to read can be challenging for many children living in poverty; there is a relationship between income level and language development (Smith, Brooks-Gunn, & Klebanov 1997). Development of a good vocabulary in the early years is important for emerging literacy. Children can learn many words about the project topic and use these words in role play and conversations. New vocabulary can be introduced during project work and definitions of familiar words refined. When project topics relate to the standard curriculum, children develop a familiarity with words they will read and study in elementary school. For example, in a project on spring gardens, children learned about bulbs and seeds and the planting process.

Teachers can use projects to strengthen young children's motivation to master a wide variety of academic skills, especially reading and writing. In a study of first grade children doing both projects and formal units, children were more involved in reading and research in the project than in the teacher-directed unit (Bryson 1994). During the Airplane Project, teachers read and discussed books about airplanes and travel. They brought in many books, charts, and magazines that helped the children extend their knowledge of airplanes. The children learned that books, magazines, and the Internet can be used as resources to increase their knowledge.

Teachers can use projects to strengthen young children's motivation to master a wide variety of academic skills.

Many opportunities for writing occur naturally in project work. Children write to record what they are observing on field-site visits or to communicate with experts. Play environments created during project work result in many literacy products. In the Airplane Project, adults modeled the writing process while taking dictation from the children for lists of materials and parts of the airplane. Children copied identification numbers and letters on the airplane at the field-site visit. They referred back to these sketches, field notes, and photos when constructing their plane.

Practical strategy 8: Maintain high expectations and standards

It is important for the teacher to maintain high standards and expectations of children. Throughout the project, teachers have many opportunities to select materials, ask questions, and provoke thought. Although it is important to remain developmentally appropriate, teachers need to guard against narrowing experiences for children who come to school with limited backgrounds. All children need to be encouraged equally to think creatively, clarify their thoughts, and stretch their minds.

References

Bryson, E. 1994. *Will a project approach to learning provide children opportunities to do purposeful reading and writing, as well as provide opportunities for authentic learning in other curriculum areas?* Urbana, IL: ERIC Clearinghouse on Elementary and Early Childhood Education.

Duncan, G.J., & J. Brooks-Gunn, eds. 1997. *Consequences of growing up poor.* New York: Russell Sage Foundation.

Grotberg, E.H. 1995. *A guide to promoting resilience in children: Strengthening the human spirit.* The Hague, The Netherlands: Bernard Van Leer Foundation.

Hart, B., & T.R. Risley. 1995. *Meaningful differences in the everyday experience of young American children.* Baltimore, MD: Brookes.

Helm, J.H., & L.G. Katz. 2001. *Young investigators: The project approach in the early years.* New York: Teachers College Press.

Helm, J.H., S. Beneke, & K. Steinheimer. 1998. *Windows on learning: Documenting young children's work.* New York: Teachers College Press.

Jones, B., G. Valdez, J. Norakowski, & C. Rasmussen. 1994. *Designing learning and technology for educational reform.* Oak Brook, IL: North Central Regional Educational Laboratory.

Katz, L.G., & S.C. Chard. 1989. *Engaging children's minds: The project approach.* Greenwich, CT: Ablex.

Smith, J.R., J. Brooks-Gunn, & P.K. Klebanov. 1997. Consequences of living in poverty for young children's cognitive and verbal ability and early school achievement. In *Consequences of growing up poor,* eds. G.J. Duncan & J. Brooks-Gunn, 132–89. New York: Russell Sage Foundation.

Snow, C.E., M.S. Burns, & P. Griffin, eds. 1998. *Preventing reading difficulties in young children.* Washington, DC: National Academy Press.

Adapted from J.H. Helm & J. Lang, "Overcoming the Ill Effects of Poverty," in *The Power of Projects: Meeting Contemporary Challenges in Early Childhood Classrooms—Strategies and Solutions,* eds. J.H. Helm & S. Beneke (New York: Teachers College Press; Washington, DC: NAEYC, 2003), 19–24. Copyright © 2003 Teachers College Press, Columbia University. Reprinted with permission.

Kathleen Fitzgerald Rice and Margot Kaplan-Sanoff

25

Growing Strong Together
Helping Mothers and Their Children Affected by Substance Abuse

Nancy speaks with the intensity of a woman two years into recovery from cocaine addiction: "For me it came down to two things. It was either the drugs or my life and my child."

附

Working with women who abuse substances, and with their children, is complicated and challenging. It also can be rewarding and life changing for all those involved. This work is very different from working with families, who have other identified stresses, such as poverty or children with special needs. We all probably have worked with hard-to-reach families, but often without understanding that the reason we may have been unable to intervene successfully was substance abuse.

For child care providers and teachers, it is critical to understand the disease of addiction: how it impacts the family; how our own feelings, attitudes, and beliefs about drugs (including alcohol) and drug use influence our interventions; and how to help families move from addiction to recovery. This article addresses the lessons learned from working with

substance-abusing women and their children by examining addiction and recovery and the role early childhood educators can play in supporting growth in both children and their mothers.

Addiction is a disease

Addiction, by definition, is a disease (Brown 1985). It is progressive and potentially fatal, with characteristic signs and symptoms. An addict compulsively uses a substance (such as alcohol), experiencing an increasing loss of control over the substance, and continues its use despite negative consequences. Addiction is not about a lack of willpower or morals. Addicts, although they chose that first drug, do not choose to have the addiction. The hallmark of addictive disease is that the drug controls the individual. The individual can no longer control the drug use. Addicts have a disease that by its very nature consumes them psychologically, physically, and spiritually.

Addiction is not confined to any one ethnic, cultural, or socioeconomic group, and it affects all ages

and both sexes. Brown (1985) describes addiction as a "family disease" with "all family members suffering the consequences of one member's addiction."

When individuals are addicted to drugs, their primary focus is on their drug of choice, to the exclusion of anything or anyone else in their lives. When mothers are addicted to drugs, their primary relationship is with their drug, not their child. Their lives become organized around getting their drug, not around caring for their children. The addiction becomes the "central organizing principle" of the family, around which relationships are developed and the family system operates (Brown 1985). Addiction prevents parents from responding appropriately to their children's needs, thus affecting children's development and sense of security (Seval Brooks et al. 1994).

Why do people become addicted?

There are many theories about why people abuse substances and develop addictions. Most useful perhaps for understanding the disease of addiction is a bio-psycho-social framework, since individuals choose their drugs and unwittingly develop addictive disease for a variety of biological, psychological, and social reasons. Biology and social learning may play a role in the disease process, as evidenced by the frequent intergenerational patterns of addiction. There may very well be a psychological component to why people use drugs—for instance, to manage symptoms of mental illness like depression or to deal with an anxiety disorder. Because an individual often develops addictive disease for a combination of these and other reasons, a bio-psycho-social framework is useful for understanding the disease.

For women, and increasingly for men, a compelling model that helps to explain addictive disease is the trauma model (Seval Brooks & Fitzgerald Rice 1997). The majority of addicted women come from backgrounds fraught with trauma and loss. Studies show from 75 percent to 90 percent of women in treatment programs report having been physically and/or sexually abused as children (Rohsenow, Corbett, & Devine 1988). There is often a history of familial substance abuse. Addicted women most likely experienced all of the chaos, fear, violence, and loss that their own children now may be experiencing. Addicted women, according to the trauma model, use substances to alleviate the pain of these early experiences of loss and trauma. They use substances to self-medicate the painful affect, shame, guilt, and extreme anxiety associated with early traumatic events, and they use substances to cope with the painful reality of their daily lives.

Addictive disease is remarkable for the intergenerational perpetuation of trauma and family dysfunction. The disease brings to each generation its own destructive brand of

© Jean-Claude Lejeune

parenting. Many addicted women had poor models for parenting and were not parented themselves; they also may have had early or frequent disruptions in care and relationships and may not know how to parent their own children differently.

As parents, addicted women may have little or no confidence in their parenting skills, limited ability to trust or develop healthy relationships, no sense of control over life events, and little self-worth. They may have tremendous difficulty identifying and coping with their own stress and intense feelings, making it nearly impossible to empathically care for their children. Substance-abusing women are often so very disconnected from themselves that their ability to recognize their own needs, choose healthy coping strategies, and keep their children safe is severely impaired.

Recovery as a developmental process

Fortunately, along with the debilitating disease of addiction comes the hope and possibility of recovery for both the family and the individual. Recovery from addiction brings its own set of challenges to the parenting relationship, so it becomes important for early childhood providers to understand what recovery is and how to support the process with both mother and child.

Recovery from addiction is best understood as a lifelong developmental process with identifiable stages (Brown 1985). Recovery is not merely a reversal of symptoms with the individual returning to a previous state of functioning. Rather, it is a dynamic process that involves significant growth and change in the individual and in the family system.

People can grow and mature, learn to experience and cope with feelings, develop self-esteem, and learn how to develop positive meaningful relationships.

In describing the stages of recovery, Brown (1985) emphasizes the shift in focus by the individual at each stage of the process. The addict begins the journey of recovery in the *transition* stage by breaking through the denial that has supported the disease process. The addict admits powerlessness and loss of control, which paradoxically allows the addict to take control of her life. The focus for the addict in this stage is on the drug itself and whether or not she is addicted. It is in this transition stage that the addict moves back and forth between thinking that maybe she has a problem and maybe not.

In the *early recovery* stage, the addict has admitted the problem and made a commitment to recovery. The focus continues to be on the drug itself and maintaining abstinence. The addict must spend a considerable amount of energy just trying to stay clean by learning a whole new way of living in and coping with the world. Little energy is left to work on relationships or parenting. Early recovery is a period of great change for women. For the first time, they experience emotions free of the numbing effects of drugs, but they can feel crippling guilt, overwhelming fear, and paralyzing anxiety. Traumatic memories may resurface. This tremendous stress sends many women relapsing into drug abuse.

As the addict builds a support system and learns new skills and ways of being in the world, she enters the *ongoing recovery* stage. Here the focus shifts from the drug and maintaining abstinence to making and keeping healthy relationships. Individuals with a stronger foothold in recovery are better able to focus on parenting, repairing old relationships, and making new, healthy ones. Ongoing recovery lasts a lifetime, requiring the individual to be ever vigilant about maintaining sobriety and her recovery.

The impact of addiction on mothers and their children

Maternal addiction and recovery take their toll not only on the women but on their children as well. It is estimated that one in eight American children has at least one alcoholic parent (MacDonald 1991). The negative impact of familial addiction is well documented. Children from substance-abusing homes may face countless risks to their development; they are at greater risk for behavior and psychological problems, abuse, neglect, low self-esteem, school failure, and substance abuse (Seval Brooks & Fitzgerald Rice 1997).

Children who are exposed in utero to drugs like cocaine or alcohol may face additional risks to their development, although there is much conflicting data about specific developmental outcomes from particular drugs. It is clear that the alarming and dismal picture of cocaine-exposed children painted in the 1980s was distorted and that these children do not suffer permanent brain damage, but this does not mean that there are no ill effects from cocaine or from other drugs such as heroin, tobacco, and alcohol (Zuckerman & Bresnahan 1991; Frank, Bresnahan, & Zuckerman 1993). The environmental impact of

Talking, Trusting, Feeling: Simple Ways to Create an Open Environment for Families

1. Post community meetings for Alcoholics Anonymous or other recovery groups on your center's bulletin board.

2. Offer a parent-workshop series on family stressors. Develop a helpful and nonthreatening workshop on familial substance abuse.

3. Create a safe, private place for parents to meet with you or talk together.

4. Know referral sources for substance-abuse treatment programs in your community.

5. Remember that a child's behavior is a message. Children don't always communicate their worries verbally. Use play and art to give children a chance to communicate their worries or concerns nonverbally.

6. Children's books about sensitive issues like family substance abuse often help children tell their own stories. Discuss when and how books might be appropriate to use with children in your program.

7. Design curriculum strategies that teach children about talking, trusting, and feeling in daily life. Talking about how it feels, for instance, to go to the doctor can begin a process for learning that may help children feel more comfortable talking about more sensitive and scary issues.

8. Children—and adults—are much more comfortable talking to and trusting familiar adults. Challenge your center's staff to think of ways that children and families can develop a long-term relationship with a primary caregiver.

living with familial addiction with all the attendant chaos and trauma can be very damaging (Seval Brooks & Fitzgerald Rice 1997). What children live with and learn in an addicted family system can impair their lives at home, in school, in relationships, and beyond.

One of the most compelling examples of what children live with and learn in an addicted family is the primary rule of the family disease: Don't Talk, Don't Trust, Don't Feel. Children are taught not to talk about the disease, ask for any help outside the family, trust anyone, and, above all, feel anything. Just as the addict numbs her feelings, her children learn to cope with their own fear, sadness, and pain by numbing themselves. The family closes around the disease, and the children are trapped inside.

How educators can help

We believe that breaking that family rule of addictive disease through family-focused intervention is one of the best ways to help children living with addiction. The first step toward family-focused intervention for providers is to recognize that the family is the target of intervention, not just the child or just the mother. Child care providers need to accept the difficult task of helping both the child and the mother move toward and stay in recovery. Each member of the family has different needs, but needs are intertwined and do not have to be viewed as conflicting. It is possible for educators to support both the mother and child with family-focused interventions that encourage talking, trusting, and feeling.

Therapeutic relationship

It becomes the dual role of the provider to model ways of interacting with children and to actively nurture the mother. Nurturing requires help-

© Jean-Claude Lejeune

ing mothers identify and label their feelings. As discussed, many women use substances to numb painful affect. Mothers can be completely out of touch with their own feelings, often substituting somatic complaints for the difficult emotions they are experiencing. Labeling these emotions and legitimizing their right to feel them is a critical first step; only then can these mothers help their children cope with their own growing emotional awareness. Mothers cannot tell children that it is all right to feel angry, sad, or confused until they have experienced and felt safe expressing their own anger, sadness, and confusion.

Setting limits

A therapeutic relationship has limits, boundaries, and explicit rules. Consequences for breaking those

rules are clear. One crucial rule is never meeting with a parent who is drunk or high. Honesty and trust are ground rules and common goals. Without shaming and punishing the mothers, child care providers need to be clear with mothers about the effects of their addiction on themselves and their children. Providers need to be honest about their dual role with families—to help in the recovery process and to keep children safe. If the mother relapses in recovery, the early childhood educator may need to involve social services to protect the child, but this should first involve an honest and open discussion with the mother. Praise and encouragement for the difficult work of parenting in recovery should be generously given, particularly to balance the more authoritative task of setting limits with the mothers.

It is critical to understand that supporting and re-parenting mothers does not mean doing the work of recovery for the mother and unwittingly allowing or enabling the substance abuse to continue. When we take the child for needed medical or educational services without involving the mother in some way, or if we do not tell the mother that she needs to attend to her or her child's physical needs and appearance, we may be encouraging the addictive behavior to continue. Providing information about the reality of addiction and its impact on children helps break down the mother's denial that fuels the disease process. Being honest with the mother, presenting her with observations of her addictive behavior, and translating the impact the addiction has on her and her child may be the wake-up call she needs to break through her denial, confront her addiction, and ask for help.

Support for educators doing the work

Grant me the serenity to accept the things I cannot change, the courage to change the things I can, and the wisdom to know the difference.

Early childhood educators working with families affected by substance abuse can learn much from these words of wisdom. The incredibly difficult work of supporting families affected by substance abuse requires much patience and careful thought. The work can be a journey filled with many detours and roadblocks, exhausting to even the most committed child care provider. Training, support, and supervision are essential for providers.

There are many barriers to working successfully with drug-involved families, barriers that make the work complicated and frustrating. These barriers include the lack of professional training about addiction and treatment; inadequate professional support and supervision; and our own feelings, attitudes, and beliefs about substance abuse.

Many child care providers and teachers don't know what to do when they suspect substance abuse in a family. If they do not know what to look for or say, or what to do if the family asks for help, providers often overlook signs of trouble, ignore the problem, or try to fix it themselves. One of the most important things a teacher can do is to ask for help in processing her concerns and turn to available supervision, consultation, and/or community supports. Providers should never try to go it alone with families. They must know the limits and boundaries of their roles and expertise, both for their own professional health and the health of the families in their care; they must look beyond their own skills and experience to find the guidance they need from other professionals.

Information and training about the disease and treatment of addiction supports child care providers by creating a solid base of knowledge from which to design and implement interventions. Connecting with other professionals can lead to invaluable professional support. Providers feel helpful, hopeful, and competent when they have the support, training, and information they need.

In most communities programs and trained professionals can bring needed expertise to the table. Child care programs can link with mental health agencies and substance-abuse treatment programs to make referrals and even receive (or offer) training and consultation. Bringing professionals together from various fields of expertise can enrich professionals and families alike. Teachers and child care providers can feel more grounded in their work when they meet with collaborating professionals about a challenging family or participate in professional training. Intra- and interagency collaboration creates opportunities for case coordination, interdisciplinary training, and professional support. It also creates opportunities for professionals to have a collective voice in advocating for families, which can be a renewing and empowering experience.

Other significant issues and potential barriers are the feelings, attitudes, and beliefs early childhood educators have about substance use and abuse. Understanding how our attitudes and feelings impact our work with families is just as important as knowing what addiction is and how to help, since our own experiences and issues color our relationships with families.

First, we must recognize that each of us has our own unique experiences with and perceptions about drug use. They come from our own histories, our present experiences, and societal and cultural beliefs and practices. These experiences and perceptions can be both helpful and harmful to our work with families. Working with addicted families can bring up painful personal issues and trigger intense anger, sadness, and confusion, emotions that can get in the way of support, compassion, and respect. On the other hand, personal experiences also can lead providers to a unique understanding of and empathy for the struggling addict. Those who have been able to grow and heal from personal experiences are some of the most skilled and caring teachers available to families.

Regardless of the path our own experiences and perceptions have put us on, we must have opportunities to process our work with families and receive supportive guidance along the way. Professional support through clinical supervision is an essential, yet vastly underused, tool for child care providers' professional support and growth. Clinical supervision is a component of most mental health programs, but it is often absent in educational programs such as child care agencies and schools, even though their educators are challenged by a host of family stresses.

Teachers and child care providers who are too burned out, too overwhelmed, and too drained cannot successfully support families. Clinical supervision that provides a safe place to vent feelings, process intense experiences, plan interventions, and promote self-exploration can be a professional lifeline. Clinical supervisors who have knowledge about mental health issues, experience working with challenging families, and training for clinical supervision can guide teachers and providers toward a new understanding of families and support our continued professional growth and maturation.

Keeping the vision

Supporting women and children affected by substance abuse is at once difficult and rewarding. To do the work well, we have to not only keep ourselves strong but also help families see and keep the vision of health and recovery for themselves. Success is measured in small steps; days are taken one at a time. Helping a mother recognize and admit she has a problem is the first step in a lifelong journey that only she can make. It is not our responsibility to take that journey for the mother or child. It is our responsibility to lend a hand and believe in the vision that a better future for everyone is possible in recovery.

References

Brown, S. 1985. *Treating the alcoholic: A developmental model of recovery.* New York: Wiley.

Frank, D., K. Bresnahan, & B. Zuckerman. 1993. Maternal cocaine use: Impact on child health and development. In *Advances in pediatrics*, Vol. 40, ed. Y.B. Barness, 65–99. St. Louis, MO: Mosby Yearbook.

MacDonald, D. 1991. Parental alcoholism: A neglected pediatric responsibility. *American Journal of Diseases in Children* 145: 609–10.

Pharis, M., & V. Levin. 1991. A person to talk to who really cares: High risk mothers' evaluation of services in an intensive intervention research program. *Child Welfare League of America* 120 (3): 307–19.

Rohsenow, D.L., R. Corbett, & D. Devine. 1988. Molested as children: A hidden contribution to substance abuse? *Journal of Substance Abuse Treatment* 5: 13–18.

Seval Brooks, C., & K. Fitzgerald Rice. 1997. *Families in recovery: Coming full circle.* Baltimore, MD: Brookes.

Seval Brooks, C., B. Zuckerman, A. Bamforth, J. Cole, & M. Kaplan-Sanoff. 1994. Clinical issues related to substance-involved mothers and their infants. *Infant Mental Health* 15 (2): 207–17.

Zuckerman, B., & K. Bresnahan. 1991. Developmental and behavioral consequences of prenatal drug and alcohol exposure. *Pediatric Clinics of North America* 38 (6): 1387–406.

Adapted from *Young Children* 53 (1): 28–33. Copyright © 1998 NAEYC.

Selected Bibliography of Children's Books

Children's literature offers a wealth of intervention material for families and professionals. The following list is a sampling of the many books that may be helpful to children who are affected by familial substance abuse. Each book should be previewed for appropriateness for the target audience. Many books require informed and careful guidance before being used with children.

Al-Anon Family Group. 1977. *What's "drunk," Mama?* New York: Author.
Told from a young girl's point of view, this book attempts to answer the questions young children have about addiction and family recovery. For ages 5–10.

Children of Alcoholics Foundation. 1994. *The feel better book.* New York: Author.
This is an activity workbook for children in grades 1–6 who might come from an alcoholic family. Reproducible worksheets and suggested activities can be used to help children deal with feelings, build self-esteem, and ask for help from trusted adults.

DiGiovanni, K. 1989. *My house is different.* Burlington, VT: Waterfront.
Joe learns through a magical dream adventure with his dog that he didn't cause his father's alcoholism and that he can't fix it, but that he can feel good about himself. For ages 4–7.

Sanford, D. 1987. *I know the world's worst secret: A child's book about living with an alcoholic parent.* Portland, OR: Multnomah.
Elizabeth's mother is an alcoholic. As young as she is, Elizabeth tries to take responsibility for caring for the family. She struggles with the pain and learns how to grow and heal, even when faced with such difficult challenges. For ages 4 and older.

Vigna, J. 1988. *I wish Daddy didn't drink so much.* Niles, IL: A. Whitman.
One of the few preschool-level titles available, this is a well-regarded story about alcoholism in a family from the perspective of a young child trying to understand it all.

William A.H. Sammons and Jennifer M. Lewis

26

What Schools Are Doing to Help the Children of Divorce

In the 1990s almost 15 million children, many under the age of 8, were told their parents were getting a divorce (National Children's Survey 1994; U.S. Bureau of Census 1998). As developmental pediatricians we have seen many children and their parents who have successfully coped with this crisis and frequently say they have been helped by the unheralded support of teachers and schools.

Educators have the advantage of being in constant touch with families of young children and of understanding developmental needs. Acting as role models, teachers often help parents understand how children's behavior and play give clues to the struggles within and hence shape the strategies adults adopt to help their children thrive.

Because divorce is so prevalent in the United States, teachers are all too familiar with the varied behaviors that children exhibit in reaction to divorce. Every day in every classroom, teachers use art projects, writing or telling stories, and reflecting back to the child their observations of his or her behavior to help the child cope

with the sadness and loss that are part of divorce. With older children the teacher is often the only adult helping a child make connections between the "how I feel" and "how I act" by wondering whether or not it was "tough to say good-bye to Dad" or by recognizing the anxiety that precedes an infrequent visit from Mom (Lewis & Sammons 1999).

As behavioral pediatricians we find that teacher observations are key to helping us determine what family situations are contributing to aggression, depression, or other marked changes in a child's actions. Ongoing hostility between parents, an inappropriate hand-over routine, a visitation schedule in which visits are too short to be enjoyable or in which the child is used as a messenger, can all contribute to behavioral changes seen in the classroom (Lewis & Sammons 1999).

Teachers often provide the insights to help other adults determine whether the child who seems to be coping well (or actually improves in terms of classroom participation or compliance with rules and overall organization) is successfully adapt-

ing or instead belongs to that worrisome group of children who, despite apparent resilience, are often most stressed and likely to show the worst possible outcome years later unless appropriate steps are taken.

Supporting the child

Since divorcing parents are often emotionally distracted, fatigued, and not functioning well as parents, teachers and early childhood specialists are frequently called upon to fill this parenting gap. Parents may not appreciate it at the time and, in fact, may even feel competition, but in looking back they see great value in the ways teachers maintain a supportive role by taking some of the following steps.

Maintaining consistency and discipline

When divorce alters the child's world, and most parents change rules and routines to accommodate new family circumstances, teachers also may be tempted to bend their well-defined expectations for behavior. On a day-to-day basis, however, many early childhood educators have told us that this approach may be misplaced kindness. They observe that altering the rules for children facing the stresses of divorce actually increases acting-out behaviors. By keeping school expectations consistent, teachers increase the child's sense of security and serve as resources for parents who may feel they are floundering.

Making kids feel competent

Teachers employ many strategies to help children feel needed and important. They allocate specific, achievable tasks and responsibilities—like watering the plants or washing the paintbrushes—with the intention of offering the child appropriate positive feedback. By focusing on competencies, rather than reminders about the need for improvement, teachers are supportive of children who, during emotional times of divorce, fall apart at the first sign of criticism as they struggle with feelings of inadequacy.

Being given permission to be a little less than perfect—to color outside the lines, spill paint, ignore an instruction—helps children. Children remember feeling reassured by the teacher who showed humor rather than disapproval. Or they smile fondly, recalling the teacher who made it seem OK to have made a mistake by poking fun at an example of his or her own forgetfulness.

In children of divorce, teachers also recognize that the desire to be good and to gain approval is driven by a fear of being unacceptable or by a misplaced guilt about causing the family breakdown. Understanding this, educators effectively model for parents ways to praise or criticize behavior rather than the child: "I like *it* when you . . . " rather than "I like *you* when you. . . . "

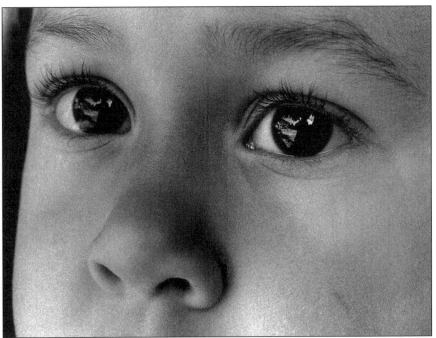

© Jean-Claude Lejeune

Listening to the child's point of view

The teacher may be the only adult in a child's life who actively encourages a child to express how he sees a situation before leaping to conclusions about his anxieties and concerns. Teachers often find that asking questions is more productive than posing answers. A question such as "Why do you think Maria is making you angry today?" at least allows the child to think about all the feelings inside him even if he cannot yet make the connection to the angry ambience at home or other events or demands he is experiencing. By offering a safe haven and simply noting the behavior in a nonjudgmental manner, teachers reassure the child that at least one adult cares enough to notice.

Being an advocate for the child

Although others may say the right words, a teacher is frequently the only adult willing to act as an advocate for the child. Aware that a child is faced with recurrent loyalty choices or is used as a messenger between hostile parents, the teacher can be one to alert both parents to the unfairness of these pressures.

Because teachers easily identify with the children in their care, they may feel angry with one or the other parent for causing so much turmoil for the child. Yet time and again we see teachers put aside personal feelings to better focus the parents' attention on the ways in which their child is responding to the changes in the family. Even if the parents cannot cooperate with each other, teachers ensure that the school and each of the parents work together in the child's best interest.

Keeping both of the parents involved

Children do best following divorce when they maintain contact with both parents (Wallerstein & Blakeslee 1989; Furstenberg & Cherlin 1991; Kelly 1993; Ahrons 1995). In contrast to the lawyers and, sadly, many family members, teach-

*In times of stress, supporting parents **and** their children is an essential task for all who have the best interests of children at heart.*

ers spend considerable effort in trying to keep fathers and mothers involved in the child's school life.

Teachers can clearly communicate the expectation that each parent should be actively involved in what takes place at school. This can be thankless work, but sending newsletters and notices to both parents, using individual conferences to offer feedback, and seeking insights from them separately about their child's progress is important.

Years later it is frequently apparent that duplicated drawings and stories or photographed art projects allowed the child's work to be shared at each home and maintained vital parent-child connections. Every child dreads losing contact with a parent. Teachers also facilitate the child's access to both parents by helping to send letters, faxes, or e-mail (Lewis & Sammons 1999).

Conclusion

Although educators may have no influence in helping parents see eye-to-eye about most issues or influencing the outcome of their relationship, teachers have considerable influence on the effect the divorce has on the children in their care. Nobody intends to "divorce" their children when they divorce a spouse. Thankfully, most parents want to maintain a strong relationship and an essential place in their children's lives, and they will value your help. In times of stress, supporting parents *and* their children is an essential task for all who have the best interests of children at heart. It's no surprise that teachers are doing it well.

References

Ahrons, C. 1995. *The good divorce.* New York: HarperCollins.

Furstenberg, F.F., & A. Cherlin. 1991. *Divided families: What happens to children when parents part.* Cambridge, MA: Harvard University Press.

Kelly, J.B. 1993. Current research on children's post-divorce adjustment. *Family and Conciliation Courts Review* 31: 45.

Lewis, J., & W.A.H. Sammons. 1999. *Don't divorce your children: Parents and children talk about divorce.* Chicago: Contemporary Books.

National Children's Survey of the National Center for Health Statistics. 1994. Washington, DC: Government Printing Office.

U.S. Bureau of the Census. 1998. *Current Population Reports* (available only online at www.census.gov).

Wallerstein, J.S., & S. Blakeslee. 1989. *Second chances.* New York: Ticknor & Fields.

Reprinted from *Young Children* 55 (5): 64–65. Copyright © 2000 NAEYC.

Books for Children

Ages 3–5

Thomas, P. 1999. *My family's changing.* Hauppauge, NY: Barron's Educational Series.

Rogers, F. 1996. *Let's talk about divorce.* New York: Putnam.

Spellman, C. 1998. *Mama and Daddy Bear's divorce.* Morton Grove, IL: Albert Whitman.

Ages 7+

Brown, L.K., & M. Brown. 1998. *My parents are divorced too: A book for kids by kids.* New York: Magination.

Danziger, P. 1995. *Amber Brown goes fourth.* New York: Putnam.

Dawson-Boyd, C. 1993. *Chevrolet Saturdays.* New York: Simon & Schuster.

V

Promoting Gender Equity, Respecting Gender Difference

In the preschool and early school years, children are becoming aware of gender and gender roles. For them to wonder and ask about gender role identity and male-female differences is healthy, and adults should respond in a natural manner, attuned to the child's age. Moreover, real gender differences crop up in every classroom, and we should feel comfortable acknowledging them, not deny they exist. At the same time, countering gender stereotypes is integral to antibias education. We want children to grow up seeing the full range of things that each of them can be or do. Gender equity and gender difference are two sides of the same coin, and as teachers we should keep both in mind in planning learning experiences and building a respectful classroom community.

Some readings in this section describe the development of gender awareness and identity (Chrisman & Couchenour; Teaching Tolerance Project). Others examine teaching strategies, classroom characteristics, and curriculum content that help to counter sexism and promote gender equity (Marshall, Robeson, & Keefe; Derman-Sparks & the A.B.C. Task Force). For instance, gender stereotypes appear in many books for young children, but there is children's literature with non-gender-stereotyped characters that teachers and parents can seek out (Roberts & Hill). Finally, since issues of sexuality and gender identity may make us uncomfortable and may be highly charged for some parents, we will do well to think through issues and concerns in this area before we find ourselves on the spot (Cahill & Theilheimer).

Nancy L. Marshall, Wendy Wagner Robeson, and Nancy Keefe

27

Gender Equity in Early Childhood Education

Many people in the United States agree that gender equity is important in elementary and secondary schools. For girls and boys to have equal access to the benefits and responsibilities of citizenship, they must have the opportunity to learn in educational environments that support learning in all academic areas and that foster the development of those skills that are necessary for adult employment and family life.

In this article we review the research and theory that support our argument that gender equity is also important in early childhood education. We then provide guidelines for a gender-equitable early childhood classroom.

The importance of gender equity

In their groundbreaking work *How Schools Shortchange Girls*, researchers at the Wellesley College Center for Research on Women (1995) chronicled the ways in which elementary and secondary schools provide unequal educational opportunities for boys and girls. The re-

search to date suggests that, while boys and girls attend the same schools, they do not have the same educational experiences.

These different educations have consequences for their adult lives. For example, women are less likely to pursue careers in science. In fact, 60 percent of all employed women work in traditionally female fields (clerical, service, or professional positions such as nursing or school teaching) (Wellesley College 1995, 7). Boys mislabeled with learning problems face limited educational and occupational opportunities. And the patterns of same-sex and cross-sex interactions formed in school have potential implications for later interactions in the family and the workplace.

In contrast, children whose educational experiences provide information about the varied roles and perspectives of men and women, and offer equal opportunities to learn, are better prepared for adulthood. In a 1985 review of more than 100 studies, Scott and Schau found that "pupils who are exposed to sex-equitable materials are more likely than others to (1) have gender-balanced knowledge of people in soci-

ety, (2) develop more flexible attitudes and more accurate sex-role knowledge, and (3) imitate role behaviors contained in the material" (1985, 228).

These issues seem far removed from the everyday lives of 3- to 5-year-olds. Yet gender equity is important in early childhood education. Before children enter elementary school, the foundation has already been laid for their understanding of what it means to be a boy or a girl. This understanding guides their participation in, or avoidance of, specific activities and settings that may be instrumental in their learning and success in later years. By promoting gender equity in early childhood education, we can broaden the horizons of all children and ensure that they are ready to learn when they enter kindergarten.

"What are little boys [and girls] made of?"

That is one of the core questions of every society. There are many theories formulated to explain the development of gender concepts and gender roles. Most reviews of the

© Jean-Claude Lejeune

research conclude that each theory has something to contribute, depending on the age of the child and the particular aspect of gender development in question (Huston 1983; Katz 1986). For questions about individual variations in gender-typing and gender-related behavior, the research of Serbin, Powlishta, and Gulko (1993) supports the usefulness of an integrative theory that incorporates cognitive-developmental, schematic-processing, and social learning theories.

In particular, this approach views the child's developing notions of gender-appropriate behavior as a function of (1) the child's use of gender as a way to categorize the self, other people, and the world around him or her (cognitive-developmental paradigm [Kohlberg & Ullian 1978]); (2) the development of *gender schemas*, networks of associated knowledge about gender that guide the cognitive processing of new information about gender (Serbin, Powlishta, & Gulko 1993); and (3) social learning (learning through observation, reinforcement, and modeling of gender-specific behaviors [Golombok & Fivush 1994]).

A child's understanding of what it means to be a boy or a girl develops between the ages of 2 and 7 years. The child must first label the self as a boy or a girl and develop an understanding of gender stability and constancy (I am a girl today and will always be a girl) (Kohlberg 1966; Fagot & Kronsberg 1982). As the child develops, he or she actively seeks out information about what makes a boy a boy and a girl a girl through the use of environmental cues (Brooks-Gunn & Matthews 1979; Archer &

Lloyd 1982). As the child processes these environmental cues, gender schemas are revised continually (Serbin, Powlishta, & Gulko 1993). It is through this process of self-socialization that children develop the gender schemas that guide their behavior (Maccoby & Jacklin 1974).

Once children develop gender constancy, they begin to exhibit a preference for same-sex playmates and same-sex toys and activities (Perry, White, & Perry 1984; Smetana & Letourneau 1984). Because young children need to value things consistent with or like the self, they develop preferences for same-sex values, people, activities, and behaviors (Kohlberg 1966; Brooks-Gunn & Matthews 1979; Martin & Halverson 1981). If a child's environment offers information that indicates that gender roles are very narrowly defined, a child's gender schema can limit his involvement in behaviors that he considers inappropriate for his gender.

What are the environmental cues that children use to build their gender schema, their sense of what it means to be a boy or a girl? Young children take their environmental cues from their parents, other significant people in their lives, the materials and images in their immediate environment, and other children. Variations in these environmental cues can contribute to the gender-related differences often found in children's abilities and talents, even in the early years (Sprafkin et al. 1983).

While family influences are very important to children's development, the educational environment can also be influential in many ways, through the materials and curriculum, through interactions with other children, and through teachers' behaviors. Gender roles and gender schema are often made more explicit and "public" in school and educational settings than in families (Lloyd

A World of Difference

& Duveen 1992). The materials children have available to them are associated with children's themes for play as well as with their social behavior (Obanawa & Joh 1995).

Gender-based preferences can also be influenced by what children believe is gender appropriate. Research studies have found that in the preschool years, girls prefer sewing, stringing beads, playing at housekeeping, painting, drawing, doing artwork, playing with dolls, and engaging in table activities while boys prefer to play with toy guns, toy trucks, carpentry, blocks, and riding toys and to engage in rough-and-tumble play (Clark, Wyon, & Richards 1969; Maccoby & Jacklin 1974; Fagot & Kronsberg 1982; Sprafkin et al. 1983).

Martin, Eisenbud, and Rose (1995) found that if gender-neutral toys were gender labeled, 4- to 6-year-old children made gender-based inferences and liked the toys less if they were attributed to the opposite sex. Smith and Zeedyk (1997) found that, while preschool girls said they preferred feminine-typed toys and neutral-typed toys, they actually played more with the neutral-typed toys. Preschool boys said they preferred both masculine-typed toys and neutral-typed toys, but spent more time playing with the masculine-typed toys.

The influence of peers in children's gender-role development is also important. Preschoolers prefer to play with children of the same sex (Fishbein & Imai 1993) and same-sex peers positively reinforce each other's gender-typed behaviors (Fagot & Kronsberg 1982; Fagot & Leinbach 1983). Positive responses from same-sex peers help to prolong the time boys spend at male-typed activities (Roopnarine 1984).

Both boys and girls receive differential treatment from teachers when playing with "gender-inappropriate" toys or activities. Although girls may be less stereotyped than boys in toy preference (Turner, Gervai, & Hinde 1993), those girls who do participate in masculine-preferred behaviors may, at worst, be ignored by same-sex peers and teachers. Boys who participate in female-preferred activities may receive negative reinforcement and criticisms both from same-sex peers and from their teachers (Fagot 1977, 1984; Etaugh 1983; Eisenberg, Tryon, & Cameron 1984; Smetana & Letourneau 1984).

Teachers can be a powerful influence in promoting play with children of the opposite sex (Eisenberg, Tryon, & Cameron 1984). Such play can broaden a child's choice of friends and provide children with more opportunities to experience various activities and develop associated skills (Asher, Oden, & Gottman 1981; Sprafkin et al. 1983; Gershener & Moore 1985). Furthermore, children act differently when playing in mixed-sex groups; boys use fewer verbal commands and girls use more contradictions (Killen & Naigles 1995).

Early childhood teachers often act and react differently to boys and girls. Teachers expect boys to be more physical, aggressive, exploratory, and independent and girls to be more docile, sociable, and dependent (Katz 1979). They respond differently to each sex when a reprimand is called for (boys often receive a loud public rebuke and girls receive a brief, soft reprimand) and give differing amounts of attention (with boys receiving more attention) (Serbin & O'Leary 1975; Carmichael 1977).

Through such teacher behavior, the classroom materials and activities available to children, and the opportunities for play with same-sex and cross-sex peers, early childhood education plays an important role in children's development. Early childhood classrooms also can help to prepare children for a more gender-equitable future. Children whose gender schemas are more varied and flexible and whose behavioral repertoire includes a range of behaviors, not just those behaviors typically associated with their gender, have the opportunity to observe, practice, and learn the skills they will need in school and in their adult lives.

What does gender equity look like in an early childhood classroom?

The first step in developing a gender-equitable classroom is to establish a set of shared goals. A gender-equitable classroom typically seeks to foster each child's

• development of a positive self-identity as a boy or girl;

• involvement in activities that support the development of a range of skills necessary for success in kindergarten and later school years, including activities that have traditionally been gender-typed for the opposite sex;

• knowledge of the full range of social and occupational roles occupied by women and men in the United States;

• opportunities to play with both same-sex and opposite-sex classmates; and,

• awareness of the negative impact of gender-based teasing and exclusion.

These goals can be achieved through a combination of the curriculum (classroom materials and activities and the organization of physical space and activities) and teachers' behavior. We believe that teachers are most likely to support gender equity when they

• are aware of gender roles in their own lives;

• are knowledgeable of gender issues in children's lives, especially in early childhood education;

• are knowledgeable of the ways in which classroom organization and curriculum activities and materials may affect children's development of gender-typed behavior;

• are knowledgeable of the ways in which their own behavior may affect children's development of gender-typed behavior;

• have access to materials and ideas for activities and teacher behavior that they can use in their classrooms and with parents; and

• are able to problem solve with other teachers some of the challenges inherent in a gender-equitable program, such as gunplay, individual differences in temperament (e.g., shyness, sociability), parents' concerns about the gender-equity goals of the program, and how to support positive gender-identity development without fostering gender-typed behavior.

The gender-equitable classroom also offers a curriculum that supports gender equity. Wilbur (1991) defines a gender-fair curriculum as one that

• acknowledges and affirms *variation,* that is, similarities and differences among and within groups of people;

• is *inclusive,* allowing both females and males to find and identify positively with messages about themselves;

• is *accurate,* presenting information that is data based, verifiable, and able to withstand critical analysis;

• is *affirmative,* acknowledging and valuing the worth of individuals and groups;

• is *representative,* balancing multiple perspectives; and

• is *integrated,* weaving together the experiences, needs, and interests of both males and females.

When gender-equitable goals are expressed in teachers' behavior and in the curriculum, we are likely to find a classroom with the following characteristics:

1. Classroom space is organized to facilitate girls' and boys' involvement in a range of activities. For example, the block corner is not segregated from other activities, and the housekeeping or dramatic play area is located in an area that encourages large-motor activity (at the top of a climbing structure, outside in the playground).

2. Classroom materials include children's books and pictures that show women and men in a range of social and occupational roles and boys and girls in activities and situations that are not gender typed.

3. Classroom materials encourage boys and girls to be involved in a range of activities. For example, Lego building materials include pieces such as people, flowers, house components, machine components; dramatic play materials include props such as men's hats and ties, women's hats, hats from a variety of occupations.

4. Over the course of the week, the program includes a range of activities, including large motor activity, dramatic play, block play, doll play.

5. Teachers model involvement in a range of activities. For example, female teachers and other women participate actively in large motor activities, block building, woodworking, Legos. Male teachers and other men participate actively in cooking, cleaning, art activities, language activities, and nurturing activities such as doll play.

6. Teachers support and reinforce behaviors without attaching gender-specific references and by valuing equally the activities traditionally associated with male or female roles.

7. Teachers encourage children to participate in a range of activities, including those activities that are typically gender typed for the opposite-sex child.

8. Teachers are as likely to have positive, one-on-one interactions with boys as with girls and are not more likely to have negative interactions with boys than with girls.

9. Teachers are as likely to ask girls questions, call on girls in group settings, and provide feedback to girls about their performance as they are to boys.

10. Teachers assign classroom chores/jobs without regard to gender (e.g., boys clean tables, girls carry "heavy" loads).

11. Teachers promote mixed-sex groups and do not foster sex segregation (e.g., do not have children line up by sex, do not designate activities as being for one sex only).

12. Teachers intervene in gender-based teasing or exclusion, including games of "cooties," "boys chase the girls" or "girls chase the boys," or "no boys allowed."

We believe that providing children with a gender-equitable early childhood education is an important first step toward ensuring equal access for all girls and boys to the rights and responsibilities of adulthood in our society. Until we can offer children such gender-fair experiences during

A gender-equitable early childhood education is an important first step toward equal access to the rights and responsibilities of adulthood in our society.

the crucial preschool years, we will not be able to understand what little boys and girls are truly "made of."

References

Archer, J., & B. Lloyd. 1982. *Sex and gender.* Harmondsworth, England: Penguin.

Asher, S.R., S.L. Oden, & J.M. Gottman. 1981. Children's friendships in school settings. In *Contemporary readings in child psychology,* eds. E.M. Hetherington & R.D. Parke. New York: McGraw-Hill.

Brooks-Gunn, J., & W. Matthews. 1979. *He and she: How children develop their sex-role identity.* Englewood Cliffs, NJ: Prentice Hall.

Carmichael, C. 1977. *Non-sexist childraising.* Boston, MA: Beacon.

Clark, A.H., S.M. Wyon, & M.P.M. Richards. 1969. Free play in nursery school children. *Journal of Child Psychology and Psychiatry* 10: 205–16.

Eisenberg, N., K. Tryon, & E. Cameron. 1984. The relation of preschoolers' social interaction to their sex-typed toy choices. *Child Development* 55: 1044–50.

Etaugh, C. 1983. Introduction: The influence of environmental factors on sex differences in children's play. In *Social and cognitive skills,* ed. M.B. Liss. New York: Academic.

Fagot, B.I. 1977. Consequences of moderate cross-gender behavior in preschool children. *Child Development* 48: 902–07.

Fagot, B.I. 1984. Teacher and peer reactions to boys' and girls' play styles. *Sex Roles* 11: 691–702.

Fagot, B.I., & S.J. Kronsberg. 1982. Sex differences: Biological and social factors influencing the behavior of young boys and girls. In *The young child,* eds. S.G. Moore & C.R. Cooper. Washington, DC: NAEYC.

Fagot, B.I., & M.D. Leinbach. 1983. Play styles in early childhood: Social consequences for boys and girls. In *Social and cognitive skills,* ed. M.B. Liss. New York: Academic.

Fishbein, H.D., & S. Imai. 1993. Preschoolers select playmates on the basis of gender and race. *Journal of Applied Developmental Psychology* 14: 303–16.

Gershener, V.T., & L. Moore. 1985. Girl play: Sex segregation in friendships and play patterns of preschool girls. In *When children play,* eds. J.L. Frost & S. Sunderlin. Wheaton, MD: Association for Childhood Education International.

Golombok, S., & R. Fivush. 1994. *Gender development.* Cambridge, England: Cambridge University Press.

Huston, A.C. 1983. Sex typing. In *Handbook of child psychology: Vol. 4. Socialization, personality, and social behavior,* ed. E.M. Hetherington. New York: Wiley.

Katz, P.A. 1979. The development of female identity. In *Becoming female,* ed. C.B. Kopp. New York: Plenum.

Katz, P.A. 1986. Modification of children's gender-stereotyped behavior: General issues and research considerations. *Sex Roles* 14: 591–602.

Killen, M., & L.R. Naigles. 1995. Preschool children pay attention to their addressees: Effects of gender composition on peer disputes. *Discourse Processes* 19: 329–46.

Kohlberg, L. 1966. A cognitive-developmental analysis of children's sex-role concepts and attitudes. In *The development of sex differences,* ed. E.E. Maccoby. Stanford, CA: Stanford University Press.

Kohlberg, L., & P.Z. Ullian. 1978. Stages in the development of psychosexual concepts and attitudes. In *Sex differences in behavior,* eds. R.C. Friedman, R.M. Richard, & R.L. Van de Wiel. Huntington, NY: Krieger.

Lloyd, B., & G. Duveen. 1992. *Gender identities and education.* Hertfordshire, Great Britain: Harvester Wheatsheaf.

Maccoby, E.E., & C.N. Jacklin. 1974. *The psychology of sex differences.* Stanford, CA: Stanford University Press.

Martin, C.L., L. Eisenbud, & H. Rose. 1995. Children's gender-based reasoning about toys. *Child Development* 66: 1453–71.

Martin, C.L., & C.F. Halverson Jr. 1981. A schematic processing model of sex typing and stereotyping in children. *Child Development* 52: 1119–34.

Obanawa, N., & H. Joh. 1995. The influence of toys on preschool children's social behavior. *Psychologia: An International Journal of Psychology in the Orient* 38: 70–76.

Perry, D.G., A.J. White, & L.C. Perry. 1984. Does early sex typing result from children's attempts to match their behavior to sex role stereotypes? *Child Development* 55: 2114–21.

Roopnarine, J.L. 1984. Sex-typed socialization in mixed-age preschool classrooms. *Child Development* 55: 1078–84.

Scott, K., & C. Schau. 1985. Sex equity and sex bias in instructional materials. In *Handbook for achieving sex equity through education,* ed. S. Klein. Baltimore, MD: Johns Hopkins University Press.

Serbin, L.A., & K.D. O'Leary. 1975. How nursery schools teach girls to shut up. *Psychology Today* 9: 57–58, 102–03.

Serbin, L.A., K.K. Powlishta, & J. Gulko. 1993. *The development of sex typing in middle childhood.* Monographs of the Society for Research in Child Development, vol. 58, 1–74. Chicago: University of Chicago Press.

Smetana, J.G., & K.J. Letourneau. 1984. Development of gender constancy and children's sex-typed free play behavior. *Developmental Psychology* 20: 691–96.

Smith, M., & M.S. Zeedyk. 1997. *What's a mother to do? Differences in children's verbal and play preferences for sex-typed toys.* Poster presented at the biennial meeting of the Society for Research in Child Development, Washington, DC.

Sprafkin, C., L.A. Serbin, C. Denier, & J.M. Connor. 1983. Sex-differentiated play: Cognitive consequences and early interventions. In *Social and cognitive skills,* ed. M.B. Liss. New York: Academic.

Turner, P.J., J. Gervai, & R.A. Hinde. 1993. Gender-typing in young children: Preferences, behavior and cultural differences. *British Journal of Developmental Psychology* 11: 323–42.

Wellesley College Center for Research on Women. 1995. *How schools shortchange girls—The AAUW Report.* New York: Marlowe.

Wilbur, G. 1991. *Gender-fair curriculum. Research report prepared for Wellesley College Center for Research on Women, August, 1991.* Cited in Wellesley College Center for Research on Women, *How schools shortchange girls—The AAUW Report* (New York: Marlowe, 1995), 111.

Gender Learning in Early Childhood

Excerpted from *Starting Small*

Gender awareness

Even before they can say the words, most toddlers become adept at pointing out girls and boys, women and men. Gender appears to be one of the first dimensions of identity that young children perceive in self and others. An understanding of the developmental processes young children undergo to acquire information and form attitudes about gender can help early childhood teachers foster gender equity in the classroom.

Children draw their earliest conclusions about gender from obvious traits such as clothing, hairstyle, body shape, and the pitch of the voice. A little later, they begin to learn about the body parts that make boys and girls different. This fascinating subject leads to serious—and sometimes startling—questions as cognitive and verbal skills develop. The time-honored game of "Doctor" and other behaviors also reflect the power of gender curiosity in early childhood.

Between the ages of 4 and 7, children come to realize that being male and being female are permanent bio-logical conditions. In turn, they comprehend that changing one's clothing, interests, or activities does not change one's gender.

Around this time, children start to expand their ideas about gender to include not just what people *are* but what they *do*. This broader sorting is first expressed nonverbally through play. Experts disagree as to the relative importance of "nature" and "nurture" in influencing boys' and girls' playing styles and activity preferences. Most parents and teachers, however, find that children are remarkably receptive to such cues, whatever their source.

According to psychologist Phyllis Katz (1987), children acquire the social "content" of gender awareness in three sequential stages. First, young children learn the culturally appropriate behavior for boys and girls; the toy, activity, and playmate choices expected of each gender. In this stage, they establish firm boundaries around gender roles, often self-segregating by gender in their play groups. It doesn't take them long to assert these patterns verbally: "Girls can't throw"; "Boys don't play with dolls."

Next children learn the expectations associated with adult male and female roles. As they attempt to interpret the adult world, many children make broad assumptions and generalizations: "Men can't cook"; "Mommies don't drive tractors."

In the third stage, children act out adult gender roles based on these concepts. For example, during pretend play, girls become mothers, nurses, and teachers, while boys are the fathers, firefighters, and doctors.

The information children use in constructing gender knowledge comes from a variety of sources— families, peers, media, teachers, children's books, and instructional materials. A significant portion of what they learn about gender occurs informally. Parents influence emerging gender concepts directly and indirectly through the toys they purchase, the roles they model in the home, and the ways they respond to gender issues in children's behavior.

Research shows that family characteristics such as structure, socioeconomic level, class, culture, race, and religion can significantly shape children's "gender learning." For example, Katz (1987) reports that young Latinas, as a group, showed a higher degree of gender stereotyping in their occupational aspirations than did White and Black girls. In the same study, girls who came from single-parent families, regardless of race or ethnicity, showed the least amount of gender stereotyping.

Researchers have confirmed Kohlberg's (1966) theory that gender stereotyping among both boys and girls ages 5 to 7 often entails a preference for the "male" role because it is more exciting and powerful (McCormick 1994). Cultural affirmation of this preference is evident in the differences in status accorded by labels such as "tomboy" and "sissy" or "Daddy's girl" and "Mama's boy." In addition, gender stereotyping can distort children's perception of nonstereotypical role models. When 5- to 7-year-olds were shown pictures of adults in nontraditional roles, such as a female physician and a male nurse, most reported that they had seen the reverse (Signorella 1987).

Such evidence suggests that gender stereotyping in children's own thinking can have an adverse effect on the social and cognitive development of both girls and boys. Teachers who model gender equity in the classroom and intervene appropriately to counteract gender bias recognize these actions as essential steps in celebrating the self-worth, abilities, and potential of all children.

Fostering gender equity

As young children develop gender awareness, they establish rigid lines around gender roles. This gender sorting is expressed in work and play through preferences in toys, playmates, and activities. To foster gender-role flexibility in their students, teachers can organize classroom environments and conduct lessons that encourage boys and girls to engage in cross-gender cooperative activities.

The following guidelines can help teachers incorporate a nonsexist model that rewards the abilities of both girls and boys. Explore and evaluate how these activities can help children expand their perception of gender boundaries.

Create a classroom environment that encourages interaction between boys and girls in all aspects of work and play. For example:

1. Integrate seating arrangements and mix genders when assigning group work.
2. Create learning areas with nonsexist materials that encourage full participation of both girls and boys.
3. Forbid derision based on gender, and encourage inclusion in all activities.

Examine curricular resources to eliminate gender bias. For example:

1. Identify and eliminate language that denies female participation (e.g., replace "fireman" with "firefighter"; avoid use of "he" as a generic pronoun).
2. Inspect books, posters, and bulletin boards for gender balance and varied gender characteristics and roles.
3. Aim for gender balance in the characters, both real and imaginary, that you discuss in class (e.g., celebrate male and female heroes).

Consider how the "hidden curriculum" encourages gender stereotypes, and take steps to counteract the process. For example:

1. Evaluate any differences in behavior expectations and discipline practices toward boys and girls.
2. Observe how you handle emotional issues with girls and boys (e.g., do you attempt to distract crying boys but reassure crying girls?).

3. Examine your use of praise (e.g., make sure that compliments for working quietly and neatly or being brave and strong apply equally to both genders).
4. Practice gender equity in the assignment of classroom duties (e.g., help boys and girls take equal responsibility for moving tables, cleaning up after snack, and dusting shelves).
5. Break down gender stereotypes through your own actions (e.g., a female teacher fixing a wagon or a male teacher mending a doll's dress gives children a broader sense of their own capacities).
6. Provide opportunities for children to engage in activities that challenge gender stereotypes (e.g., as a mixed gender group, design and build a simple bookcase, or make chef hats and have everyone cook a feast).
7. Arrange for adults to visit the classroom to model nontraditional roles (e.g., invite female carpenters and male nurses to talk about what they do).

References

Katz, P.A. 1987. Variations in family constellations: Effects on gender schemata. *New Directions for Child Development* 38: 39–56.
Kohlberg, L. 1966. A cognitive-developmental analysis of children's sex-role concepts and attitudes. In *The development of sex differences*, ed. E.E. Maccoby, 82–173. Stanford, CA: Stanford University Press.
McCormick, T.M. 1994. *Creating the nonsexist classroom: A multicultural approach.* New York: Teachers College Press.
Signorella, M.L. 1987. Gender schemata: Individual differences and context effects. *New Directions for Child Development* 38: 23–38.

Developing Concepts of Gender Roles

Excerpted from *Healthy Sexuality Development*

By age 3, many children can tell you, "I am a boy" or "I am a girl." However, few of them understand facts on which this sexual identity is based. Their information typically comes from parents who have provided the labels "girl" and "boy."

Children who are supported in their own play interests and styles are given a good beginning for healthy development. Adults who provide girls and boys alike both active and quiet play, as well as a variety of toys and materials, are setting the most optimal foundation for healthy sexuality development.

Emotional development comprises a child's ability to understand herself or himself, self-esteem, expression of emotions, and appropriate demonstrations of affection. Before children reach kindergarten age, they often have identified traditionally gender-related activities and toys and often choose to play only with children of the same gender.

Mr. Zane, a first grade teacher, told about a girl in his class, Zoë, who came to school with a very special toy her mother had gotten for her over the weekend. When this male teacher asked the child where she got it, adding that he would like to have one, she said, "Oh, Mr. Z, these are only for girls." Expand-

ing children's understanding of gender roles is an ongoing task for teachers.

Although it is important for children to develop a strong sense of self and incorporate what it means to be a girl or a boy, adults must help children to see that nei-

© Jean-Claude Lejeune

A World of Difference

A Young Child's Healthy Sexuality Development
Relates to All Areas of Development

Physical development and behavior

Is interested in and explores body parts

Gains control over body functions

Experiences changes in the body as he or she grows older

Touches genitals or masturbates

Cognitive development

Learns about body parts and functions

Understands self as boy or girl

Understands others as girls, women, boys, or men

Is curious about and understands concepts about reproduction and other biological systems

Understands similarities and differences among humans

Social development

Is nurtured by loving adults

Makes friendships

Classifies behaviors according to gender roles

Develops basic awareness of morality

Responds to limits set by adults

Demonstrates assertiveness

Emotional development

Displays self-esteem and awareness of gender identity

Expresses affection and caring

Shows empathy

Shows respect for others

Manages anger, sadness, and joy appropriately

---

ther girls nor boys should be limited by gender roles. A teacher might ask Zoë why she believes that this toy is only for girls. Approaches that use stories or scenarios with puppets or props often help older preschool or primary-age children to better understand how boys and girls may play with the same toys and have the same interests. Some important reasons for assisting children in this understanding include the following:

• **Strict gender roles can limit friendships.** When Zoë is playing with her special toy, she is likely to deny boys access to it simply because she mistakenly thinks that only girls can play with that toy.

• **Strict gender roles can affect our feelings about ourselves.** Zoë is likely to believe that if her toy is only for girls, then some other toys are only for boys. She will refrain from playing with these toys and, perhaps, will miss out on some area of competence or interest.

• **Strict gender roles can promote homophobia, and homophobia can promote the supporting of strict gender roles.** Zoë may get the message that boys who want to play with her toy are probably gay and that she should be wary of homosexuality (Cyprian 1998).

Reference

Cyprian, J. 1998. *Teaching human sexuality: A guide for parents and other caregivers.* Washington, DC: Child Welfare League of America.

Adapted from K. Chrisman & D. Couchenour, *Healthy Sexuality Development: A Guide for Early Childhood Educators and Families* (Washington, DC: NAEYC, 2002), 11–13, 28. Copyright © 2002 NAEYC.

Expanding Awareness of Gender Roles

Excerpted from *Anti-Bias Curriculum*

Young children have already learned many things about the importance of gender in society. Engaging children in activities about different types of families and the various things that people of both sexes can do helps to foster a healthy understanding of gender roles amongst children.

• Read books about boys and girls that contradict gender stereotypes, such as *William's Doll* (by C. Zolotow; Harper & Row, 1972). [More titles are listed in reading #32 in this volume.]

• Have the children find and cut out magazine pictures of boys and girls, men and women, showing the diversity of looks, dress, activities, and emotions. Make books with the pictures: "About Girls and Women," "About Boys and Men."

• Create a display of photos and pictures of women and men doing the same kinds of tasks "in the home" and "in the world of work." Make sure there are racial and ethnic diversity and images of differently abled people. Use this to talk about the different tasks the children's family members do, and talk about what kinds of tasks the children do and would like to do when they grow up.

• As the teacher, role model learning new skills and sharing tasks in the classroom in nonsexist ways.

• Read books about different ways families are organized: two parents; single parents; children living with family members other than parents; two-parent families and a live-in grandparent; adopted two-parent, single-parent, same-race, different-race families; "blended" families; gay or lesbian families (two daddies or two mommies—you may decide not to use the words *gay* and *lesbian*, but the child deserves calm recognition of the reality of the composition of his family); only child; many children; cousins living as a family; families without children; single adults who do not live with their families. These last two family types are very hard for children to understand. And don't forget foster families; we usually do. Talk about the different kinds of families of the children and staff.

• Make a picture display of different kinds of families called "Beautiful Families Come in Many Different Ways." Help children understand that all families serve the same functions—to provide a home, to take care of children and adults in the family, and so on.

• Invite members of the children's families (including extended family) who do nontraditional jobs to visit and talk with your class (male flight attendant, nurse, secretary; female construction worker; and so on).

• Support children's dramatic play in nontraditional roles and about different kinds of families.

• Insist that all children take equal responsibility in carrying out the necessary jobs for maintaining the classroom or child care center. Rotate tasks so that girls and boys carry out all tasks.

• Using dolls, tell stories that support nontraditional behaviors and describe the conflicts children sometimes feel when acting in ways that challenge stereotypic gender roles.

Finding a balance

Two issues affect how learning about gender identity is implemented in different settings:

1. Expectations about gender roles are not only affected by the general sexism in our society; ethnic and cultural background also influences people's beliefs about gender behavior. This is one area where the creative tension between respecting diversity and countering sexism can be very apparent. Teachers must be careful not to act in racist ways while trying to be antisexist. This requires: (a) doing activities about gender roles within the context that there are many choices, rather than making some choices superior to others; and (b) finding alternative ways to promote each child's full development.

For example, if a family really doesn't want girls in pants, see if you can agree to special times in the school day when pants are worn for specific large motor physical activities, or for constructing and painting a new piece of equipment. Provide smocks so that good clothes do not get dirty. If a family really doesn't want a boy encouraged to cry, find other ways for that child to express his feelings (dictating/writing a story).

2. Some adults fear that encouraging nontraditional gender behavior (boys who play with dolls or who cry; girls who prefer large motor activities or don't like to wear dresses)

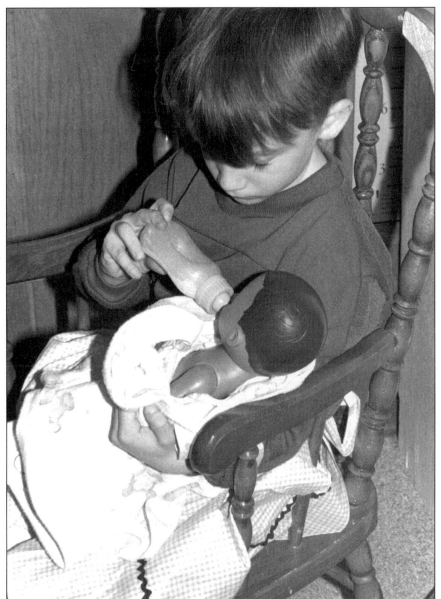

© Marilyn Nolt

leads to homosexuality. There is no research evidence that nontraditional gender behavior creates homosexuality. Nevertheless, teachers may need to spend time in educational discussions with parents who are frightened by their children participating in certain activities, and may have to make choices about

what activities they will stand up for and which they will modify or let go.

Reprinted from Louise Derman-Sparks and the A.B.C. Task Force, *Anti-Bias Curriculum: Tools for Empowering Young Children* (Washington, DC: NAEYC), 53–54. Copyright © 1989 Louise Derman-Sparks. Reprinted with permission.

Betsy J. Cahill and Rachel Theilheimer

31

"Can Tommy and Sam Get Married?"

Questions about Gender, Sexuality, and Young Children

Over lunch, 5-year-old Tommy announced that when he grows up he is going to marry his best friend Sam. "Can Tommy and Sam get married?" Ethan asked his teacher. Ethan was fairly sure that only men and women could marry each other.

The children's teacher was stumped. She approached a colleague who is a lesbian, told the story, and said, "Here's one for you, Laura. I have no idea what to say." This was a sexuality issue that this heterosexual teacher felt was out of her domain. She turned to Laura believing a lesbian would know how to approach it.

Both of them could seek resources. Practical articles inform teachers about talking to children about sexuality (Lively & Lively 1991) and about including gay and lesbian family members in programs (Clay 1990; Corbett 1993; Wickens 1993; Casper et al. 1996). Wickens (1993) even addresses a situation similar to that of Tommy, Sam, and Ethan. She advises teachers who are worried about their job security when responding to children's questions that adults perceive to be related to

lesbian and gay issues. There are also materials that examine how a child develops a homosexual orientation (see Bailey & Zucker 1995; Frieman, O'Hara, & Settel 1996).

This article adds to these resources by helping teachers as they work with children and families. The story of Tommy, Sam, and Ethan raises four questions:

• How can teachers become more comfortable with questions asked about sexual orientation and social conventions?

• What does research tell us about children's developing sexuality, and how can that information be useful to the teachers of young children?

• How can teachers respond when issues of young children's developing sexuality arise in classrooms?

• What are some appropriate ways to talk to families about sexual orientations and societal mores?

Comfort and discomfort with issues of sexuality

"Is my child gay?" Charles's father asked. "He only likes to play with

girls." This parent-to-teacher question is not uncommon in early childhood settings (see Casper et al. 1996). Often teachers respond by reassuring parents that dressing up, pretending, or playing only with friends of the opposite sex is normal for young children. This response puts families at ease and enables the children to continue to play as they choose.

It does not directly answer the question, however, and some parents and teachers may be left feeling unsettled. Mulling it over, teachers may wonder about their own underlying feelings about gay and lesbian issues. The explicit message to Charles's father was, "Don't worry," but the implicit one may be that homosexuality is not normal and could be something to worry about, just not with very young children. A more direct answer might be that we do not know if Charles will be gay or not, but his play choices are probably not indicators of his future sexual orientation.

In their constructions of gender roles, adults often assume (perhaps as Charles's dad did) that boys are masculine and girls are feminine

(Martin 1990). A gender role has many components, including activity choice, interests, skills, dress, and sexual partner (Yorburg 1974).

Many early childhood educators, however, believe that both girls and boys deserve to participate in the full range of activities with friends of their choice regardless of traditional gender designations (Sprung 1975; Derman-Sparks & the A.B.C. Task Force 1989). For example, they believe that girls' active explorations should be encouraged, boys' nurturing behavior should be fostered, and children of both sexes can be playmates.

Yet boys who repeatedly play with dolls or cry and girls who consistently play with trucks or refuse to wear dresses may introduce a new theme (Honig 1983; Lloyd & Duveen 1992). A child's play activities and other behaviors may cause the teacher to question that child's potential sexual orientation. The teacher, even when committed to an antibias approach, may then experience discomfort. In such cases, the teacher may become as concerned as Charles's dad was about the reasons behind the child's behaviors or choice of activities and what they mean.

The first step for teachers who are worried about a child's gender behavior is to acknowledge that their discomfort could stem from what may seem to be the child's developing lesbian or gay orientation. If teachers realize that this is at the root of their concern, they can begin to analyze their feelings about homosexuality and consider the impact their beliefs can have on the children and families with whom they work.

A second step teachers can take to become more comfortable with issues related to homosexuality is to interact with people who are lesbian or gay or have thought a lot about lesbian and gay issues. Local organizations such as a chapter of Parents,

Family, and Friends of Lesbians and Gays (PFFLAG) can serve as a resource to teachers. Ethan's teacher turned to Laura as a resource. She knew Laura and could compare information, including myths and stereotypes, with what she had learned from their professional relationship. Although Laura may not have had a ready answer to Ethan's question, together these teachers could talk openly and from different perspectives to gain an understanding from the challenge Ethan posed.

Third, teachers can proceed to learn more—about children's developing sexuality in general and about the particular child's situation. With knowledge can come more understanding and, subsequently, increased comfort with children's behavior and children's and parents' questions.

Children's developing sexuality

In another classroom, this one for infants and toddlers, Janice called to 18-month-old Maria, "Go hold your boyfriend's hand."

"Are you assuming a norm of heterosexuality?" asked her coworker Bill. "Maria may grow up to have a girlfriend instead."

Janice didn't know what Bill was talking about. She was just getting the children ready to go outside. According to Bill, Janice was making the assumption that Maria would naturally have a boyfriend rather than a girlfriend; she was working from an underlying notion that all children are heterosexual.

Many early childhood teachers, like Janice, have little information about the development of human sexuality. According to Lewis (1987) human sexuality has received almost no attention in the child development literature because prior to puberty the constructs of sexual attrac-

tion and choice of sexual partner cannot be studied. Yet it is misleading to infer from Lewis that children are not developing an understanding of and feelings about sexuality. As the new guidelines for developmentally appropriate practice state,

> From birth, children are actively engaged in constructing their own understandings from their experiences, and these understandings are mediated by and clearly linked to the sociocultural context. (Bredekamp & Copple 1997, 13)

The messages Maria receives from Janice, Bill, and the other adults and children who are part of her sociocultural context will contribute to Maria's construction of herself as a sexual being.

Lively and Lively discuss how sexuality develops. They maintain that the nature of human sexuality starts at birth or even in utero, forming "the base on which the evolution of children to adolescence is built" (1991, 14). Several external factors also influence children's sexuality. The care they receive during infancy has an impact on their attitudes toward their bodies as sources of pleasure and pride. Early relationships, including the physical dimensions of touching and responding to touch, ground all development, including sexual development. In addition, children observe relationships around them, expressions of feelings, and physical interactions. These findings indicate that how caregivers and families behave toward children can have a lasting influence on how children later feel about their sexual identities (Lively & Lively 1991).

There are no consistent findings in the literature on how a child develops a heterosexual or homosexual orientation. Sexual orientation appears to be formed by a complex interplay among psychological, biological, and social situations (Strickland 1995). Although we do not know at what age or how children develop their sexual orientation, we can be sure young children are developing images of themselves as sexual beings that influence their understandings and acceptance of their sexuality (Lively & Lively 1991). How their caregivers interact with them and the messages the caregivers give about sexuality do matter to the ways in which children perceive themselves.

Janice took a heterosexual world for granted and was surprised when Bill took issue with her assumption that Maria would naturally have a boyfriend. Janice had not considered that Maria was developing a sexual orientation. As a conscientious and caring teacher, Janice did not want to hurt Maria. She did not know that what she had said without thinking could negatively affect a child's perception of herself.

Responding to children

Maria and Janice's story helps one think about how teachers' language and behavior can affect how children look at themselves. Charles's father's story raises questions about how teachers might think about their reactions to children's behavior and children's potential sexual orientation. The story involving Ethan, Tommy, and Sam raises a still-unanswered question for teachers: How should they respond when children ask questions that adults believe are linked to gay and lesbian issues?

We do not know what Tommy and Sam had in mind when they said they planned to get married. Perhaps because they are best friends they think about marriage as the ultimate attestation to deep friendship.

© Mark Klein

They may grow up to be gay, or one or both of them may become heterosexual adults. Not knowing how their sexual orientations are developing and wanting to be inclusive of all that children are and will become, Ethan's teacher must respond thoughtfully.

Some teachers' first inclination might be to ignore Ethan's question. Teachers who feel uneasy with the issues may not want to place themselves in an uncomfortable situation or may not want to transmit their discomfort to the children. While both of these reasons are understandable, ignoring the child's question lends the mystique of taboo to the issue and devalues children's thinking. Since children really do raise questions related to gay and lesbian issues, as Tommy, Sam, and Ethan did, teachers who are not comfortable with the questions must be prepared to respond nonetheless.

Some teachers may feel such discussions belong in the home, handled by families. Sexuality, like religion and death, is a topic about which many families have strong beliefs. Teachers may want to say, "Go ask your parents." The child, however, has asked the teacher and awaits a response. Sending the child to her parents gives the message that the teacher is avoiding the issue. Although parents should know about their child's questions and how a teacher handled them, the responsibility for answering those questions remains with the teacher.

Other teachers may worry that they cannot answer a question about same-sex marriages at a level that children can understand. Sometimes a simple, honest answer suffices. One teacher response might be, "Tommy and Sam can choose to live together when they grow up. There are men who prefer to make a family with another man instead of with a woman. And they love each other just like other families. They can

A World of Difference

even have a wedding ceremony if they want." This is a clear and factual response that answers the question directly, although it does not raise new questions about the complexities of laws about and societal attitudes toward lesbians and gays. Some children will be satisfied; others will have more comments and questions.

How can the teacher know exactly what 5-year-old Ethan had in mind when he asked his question? Even a simple answer may be off the mark if the question meant something else to the child. To gain better insight into Ethan's thinking, his teacher can ask him some careful questions.

The teacher might respond, "Ethan, what do *you* think? Can two men marry each other?" The teacher might draw Tommy and Sam into the discussion to have the benefit of more views as children and teacher think about the issue together. Eliciting Ethan's understandings will help his teacher become more certain of his meaning and enable Ethan to construct his own knowledge on the subject. The teacher can then elaborate and clarify instead of providing information that might be off target.

A class meeting can be a forum for everyone's ideas and can enable children to socially construct an understanding of the complex interrelated issues involved. One such meeting in a class of 5- and 6-year-olds began when the teacher wrote this question on the morning meeting chart: "Can a man marry a man? Can a woman marry a woman?" (Wolkenberg 1993). The teacher described to the children how the question arose when the children were on a class trip. The subsequent discussion, with very little teacher intervention, touched on marriage in contrast to living together, marriage rituals such as weddings and the accompanying conventions, parenting and children, adoption, laws in the United States and elsewhere, love, and divorce.

Children asked each other to define terms such as "gay." In this situation the teacher raised an issue to all the children, including those who did not bring it up. Yet more views led to a richer discussion.

How Ethan's teacher should handle his question depends on the community she serves, what she already knows about the children and families, and her beliefs and classroom practices. She must also keep in mind that what she says—and does not say—affects what the children are learning about their own and other people's sexuality. The points raised here can help her as she strives to be responsive to all children:

• Ignoring a child's question is disrespectful to the child

• Children's questions deserve clear and honest responses

• Teachers should delve into the meaning of a child's question

• As children talk about their views, teachers are responsible for elaborating and elucidating

• Different perspectives from a group of children enrich discussion and the knowledge constructed through it

Because discussions of gay and lesbian issues grow out of many adult feelings and a history of avoidance, teachers have a special responsibility to answer and discuss children's questions openly and honestly. Teachers cannot expect questions to be resolved immediately; as with other complex topics, issues may emerge again to be examined repeatedly by the children.

Talking to parents

If Ethan's teacher planned to gather the children for a discussion of Ethan's question, she might inform their families in advance. She might write a note for children to take home that evening. Here is a sample of such a letter:

Dear Families,
One of the children raised a question today. He asked if two men could marry each other. Tomorrow we will discuss it as a group. I anticipate that the children will have many interesting ideas and questions. Please join us for the discussion at 10 A.M. if you can. You might also want to talk to your child about the conversation and continue it at home. If you have any questions, please give me a call.

Some parents probably will want to talk to the teacher. For example, Takisha's father might want to know what happened that precipitated a classroom discussion related to lesbian and gay issues. After the discussion, he may want to hear the details of what the teacher and the children said. Together the teacher and Takisha's father could talk about the discussion—what it meant for Takisha, the other children, and the teacher, and what it means now for the parent.

On the other hand, some parents may be angry. Guy's grandmother might be concerned that the school is overstepping its bounds by discussing a topic that she did not want discussed with Guy or that she felt belonged exclusively in their home. She and the teacher would need an in-depth conversation away from the children to communicate effectively with each other. There they would have the chance to understand each other's perspectives and discuss their ideas for handling Guy's questions. Families and teachers may have to negotiate with one another to arrive at responses with which they are comfortable (Berger 1995). During the conversation the teacher could explain that her goal is for the children to grow up feeling comfortable with themselves and each other, accepting who they are and who they are becoming in all areas of their development.

Conclusion

Lee was 6 and had decided she was a boy. The other children knew she was a girl but accepted her gender choice and often referred to her as "he." Lee wore short hair and overalls and played mostly with boys. Although Lee's parents were not concerned, her teachers wanted to find out why Lee seemed confused about her gender.

Lee's teachers followed the process outlined in this article. Their first step was to examine their concerns. Talking it over, they realized they felt there was something wrong when a 6-year-old seemed not to know her biological sex. Six seemed too old for Lee not to know she was a girl. This delay worried them, although Lee did not seem to have lags in any other areas. As they talked to each other, they realized that Lee's nonstereotypical gender role behavior made them wonder if she would grow up to be a lesbian. They talked about how each of them felt about this possibility.

Next the teachers tried to learn more about what was really going on. They decided to read about children's developing gender identity and its relationship to children's developing sexual identity. They also spent more time with Lee. Talking to her and her friends revealed that Lee believed girls and boys could be whatever they wanted to be when they grew up. However, Lee said, girls could not be daddies. Her father was a very important person in her life, and projecting herself into the future, Lee did not want to rule out the possibility of being just like him.

Families and teachers may have to negotiate with one another to arrive at responses with which they are comfortable.

Lee's teachers stopped worrying. She had explained to them that she knew she was a girl and was pretending to be a boy. The teachers appreciated her desire to be like her mom *and* her dad. In this case their response to the child was to accept her behavior.

They also shared their discoveries about Lee with her parents. Although Lee's parents had not expressed any concern about their daughter, they were pleased to know what the teachers had learned: Lee adored her father.

The teachers in Lee's story thought about their own feelings regarding the issues Lee raised for them. They sought information from their reading and from the child herself. Then they responded to Lee and communicated with her parents. In this process the teachers made no assumptions about children's developing sense of self. By understanding Lee and some of the issues she raised for them, these teachers were working to create a community of respect for all children.

References

Bailey, M.J., & K.J. Zucker. 1995. Childhood sex-typed behavior and sexual orientation: A conceptual analysis and quantitative review. *Developmental Psychology* 31 (1): 43–55.

Berger, E.H. 1995. *Parents as partners in education: Families and schools working together.* Englewood Cliffs, NJ: Merrill.

Bredekamp, S., & C. Copple, eds. 1997. *Developmentally appropriate practice in early childhood programs.* Rev. ed. Washington, DC: NAEYC.

Casper, V., H.K. Cuffaro, S. Schultz, J.G. Silin, & E. Wickens. 1996. Toward a most thorough understanding of the world: Sexual orientation and early childhood education. *Harvard Educational Review* 66 (2): 271–93.

Clay, J. 1990. Working with lesbian and gay parents and their children. *Young Children* 45 (3): 31–35.

Corbett, S. 1993. A complicated bias. *Young Children* 48 (3): 29–31.

Derman-Sparks, L., & the A.B.C. Task Force. 1989. *Anti-bias curriculum: Tools for empowering young children.* Washington, DC: NAEYC.

Frieman, B.B., H. O'Hara, & J. Settel. 1996. Issues in education: What heterosexual teachers need to know about homosexuality. *Childhood Education* 73 (1): 40–42.

Honig, A. 1983. Sex role socialization in early childhood. *Young Children* 44 (4): 61–75.

Lewis, M. 1987. Early sex role behavior and school age adjustment. In *Masculinity/femininity: Basic perspectives*, eds. J.M. Reinisch, L.A. Rosenblum, & S.A. Sanders, 202–26. New York: Oxford University Press.

Lively, V., & E. Lively. 1991. *Sexual development of young children.* Albany, NY: Delmar.

Lloyd, B., & G. Duveen. 1992. *Gender identities and education.* New York: Harvester Wheatsheaf/St. Martin's Press.

Martin, C.L. 1990. Attitudes and expectations about children with nontraditional and traditional gender roles. *Sex Roles* 22: 151–65.

Sprung, B. 1975. *Nonsexist education for young children.* New York: Citation.

Strickland, B.R. 1995. Research on sexual orientation and human development: A commentary. *Developmental Psychology* 31 (1): 137–40.

Wickens, E. 1993. Penny's question: I will have a child in my class with two moms—What do you know about this? *Young Children* 48 (3): 25–28.

Wolkenberg, D. 1993. David's discussion: Who can marry? Transcript distributed at the Reconceptualizing Research in Early Childhood Education Conference, October, Ann Arbor, Michigan.

Yorburg, B. 1974. *Sexual identity: Sex roles and social change.* New York: Wiley.

Lisen C. Roberts and Heather T. Hill

32

Using Children's Literature to Debunk Gender Stereotypes

Pinky is a 7-year-old boy who likes the color pink and is best friends with Rex, a girl who likes dinosaurs. In *Pinky and Rex and the Bully,* he tells the antagonist, "It's none of your business what I like or who I play with. I'm not a sissy, and I'm not a girl."

In the list on page 127, we present *Pinky and Rex and the Bully* and 21 other books for 4- to 6-year-olds that break gender role stereotypes. Why do we need such a list?

Sex is biologically determined, but gender is a social construct—the behaviors, attitudes, roles, and activities typically associated with, assigned to, or expected of one sex. The terms are not interchangeable. By age 3, most children can identify themselves as girls or boys, but they are still sorting out the concept of gender. Most, for example, will not understand until the age of 6 or 7 that sex is permanent and determined by anatomy rather than external characteristics such as clothing, hairstyle, or toy choice.

The early childhood years are crucial for learning about gender. Young children are strongly influenced by our society's traditional gender role norms. To reach their individual potential, unbound by gender role constraints, young children need adults to challenge society's gender role stereotypes (Derman-Sparks & the A.B.C. Task Force 1989; Wellhousen 1996).

Children's books, in addition to promoting language skills and entertaining children, also socialize children to our cultural norms. Gender is one important component of that socialization. The images of gender roles presented in children's literature contribute to children's understanding of gender in our society (Peterson & Lach 1990; Singh 1998).

Despite the increasing cultural awareness of changing gender roles, much of children's literature continues to present traditional stereotypes (Rudman 1995). Many children's books present, for example, boys as adventurous, independent, and capable, and girls as dependent, naïve, and passive (Singh 1998). In a study of nearly one thousand titles listed in *The Horn Book Guide* (Ernst 1995) that referred to one gender or the other, male-oriented titles appeared 55 percent more often than female-

oriented titles. Studies of recent award-winning (Caldecott, Newbery) literature similarly find more male presence than female in titles and in frequency of picture representations, main characters, and supporting characters (Ernst 1995; Turner-Bowker 1996; Nilges & Spencer 2002). An examination of the books kindergarten teachers perennially read to children revealed nearly twice as many male images as female (Narahara 1998).

Not only are male images far more dominant in children's literature, there is also a discrepancy in the images themselves. Male characters tend to be described as more active than female characters (Turner-Bowker 1996). Female characters are more likely to be engaged in traditional household tasks such as food preparation and cleaning, while male characters are more likely to be engaged in traditional production tasks such as agriculture and construction (Crabb & Bielawski 1994). Male characters tend to be presented as active problem solvers, while female characters are passive followers (Ernst 1995).

© Marilyn Nolt

We must critically examine children's books and select non-gender-stereotyped literature. The Council on Interracial Books for Children (CIBC 1990) provides a checklist for analyzing children's books for sexism. For example, it says to check the illustrations:

Look for stereotypes such as the domestic mother or wicked stepmother.

Look for tokenism. Is there just one female character surrounded by males?

Examine who is doing what. Are males depicted as active and females as passive? Who is in a leadership role and who is subservient?

Second, check the storyline:

Is a particular problem faced by a female resolved through the benevolent intervention of a male?

Are the achievements of female characters based on their own initiative and intelligence?

Could the same story be told if the gender roles were reversed?

Further guidelines for positive non-gender-stereotyped literature include checking that the characters are portrayed as individuals; that male and female characters are engaged in similar activities, occupations, and household chores; and that there is cooperation rather than competition between the sexes (CIBC 1990; Rudman 1995).

We can also discuss literature with children to promote antibiased thinking (Derman-Sparks & the A.B.C. Task Force 1989). Temple (1993) presents a classroom dialogue with second- and third-graders on the gender-stereotyped story "Beauty and the Beast." The teacher

poses questions such as, "What if Beauty had been kind and clever but not pretty?" and "What if Beauty had been a boy and the Beast a girl?" Teachers can ask similar questions with any book they present to the class. Temple urges teachers to promote children's active examination of literature, rather than passive acceptance.

Certain children's books counteract our society's lingering emphasis on traditional roles for each gender and present the female perspective more frequently. Sharing these non-gender-stereotyped books with children increases individual self-esteem and attitudes of gender equity in early childhood (Ochman 1996; Trepanier-Street & Romatowski 1999).

Because there are so many children's books available that present stereotypical roles and behaviors and an imbalance of the two genders, teachers should make a conscious effort to introduce books to young children that are free of gender stereotypes. We need to read books with young children that present girls as creative, capable, and intelligent and boys as nurturing, artistic, and compassionate (Derman-Sparks & the A.B.C. Task Force 1989; Fox 1993; Wellhousen 1996; Odean 1997, 1998; Singh 1998). We need to share books with strong characters and good plots that treat both genders with respect for the complexity of real lives (Rudman 1995; Carden 1998). Two sources for finding such books are Odean's *Great Books for Girls* (1997) and *Great Books for Boys* (1998), which each present about 600 books for young people of all ages. The librarian at your local library can be a resource too.

We have compiled our own list of 22 favorites for 4- to 6-year-old children in particular, some of which also appear in Odean's guides. In most cases, the citations refer to the current hardcover editions.

A World of Difference

Children's Books that Break Gender Role Stereotypes

Amazing Grace. By Mary Hoffman. Illustrated by Caroline Binch. 1991. New York: Dial Books for Young Readers.

Grace loves to act out stories. She eventually overcomes restrictions of gender and race to play the part of her dreams, Peter Pan, in the school play.

Anna Banana and Me. By Lenore Blegvad. Illustrated by Erik Blegvad. [1987] 1999. Distributed by Econo-Clad Books.

Anna Banana is a fearless young girl. When she plays with a timid boy, he eventually becomes as brave as his friend.

The Art Lesson. Written and illustrated by Tomie DePaola. 1999. New York: Putnam. Distributed by Econo-Clad Books.

Tommy loves to draw but feels constrained in art class. A new teacher finally strikes a compromise to allow for Tommy's creativity.

Boy, Can He Dance! By Eileen Spinelli. Illustrated by Paul Yalowitz. [1993] 1999 Lib ed. Bt Bound.

Tony doesn't want to become a chef like his father. Instead, he wants to dance.

The Chalk Box Kid. By Clyde Bulla. Illustrated by Thomas B. Allen. 1987. New York: Random House.

Gregory does not have anywhere to grow a garden, so he creates one of his own.

Christina Katerina and the Box. By Patricia Lee Gauch. Illustrated by Doris Burn. 1998. New York: PaperStar/Putnam's Sons.

An innovative young girl finds a number of uses for a large box.

Ira Sleeps Over. Written and illustrated by Bernard Waber. 1973. Boston: Houghton Mifflin.

When Ira is invited to sleep over at Reggie's house, he must decide whether to take his beloved teddy bear. In the end, he learns that it is acceptable for boys to have teddy bears.

Little Granny Quarterback. By Bill Martin Jr. and Michael Sampson.

Illustrated by Michael Chesworth. 2001. Honesdale, PA: Boyds Mills Press.

Granny, who was a star quarterback in her youth, leaps into her television to assist her favorite team with the winning touchdown.

Mama and Me and the Model T. By Faye Gibbons. Illustrated by Ted Rand. 1999. New York: Morrow Junior Books/HarperCollins.

When the Model T arrives, Mama proves that she, like the men, can drive.

Mermaid Janine. By Iolette Thomas. Illustrated by Jennifer Northway. 1993. New York: Scholastic Trade.

Janine takes swimming lessons and becomes determined to swim the length of the pool. With practice and attention to her body's strength, she finally does.

Mirette on the High Wire. Written and illustrated by Emily McCully. 1992. New York: Putnam Group Juvenile.

Mirette learns to walk the tight rope, taught by Monsieur Bellini, who himself has withdrawn from performance due to fear.

More Than Anything Else. By Marie Bradby. Illustrated by Chris K. Soentpiet. 1995. New York: Orchard Books.

This is based on the childhood of Booker T. Washington, a boy who wants more than anything else to learn how to read.

Nessa's Fish. By Nancy Luenn. Illustrated by Neil Waldman. 1999. Econo-Clad Books.

When Nessa's grandmother becomes ill on a fishing excursion, Nessa defends her and their catch against wild animals.

The Paper Bag Princess. By Robert Munsch. Illustrated by Michael Martchenko. 1988. Annick Press.

Princess Elizabeth rescues her prince from a fire-breathing dragon. When he doesn't appreciate her efforts, she decides not to marry him after all.

Pinky and Rex and the Bully. By James Howe. Illustrated by Melissa Sweet. 1996. The Pinky and Rex series. New York: Atheneum.

A boy who loves the color pink defends himself and his choice for a best friend, a girl who loves dinosaurs.

Sam Johnson and the Blue Ribbon Quilt. Written and illustrated by Lisa Campbell Ernst. 1983. William Morrow/HarperCollins.

Sam isn't welcome into the women's quilting club so he organizes a men's quilting group. Eventually the men and women join to make a quilt together.

The Story of Ferdinand. By Munro Leaf. Illustrated by Robert Lawson. 1987. New York: Viking.

This classic about the value of peace presents Ferdinand, a young bull who prefers smelling flowers to butting heads.

Tonio's Cat. By Mary Calhoun. Illustrated by Edward Martinez. 1996. New York: Morrow Junior Books/HarperCollins.

Tonio is new in town and wants to make friends. At the risk of making himself an outcast, he defends Toughy, a stray cat, against the other kids.

Tough Boris. By Mem Fox. Illustrated by Kathryn Brown. 1994. San Diego: Harcourt Brace.

Boris is tough, but in the end, when his parrot companion dies, he—like all pirates—cries.

When Sophie Gets Angry, Really, Really Angry. Written and illustrated by Molly Bang. 1999. New York: Scholastic Trade.

Sophie gets angry and deals with her strong feelings by climbing trees.

White Dynamite and Curly Kidd. By Bill Martin Jr. and John Archambault. Illustrated by Ted Rand. 1996. New York: Henry Holt.

A child excitedly watches Dad ride the rodeo bull and wants to grow up to be a bull rider like him. The twist is that she's a girl.

Will I Have a Friend? By Miriam Cohen. Illustrated by Lillian Hoban. 1989. New York: Alladin. Distributed by Econo-Clad Books.

Jim worries about the first day of school until he connects with another boy.

References

Carden, K. 1998. Mining for gold in children's books. *Christian Science Monitor*, June 23, B8.

CIBC (Council on Interracial Books for Children). 1990. *Guidelines for selecting bias-free textbooks and storybooks*. New York: Author. Also available online as "10 quick ways to analyze children's books for racism and sexism" at www.birchlane.davis.ca.us/library/10quick.htm.

Crabb, P.B., & D. Bielawski. 1994. The social representation of material culture and gender in children's books. *Sex Roles* 30: 69–79.

Derman-Sparks, L., & the A.B.C. Task Force. 1989. *Anti-bias curriculum: Tools for empowering young children*. Washington, DC: NAEYC.

Ernst, S.B. 1995. Gender issues in books for children and young adults. In *Battling dragons: Issues and controversy in children's literature*, ed. S. Lehr, 66–78. Portsmouth, NH: Heinemann.

Fox, M. 1993. Men who weep, boys who dance: The gender agenda between the lines in children's literature. *Language Arts* 70 (2): 84–88.

Narahara, M. 1998. *Gender bias in children's picture books: A look at teachers' choice in literature*. ERIC, ED 419247.

Nilges, L.M., & A.F. Spencer. 2002. The pictorial representation of gender and physical activity level in Caldecott medal winning children's literature: A relational analysis of physical culture. *Sport, Education & Society* (7): 135–51.

Ochman, J.M. 1996. The effects of nongender-role stereotyped same-sex role models in storybooks on the self-esteem of children in grade three. *Sex Roles* 35: 711–35.

Odean, K. 1998. *Great books for boys*. New York: Ballantine.

Odean, K. 1997. *Great books for girls*. New York: Ballantine.

Peterson, S.B., & M.A. Lach. 1990. Gender stereotypes in children's books: The prevalence and influence on cognitive and affective development. *Gender and Education* 2 (2): 185–98.

Rudman, M.K. 1995. *Children's literature: An issues approach*. 3d ed. White Plains, NY: Longman.

Singh, M. 1998. *Gender issues in children's literature*. ERIC, ED 424591.

Temple, C. 1993. "What if Beauty had been ugly?" Reading against the grain of gender bias in children's books. *Language Arts* 70 (2): 89–93.

Trepanier-Street, M.L., & J.A. Romatowski. 1999. The influence of children's literature on gender role perceptions: A reexamination. *Early Childhood Education Journal* 26 (3): 155–59.

Turner-Bowker, D.M. 1996. Gender stereotyped descriptors in children's picture books: Does "Curious Jane" exist in the literature? *Sex Roles* 35: 461–88.

Wellhousen, K. 1996. Girls can be bull riders, too! Supporting children's understanding of gender roles through children's literature. *Young Children* 51 (5): 79–83.

Reprinted from *Young Children* 58 (2): 39–42. Copyright © 2003 NAEYC.

VI

Creating an Inclusive Classroom

Because many families are eager for their children to participate in early childhood programs alongside their typically developing peers, children with disabilities are participating in such programs in substantial numbers. As early childhood educators we face both challenges and rewards in creating high-quality, inclusive classrooms and in working collaboratively with families and other professionals (Allred, Briem, & Black).

As in other areas of diversity, children begin early to learn attitudes toward others, and carry these with them as they mature (Diamond & Stacey). Not surprisingly, the greatest influence on these attitudes is how children see adults respond to children who have disabilities. Do we respond to children with disabilities with openness and acceptance, for example, or with nervousness and discomfort (McDermott)? An essential step for every program that includes a child with a disability is considering that child's specific abilities and needs and planning how to respond to them (Flynn & Kieff). By compelling us to plan carefully for the children with disabilities, inclusion continually reminds us that thoughtful individualized planning has great value for every child in our class.

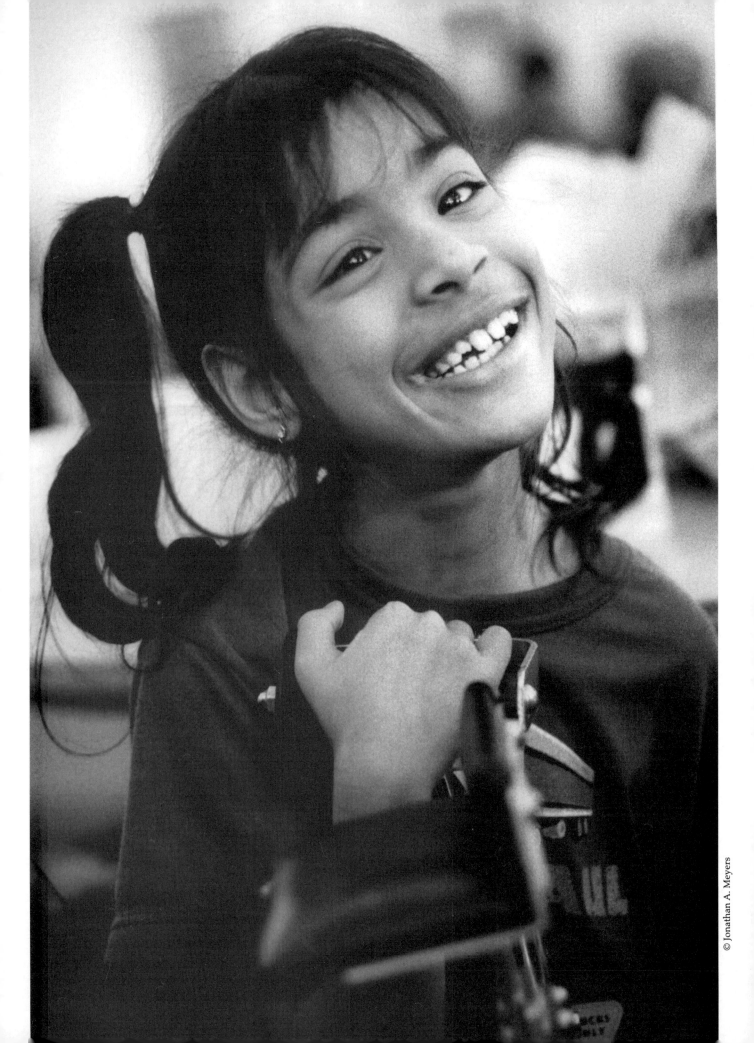

Keith W. Allred, Raquel Briem, and Sharon J. Black

33

Collaboratively Addressing Needs of Young Children with Disabilities

Increasing numbers of parents of young children with disabilities are placing their children in neighborhood preschools, play groups, and child care rather than obtaining services in segregated facilities. Although integrating such children in the environments in which they would typically participate if they did not have disabilities is considered by many to be best practice (Salisbury 1991; Chandler 1994; Wolery & Wilbers 1994), this approach can place heavy demands on early childhood teachers, caregivers, and parents (Cripe & Crabtree 1995; Bricker & Widerstrom 1996).

To designate the services, service locations, and responsible persons involved in caring for a child with a disability, an Individualized Family Service Plan (IFSP) is developed by an interdisciplinary team that may include early intervention professionals, therapists, caregivers, preschool teachers, and health care providers, in addition to the child's parents (DeHaas-Warner 1994; Wolery & Wilbers 1994; Cohen 1995).

If the plan is developed collaboratively by this group of concerned participants and is implemented naturally but purposefully into the child's daily routines, all of those involved in the care and education of the child will find that the demands of working with the child in natural settings will present fewer uncertainties and challenges.

Organizing and collaborating

Professionals from several disciplines bring to the IFSP the insights and objectivity that result from professional knowledge and experience (McCormick & Feeney 1995). They work with the parents of the child to set goals that are feasible and functional for the specific child (Dunst 1991). Such goals should reflect not only the professionals' knowledge and experience but, most important, the family's needs, concerns, priorities, and values.

The Division for Early Childhood Task Force on Recommended Practices (1993) states that the IFSP should be individualized to the needs of the family, respectful and supportive of the family, and responsive to individual and family change. Parents who feel ownership of the child's goals are more likely to consider these goals as top priorities in their family routine, rather than as additional burdens that must be imposed on top of a full slate of family responsibilities (Winton, McCollum, & Catlett 1997).

As parents need the guidance and support of early childhood professionals, the professionals need the input and support of the family as well. Family members provide insights into the individual strengths and weaknesses of a child with a disability. Their knowledge of and intimate relationship with the child can help professionals to make efficient use of their time, resources, and capabilities so that their already demanding schedules will not be overly stretched (Cripe & Crabtree 1995).

© Michael Siluk

Identifying existing routines

Routines within the family

Most families develop routines and rituals that provide structure, stability, and efficiency in their daily lives. With guidance from professionals, IFSP goals can be worked into a family's daily schedule in ways that utilize the family's unique resources (Brotherson & Goldstein 1992).

Professionals can help parents identify what the child needs to do to participate more fully in each aspect of the family's routine and derive the greatest benefit from that participation (Bricker & Cripe 1989; Johnson, McGonigel, & Kaufmann 1989). The functions involved in daily activities such as bath time, diapering, cleaning, or mealtime offer opportunities for the child's skill development that parents may not recognize because the routines have become mundane.

Routines within the professional setting

Most professionals develop routines for the same reasons families do. A child care facility or preschool may have a routine snacktime, circle time, naptime, and so forth. As with family routines, these activities provide rich opportunities to carry out ecologically functional goals (Hobbs 1975; Bricker & Cripe 1992; Fox & Hanline 1993). When interventions are implemented within activities that exist in the environment, the skills the child learns will be functional and more easily generalized to additional settings (Diamond, Hestenes, & O'Connor 1994).

In adapting these routines, professionals are able to apply the underlying principles of developmentally appropriate practice as a framework for forming IFSP goals that are ecologically based (Hobbs 1975; Bronfenbrenner 1979).

Developing child and family goals

Listening to each other

Parents and professionals may have different perceptions regarding what the child's needs are and what the goals should be (Bailey 1987; Kaiser & Hemmeter 1989). When differences occur, it is important for team members to respect each other's perspectives and contributions. All members of the IFSP team need to understand what the parents want for their child (Bernheimer, Gallimore, & Weisner 1990).

Parents should describe what the child needs in order to participate more fully in family life. For example, if the family eats several meals a day together and the child is unable to handle a utensil, a high-priority goal would be to work on helping the child to eat independently. While the professionals may have a more objective view of priorities and objectives that are appropriate for a child with a particular disability, they should *suggest* objectives to parents, explaining how each relates to more long-term goals.

Incorporating goals with routines

When goals and objectives have been selected, the IFSP team should reexamine routines and brainstorm to identify additional opportunities in the child's various environments for working on the chosen objectives and goals (Seibert 1987). For example, if encouraging the child to make more eye contact has been chosen as a goal, a child care worker could work on this goal while greeting the child each morning and during the daily singing time. In addition, parents could be encouraged to work on eye contact during family meals.

Making goals visible

Many people find it easier to remember to work goals into routines if the goals are visible. Parents may want to post signs in areas of the home where the routines naturally occur. For example, this chart might be placed in the bathroom:

Washup/bathtime

• Sign the words *bath, bubbles, soap, wet, dry*

• Poke bubbles, shaving cream

- Turn faucet on and off
- Climb into tub
- Point to nose, eyes, ears while looking in mirror

If preschool teachers or child care providers want to post goals, they ensure that the child with a disability is not singled out. A goal such as making eye contact could be listed as "making eye contact with each individual in the class during daily singing time."

Arranging and adapting goals creatively

A variety of opportunities for naturalistic teaching can be discovered with a little ingenuity and foresight (Hanline & Fox 1993; Noonan & McCormick 1993), if the IFSP team works collaboratively to identify them.

When?

Although goals for a young child with a disability should be integrated with existing routines whenever possible, opportunities to practice skills and competencies should not be limited to daily routines. For example, dressing independently fits smoothly into the morning routine of dressing to prepare for the day, but additional practice might occur when the child is putting on a jacket before playing outside on a cool day or putting on shoes after taking a nap.

Engaging in make-believe activities such as dressing up provides additional practice activities for a child capable of symbolic/dramatic play. The teacher could also encourage parents to provide these same opportunities at home by reminding them how much young children enjoy dressing up in mom's and dad's clothes. Taken a step further, if parents and older siblings engage in dress-up games, the young

child is more likely to imitate and thus participate in additional practice opportunities.

Who?

Another way to work in additional practice is for significant individuals other than the mother and the preschool teacher to find opportunities to work with the child. Fathers of children with disabilities are sometimes neglected during planning by professionals (Davis & May 1991; Allred 1992). An alert IFSP team will find that the timing of routines such as dressing can be arranged to fit with a father's schedule as well as a mother's. Older siblings also can participate. In addition to the child's teacher, school personnel such as a school bus driver, cafeteria worker, or custodian may be able to participate in practicing self-help and independence goals.

How?

As Diamond, Hestenes, and O'Connor point out, "A critical element of activity-based intervention strategies involves embedding in all types of classroom activities teaching that is related to children's individual goals and objectives" (1994, 72). For experienced teachers such embedding occurs naturally, but parents often find it difficult. If a child's goal is to squat and return to standing position, then the teacher may structure activity time, singing, snacktime, and so forth such that the child is repeatedly involved in squatting. To illustrate, both fine and gross motor activities such as tossing a bean bag are easily adapted to meet the goal.

The same goal could be addressed at home by the parents setting out a number of bath toys on the floor, then, prior to bathing the child, encouraging her to pick up the objects individually and place them in the bathtub. Parents who can observe professionals integrating their

child's goals into daily routines at preschool and in other naturalistic settings find similar integration easier to practice in the home.

Ensuring functionality of goals

A timely and functional goal for a young child with a disability should contribute to the child's being successful in his or her natural environment (Brown, Nietupski, & Hamre-Nietupski 1976; LeBlanc, Etzel, & Domash 1978). Therefore, a goal that does not fit naturally into a child's routine should be reconsidered to determine if it is necessary or practical for the child, family, or preschool situation at the time (Notari-Syverson & Shuster 1995). If the goal is not related to current routines but is a prerequisite for further skills, it may need to be practiced in isolation.

If it is not useful or practical, a goal may need to be eliminated in favor of one that is more appropriate (Brinker 1985; Bricker 1986). For example, a goal to have a child put on a coat independently before going outside is functional in January; but in July it might be more appropriate for the child to learn to remove shoes before going into a swimming pool.

Sometimes a skill is necessary, but the specific goal is superfluous. For example, a child who needs to learn to stack objects is sometimes assigned to practice stacking one-inch cubes. But how many families routinely practice stacking one-inch cubes? The skill would be more meaningful and easier to practice if the IFSP team were to look for ways in which stacking might be a natural part of a family's day. Perhaps a brother or sister could invite the child to join in building a block fort or tower. The mother might help the child stack Jello boxes as she unloads groceries, or the father might invite the child to stack crackers that are being arranged for a snack. Such family collaboration contributes to both improved child outcomes and increased family satisfaction (Dunst et al. 1991; Dunst et al. 1993).

Conclusion

Each family, preschool, and other care setting has unique strengths and resources that can be adapted for the training and education of a young child with a disability. If early childhood professionals, preschool teachers, and parents work collaboratively in designing an Individualized Family Service Plan, services to the child will be maximized, and both professionals and family members will find it easier to meet the child's needs without overextending their own energy and time.

Working together and considering each other's priorities and needs, the IFSP team should identify routines that are a part of the child's natural environments, select appropriate goals that will help the child function successfully in those environments, and incorporate the goals within the daily routines of the family and school. If team members are creative, they can find additional opportunities for the child to practice skills with different people in a variety of circumstances.

Above all, team members must continually reexamine and reevaluate the child's goals to be sure that they are functional and realistic for the particular child, family, and preschool or other environment. Such parent-professional collaboration is the cornerstone of family-centered services, and especially relevant when a young child has a disability.

References

Allred, K.W. 1992. Research review: Fathers of young children with disability. *DEC Communicator* 18 (3): 6–7.

Bailey, D.B. 1987. Collaborative goal-setting with families: Resolving differences in values and priorities for services. *Topics in Early Childhood Special Education* 7 (2): 59–71.

Bernheimer, L.P., R. Gallimore, & T.S. Weisner. 1990. Ecocultural theory as a context for the individual family service plan. *Journal of Early Intervention* 14 (3): 219–33.

Bricker, D. 1986. *Early education of at-risk and handicapped infants, toddlers, and preschool children.* Glenview, IL: Scott Foresman.

Bricker, D., & J. Cripe. 1989. Activity-based intervention. In *Early education of at-risk and handicapped infants, toddlers, and preschool children* (2d ed.), ed. D. Bricker, 251–74. Palo Alto, CA: Vort.

Bricker, D., & J.J.W. Cripe. 1992. *An activity-based approach to early intervention.* Baltimore, MD: Brookes.

Bricker, D., & A. Widerstrom, eds. 1996. *Preparing personnel to work with infants and young children and their families.* Baltimore, MD: Brookes.

Brinker, R.P. 1985. Curricula without recipes: A challenge to teachers and a promise to severely mentally retarded students. In *Severe mental retardation: From theory to practice,* eds. D. Bricker & J. Filler, 208–29. Reston, VA: Council for Exceptional Children.

Bronfenbrenner, U. 1979. *The ecology of human development: Experiments of nature and design.* Cambridge, MA: Harvard University Press.

Brotherson, M.J., & B.L. Goldstein. 1992. Time is a resource and constraint for parents of young children with disabilities: Implications for early intervention services. *Topics in Early Childhood Special Education* 12 (14): 508–27.

Brown, L., J. Nietupski, & S. Hamre-Nietupski. 1976. The criterion of ultimate functioning. In *Hey, don't forget about me,* ed. M.A. Thomas, 2–15. Reston, VA: Council for Exceptional Children.

Chandler, P.A. 1994. *A place for me: Including children with special needs in early care and education settings.* Washington, DC: NAEYC.

Cohen, A.J. 1995. From our readers. It is important that child care providers understand the legal framework that governs the rights of individuals with disabilities. *Young Children* 50 (2): 4–5.

Cripe, J.J.W. (producer), & J. Crabtree (director). 1995. *A family's guide to the individualized family service plan.* Video. (Available from Paul H. Brookes Publishing, P.O. Box 10624, Baltimore, MD 21285-0624.)

Davis, P.B., & J.E. May. 1991. Involving fathers in early intervention and family support programs: Issues and strategies. *Children's Health Care* 20 (2): 87–92.

DeHaas-Warner, S. 1994. The role of child care professionals in placement and programming decisions for preschoolers with special needs in community-based settings. *Young Children* 49 (5): 76–78.

Diamond, K.E., L.L. Hestenes, & C.E. O'Connor. 1994. Integrating young children with disabilities in preschool: Problems and promise. *Young Children* 49 (2): 68–75.

Division for Early Childhood Task Force on Recommended Practices. 1993. *DEC recommended practices: Indicators of quality in programs for infants and young children with special needs and their families.* Reston, VA: Council for Exceptional Children.

Dunst, C.J. 1991. Implementation of the individualized family service plan. In *Guidelines and recommended practices for the individualized family service plan* (2d ed.), eds. M.J. McGonigel, R.K. Kaufmann, & B.H. Johnson, 67–78. Bethesda, MD: Association for the Care of Children's Health.

Dunst, C.J., C. Johanson, C.M. Trivette, & D. Hamby. 1991. Family-oriented early intervention policies and practices: Family-centered or not? *Exceptional Children* 58: 115–26.

Dunst, C.J., C.M. Trivette, A.L. Starnes, D.W. Hamby, & N.J. Gordon. 1993. *Building and evaluating family support initiatives: A national study of programs for persons with developmental disabilities.* Baltimore, MD: Brookes.

Fox, L., & M.F. Hanline. 1993. A preliminary evaluation of learning within the context of play. *Topics in Early Childhood Special Education* 13: 308–27.

Hanline, M.F., & L. Fox. 1993. Learning within the context of play: Providing typical early childhood experiences for children with severe disabilities. *Journal of the Association for Persons with Severe Handicaps* 18: 121–29.

Hobbs, N. 1975. *The future of children.* San Francisco, CA: Jossey-Bass.

Johnson, B., M. McGonigel, & R. Kaufmann, eds. 1989. *Guidelines and recommended practices for the individualized family service plan.* Washington, DC: U.S. Department of Education and U.S. Department of Health and Human Services.

Kaiser, A.P., & M.L. Hemmeter. 1989. Value-based approaches to family intervention. *Topics in Early Childhood Special Education* 8 (4): 72–86.

LeBlanc, J., B. Etzel, & M. Domash. 1978. A functional curriculum for early intervention. In *Early intervention: A team approach,* eds. K. Allen, V. Homes, & R. Schiefelbusch, 331–81. Baltimore, MD: University Park Press.

McCormick, L., & S. Feeney. 1995. Modifying and expanding activities for children with disabilities. *Young Children* 50 (4): 10–17.

Noonan, M.J., & L. McCormick. 1993. *Early intervention in natural environments.* Pacific Grove, CA: Brooks/Cole.

Notari-Syverson, A.R., & S.L. Shuster. 1995. Putting real-life skills into IEP/IFSPs for infants and young children. *Teaching Exceptional Children* 27 (2): 29–32.

Salisbury, C.L. 1991. Mainstreaming during the early childhood years. *Exceptional Children* 58 (2): 146–54.

Seibert, J.M. 1987. The Scales in early intervention. In *Infant performance and experience: New findings with the Ordinal Scales,* eds. I.C. Uzgiris & J. McV. Hunt, 340–70. Urbana: University of Illinois Press.

Winton, P., J. McCollum, & C. Catlett. 1997. *Reforming personnel preparation in early intervention.* Baltimore, MD: Brookes.

Wolery, M., & J.W. Wilbers, eds. 1994. *Including children with special needs in early childhood programs.* Washington, DC: NAEYC.

Reprinted from *Young Children* 53 (5): 32–36. Copyright © 1998 NAEYC.

Karen E. Diamond and Susan Stacey

34

The Other Children at Preschool

Experiences of Typically Developing Children in Inclusive Programs

Excerpted from *Natural Environments and Inclusion*

Why is it important that we pay attention to the experiences of typically developing children in inclusive programs? Inclusion is a lifelong process that has the goal of full participation for children and adults within education, community activities, and work (Kliewer 1999). Twenty years after they leave preschool, typically developing children (now adults!) will be members of communities that include adults with disabilities. There is ample evidence that attitudes toward others are learned, and that the development of attitudes begins during the preschool years (Ramsey & Myers 1990).

If children's experiences in inclusive preschool programs are positive ones, these experiences support the development of positive attitudes toward people with disabilities. Similarly, negative experiences in inclusive preschool settings may be precursors to later, more rigid, prejudices about people with disabilities (Stoneman 1993). For people with disabilities, negative attitudes may be just as effective as physical, architectural barriers in limiting opportu-

nities to participate fully in schools, jobs, and communities.

Prior experience, it seems, may have an effect on typically developing children's subsequent responses to classmates with disabilities. In this article, we examine research on the development of children's ideas about people with disabilities. The examples in this article come from our observations at Purdue University's Child Development Laboratory School which offers inclusive programs for 3-, 4-, and 5-year-old children.

Greg and Brittany are typically developing 4-year-olds. One of their classmates, Tara, has significantly delayed motor and language skills. Greg appears fascinated by Tara's wheelchair; he often stands nearby and watches intently as a teacher helps Tara to participate in classroom activities. Brittany, on the other hand, is very matter-of-fact about Tara's disability. Her older brother had severe multiple disabilities, and she is used to being with children who cannot walk or talk. Sometimes Brittany offers to help so that Tara can participate in an activity.

Children's understanding of disabilities

What is it like for typically developing children to have a classmate with a disability? Research has demonstrated that preschool children know quite a lot about physical and sensory disabilities, particularly when a child uses adaptive equipment, regardless of children's experiences with people with these disabilities.

For instance, we found that most 3- and 4-year-olds thought that someone who used a wheelchair or was blind would have trouble walking, and that someone who wore a hearing aid would have trouble hearing. Children held these ideas even if they had never been in a class with a child with a disability. Having equipment that they can see seems to make it easier for children to understand a disability (Diamond et al. 1997). Adaptive equipment can also be confusing. When we talked with one 5-year-old about what it might be like to be deaf, he suggested that someone who is deaf "can't hear because he has those things [hearing aids] in his ears. He could hear if he took them out" (Diamond & Hestenes 1994). Having classmates with special needs promotes typically developing children's appreciation for the capabilities of each classmate.

Now that they've been together for several months, the kids know that Tara has a sense of humor and will tease; they know Robin can read anything (and sometimes look to her if they are stumped); and they know that Brian is the most helpful child in class when it comes to finding lost shoes and socks.

Mental retardation and emotional disturbance are disabilities that are more difficult for children to understand. We have found that when preschool children look at photographs, they do not appear to notice the facial characteristics that are unique to children with Down syndrome (Diamond & Hestenes 1996; Innes & Diamond 1999). This is in contrast to older children who rely on facial characteristics to identify others as "retarded" or "not retarded" (Goodman 1989). Thus, unlike older children, preschoolers may be initially unaware of the disabilities of some of their classmates, particularly if the classmate uses no specialized equipment. In fact, research suggests that young children are not even aware of the possibility that someone might have a disability that is related to difficulties in thinking, such as mental retardation or emotional disturbance (Conant & Budoff 1983; Diamond & Hestenes 1996).

Even young children develop a more complex understanding of disabilities when they attend an inclusive program. We found, for example, that preschool children who had a classmate who was deaf had a much better understanding of sign language, and of the connection between hearing and talking, than did children without this experience. In addition, children developed a bet-

Young children develop a more complex understanding of disabilities when they attend an inclusive program.

ter understanding that disabilities do not disappear—that a child with cerebral palsy is likely to have a disability as an adult—when they had classmates with disabilities.

Young children use knowledge that they already possess (for example, that you can be hurt in an accident or that babies do not talk) to explain something they are only beginning to understand (a child's disability). Children often attributed a classmate's braces, walker, or wheelchair to an accident in which "he broke his leg," or explained a peer's difficulty talking by saying, "he can't talk because he's a baby; when he gets older, he'll be able to talk just like me." In addition, children often focus on one or two important features (such as equipment or significantly delayed skills) in determining whether or not a child has a disability. Children may use this awareness to judge how similar or dissimilar a child with a disability is to him- or herself.

Children's acceptance of others

What do children learn from experiences in inclusive preschools? According to parents, preschool children become more accepting of human differences, more aware of the needs of others, show less discomfort with people with disabilities, are less prejudiced, have fewer stereotypes about people who are different, and are more responsive and helpful to other children after their enrollment in an inclusive program (Peck, Carlson, & Helmstetter 1992).

When we asked children about how they might solve a series of hypothetical classroom dilemmas that included a child with a disability, we found that children in inclusive classes had significantly more ideas about how they might be helpful, and were significantly more likely to refer to a child's disability, than were children in classes with only typically developing classmates (Diamond & Carpenter 2000). These qualities are evident in our observations of children's interactions in the spring of the school year.

The children no longer pay much attention to all the adaptive equipment Tara uses, and will sometimes go get it for her, or go with her to get her other chair. Just the other day, Greg commented that Tara liked to play with tools and "fix" things. He spontaneously got a screwdriver and "fixed" her wheelchair.

Brittany laid down on the floor and began doing exercises while the physical therapist was doing stretches with Tara. Once Brittany started this, several other children joined in. Another child, recognizing that Tara hates doing stretches, sometimes brings her a book to look at, or gets the tape recorder so she can listen to music.

Children's interactions

Research has consistently demonstrated that children with disabilities are included less often in interactive play activities than are their typically developing peers. Although the degree of social separation between peers with and without disabilities appears to vary with the severity of the child's delays, even children with mild delays are less accepted as playmates than are their typically developing classmates (Guralnick et al. 1996). In an observational study, Brown and his colleagues (1999) found that typically developing children were significantly more likely to direct interactions toward typically developing classmates than toward classmates with disabilities. Despite this, children with disabilities interacted frequently with their typically developing peers in both of these studies.

If the idea of "playing together" is expanded to include parallel play activities in addition to more complex social interactions, research suggests that children with disabilities are included in common events in preschool classrooms, although their level of social participation tends to be less than for typically developing children (Okagaki et al. 1998; Brown et al. 1999).

The children play alongside Robin even if they themselves are capable of cooperative play. They seem to realize that she is not. For instance, Robin loves Marbleworks. One day, Sara approached her very quietly, didn't speak or ask for anything, picked up an occasional marble and rolled it down, waiting for Robin to look and take a turn. In this way, they were able to take turns, unusual for Robin.

Teachers and parents as models

We know little about the ways in which teachers' behaviors affect the development of children's ideas about, and attitudes toward, people with disabilities. Research suggests, however, that when children are divided into groups based on whether or not they have a disability, this may encourage typically developing children to think about their classmates with disabilities as different

from themselves (e.g., Bigler, Jones, & Lobliner 1997).

For example, Schnorr (1990) studied typically developing first-graders' perceptions of Peter, a child with Down syndrome who was included in their class for part of each school day. While teachers and parents thought that this part-time inclusion was quite successful, these first-graders thought that Peter was different from themselves. They attributed his "difference" to factors that separated him from his classmates: He left the classroom for specialized services, did different work, and rode a different bus. More recently, Janko and her colleagues (1997) identified a number of practices in inclusive preschool programs that separated children with disabilities from their classmates. In one school district, children with disabilities were transported to school by a district school bus, while children without disabilities were transported by their families (a common practice in many programs). Children ques-

tioned "the difference between the 'car kids' and the 'bus kids'" (293) who not only rode a bus but also stayed at school for lunch. For these children, whether or not you rode a bus was an important characteristic that divided them into children with disabilities (bus kids) and children without disabilities (car kids).

Conversely, in another child care classroom, each child had an assigned chair, not just the child with Down syndrome whose chair had been modified by the physical therapist. By using this strategy, teachers met one child's need for a chair that provided more support without marking that child as different from the rest of the group. Similarly, integrated rather than pull-out therapies that allow children with disabilities to remain part of the classroom group may facilitate children's views of their classmates with disabilities as important members of their class (Diamond & Cooper 2000; McWilliam 1996).

© Ellen B. Senisi

"I wonder if Robin knows?" She will usually read it for the child. If we can find more things that she can do . . . then I think they might see her as a capable person who understands what is going on.

Parents of children with disabilities play an important role in promoting children's understanding of their child (Turnbull, Pereira, & Blue-Banning 1999). One strategy that has been used by parents of children with disabilities in our inclusive program is to provide other parents with specific information about their child's disability. This serves many purposes. It gives the parents of a child with a disability an opportunity to talk about their child with other parents; it helps to answer other parents' unasked questions about a child's disability; and it gives parents the information they may need when responding to their child's questions. In addition to communicating with other parents, parents of children with disabilities often have opportunities to talk about their child's disability with his or her classmates (Turnbull & Turnbull 1991). Sometimes this is done while explaining about special equipment.

Discussions between children and parents about classmates with disabilities are likely to be common. The ways in which parents respond to children's questions are important in promoting children's acceptance of their classmates (Okagaki et al. 1998).

To the extent that classroom experiences promote more opportunities for all children to work and play together, and fewer opportunities for children with disabilities to be seen as members of an "out-group" who are "not like me," such experiences may also promote the development of more positive attitudes toward classmates with disabilities. This is evident in the following comment from Robin's teacher.

Sometimes we'll try to point out a particular skill. For instance, Robin is the only child in her class who knows how to read. At Large Group, when children are learning to read their names and the names of their classmates, if someone is stuck, we'll say,

Suggestions for practice

There is evidence that the structure of the classroom may influence children's ideas about their peers with disabilities (Schnorr 1990). The following suggestions for practice reflect results from research and are ones that we have implemented in our program.

A World of Difference

- Work with specialists so that therapies are provided within the classroom.
- Encourage therapists to include typically developing children in the therapy session.
- Encourage children's interests in adaptive equipment and develop ways that they explore and help set up equipment.
- Ensure that children sit together *in similar seating* for social events such as snack, lunch, or group time. In our program, therapists have developed a variety of adapted seating arrangements so that children who need additional support are able to sit with their peers for group events.
- Find out what each child can do and emphasize this with other children.
- Draw attention to positive personality traits that are shared among all children.
- Assign "buddies" for some activities so that all children have an opportunity to play with each of their classmates.
- Take advantage of children's shared interests and prompt interactions between classmates.

Research suggests that typically developing children's attitudes toward people with disabilities will be closely associated with children's awareness of disability, the ways in which teachers and parents foster the inclusion of children with disabilities in school and community settings, and the quality and extent of children's interactions with classmates with disabilities during the early school years. When children accept the responsibility for ensuring that a classmate with a disability is included in classroom activities (Salisbury & Palombaro 1998), wait for a classmate in a wheelchair to "catch up" with the group (Janney & Snell 1996), or offer assistance to a classmate (Richardson & Schwartz 1998), these behaviors tell us that

children both are aware of a child's disability-related limitations and think of that child as part of their peer group.

References

Bigler, R.S., L.C. Jones, & D.B. Lobliner. 1997. Social categorization and the formation of intergroup attitudes in children. *Child Development* 68: 530–43.

Brown, W.H., S.L. Odom, S. Li, & C. Zercher. 1999. Ecobehavioral assessment in early childhood programs: A portrait of preschool inclusion. *The Journal of Special Education* 33: 138–53.

Conant, S., & M. Budoff. 1983. Patterns of awareness in children's understanding of disability. *Mental Retardation* 21: 119–25.

Diamond, K.E., & C. Carpenter. 2000. The influence of inclusive preschool programs on children's sensitivity to the needs of others. *Journal of Early Intervention* 23: 81–91.

Diamond, K.E., & D. Cooper. 2000. Children's perspectives on the roles of teachers and therapists in inclusive early childhood programs. *Early Education and Development* 11: 203–16.

Diamond, K.E., & L. Hestenes. 1994. Preschool children's understanding of disability: Experiences leading to the elaboration of the concept of hearing loss. *Early Education and Development* 5: 301–9.

Diamond, K.E., & L. Hestenes. 1996. Preschool children's conceptions of disabilities: The salience of disability in children's ideas about others. *Topics in Early Childhood Special Education* 16: 458–75.

Diamond, K.E., L. Hestenes, E. Carpenter, & F. Innes. 1997. Relationships between enrollment in an inclusive class and preschool children's ideas about people with disabilities. *Topics in Early Childhood Special Education* 17: 520–36.

Goodman, J. 1989. Does retardation mean dumb? Children's perceptions of the nature, cause, and course of mental retardation. *The Journal of Special Education* 23: 313–29.

Guralnick, M.J., R. Connor, M. Hammond, J.M. Gottman, & K. Kinnish. 1996. Immediate effects of mainstreamed settings on the social interactions and social integration of preschool children. *American Journal on Mental Retardation* 100: 359–78.

Innes, F., & K.E. Diamond. 1999. Typically developing children's interactions with peers with disabilities: Relationships between mothers' comments and children's ideas about disabilities. *Topics in Early Childhood Special Education* 19: 103–11.

Janko, S., I. Schwartz, S. Sandall, K. Anderson, & C. Cottam. 1997. Beyond micro systems: Unanticipated lessons about the meaning of inclusion. *Topics in Early Childhood Special Education* 17: 286–306.

Janney, R.E., & M.E. Snell. 1996. How teachers use peer interactions to include students with moderate and severe disabilities in elementary general education classrooms. *Journal of the Association for Persons with Severe Handicaps* 21: 72–80.

Kliewer, S. 1999. Seeking the functional. *Mental Retardation* 37: 151–54.

McWilliam, R.A. 1996. A program of research on integrated vs. isolated treatment in early intervention. In *Rethinking pull-out services in early intervention: A professional resource*, ed. R.A. McWilliam, 71–102. Baltimore, MD: Brookes.

Okagaki, L., K.E. Diamond, S. Kontos, & L. Hestenes. 1998. Correlates of young children's interactions with classmates with disabilities. *Early Childhood Research Quarterly* 13: 67–86.

Peck, C.A., P. Carlson, & E. Helmstetter. 1992. Parent and teacher perceptions of outcomes for nonhandicapped children enrolled in integrated early childhood programs: A statewide study. *Journal of Early Intervention* 16: 53–63.

Ramsey, P.G., & L.C. Myers. 1990. Salience of race in young children's cognitive, affective, and behavioral responses to social environments. *Journal of Applied Developmental Psychology* 11: 49–67.

Richardson, P., & I.S. Schwartz. 1998. Making friends in preschool: Friendship patterns of young children with disabilities. In *Making friends: The influences of culture and development*, eds. L.H. Meyer, H.S. Park, M. Grenot-Scheyer, I.S. Schwartz, & B. Harry, 65–80. Baltimore, MD: Brookes.

Salisbury, C., & M. Palombaro. 1998. Friends and acquaintances: Evolving relationships in an inclusive elementary school. In *Making friends: The influences of culture and development*, L.H. Meyer, H.S. Park, M. Grenot-Scheyer, I.S. Schwartz, & B. Harry, 81–104. Baltimore, MD: Brookes.

Schnorr, R. 1990. "Peter? He comes and goes. . . .": First graders' perspectives on a part-time mainstream student. *Journal of the Association for Persons with Severe Handicaps* 15: 231–40.

Stoneman, Z. 1993. Attitudes toward young children with disabilities: Cognition, affect, and behavioral intent. In *Integrating young children with disabilities in community programs: From research to implementation*, eds. C. Peck, S. Odom, & D. Bricker, 223–48. Baltimore, MD: Brookes.

Turnbull, A.P., L. Pereira, & M.J. Blue-Banning. 1999. Parents' facilitation of friendships between their children with a disability and friends without a disability. *Journal of the Association for Persons with Severe Handicaps* 24: 85–99.

Turnbull, R., & A.P. Turnbull. 1991. Including all children. *Children Today* 20 (2): 3–5.

Adapted from K. Diamond & S. Stacey, "The Other Children at Preschool: Experiences of Typically Developing Children in Inclusive Programs," in *Natural Environments and Inclusion*, 59–68, Young Exceptional Children Monograph Series, eds. S. Sandall & M. Ostrosky, no. 2 (Denver, CO: Division for Early Childhood, 2000). Copyright © 2000 Division for Early Childhood of the Council for Exceptional Children (406-243-5898). Reprinted with permission.

Jeanne McDermott

35

A Letter to Teachers of Young Children

It's fall, the beginning of a new school year, a time of hope and promise. You plan to create an inclusive classroom where young children address their differences with care and respect.

On the first day of school, before you even know everyone's names, a 3-year-old points at my son and says loudly, "That boy looks like a space alien." You've got to break some eggs to make an omelet, and you've got to expect some uncomfortable and insensitive moments when young children are learning about each other's differences.

Most children—including my son, who was born with a craniofacial condition—have a rude "point and shout" moment in public. It is to be expected when children are first noticing bodies, mastering language, and making sense of themselves as social beings. Unfortunately, for young children, different usually means bad.

What is a teacher of young children to do? First, be aware that every beginning presents a social hurdle for a child who acts or looks in a way that differs from the major-

ity. The curiosity kindled by this difference will disappear in time as children build relationships, and it has been my experience that the majority of young children make no comment. But do not assume that they have failed to notice. Many children will say something like this to you or to their parents:

"There's a weird-looking kid at school."
"He has a fat head."
"He looks like a zombie."
"He looks like a squid."
"He doesn't talk right."
"Why can't he close his mouth?"
"He looks bad."
"What's wrong with his fingers?"
"What's wrong with him?"

These are all comments we've heard directly or indirectly about our son.

The most important thing for you to model is comfort and acceptance. Children pay more attention to your emotions than your words. If you are nervous or afraid, it comes across in your body language and tone of voice. One adult responded to a child's awkward question about my son by saying, "Oh, he has hydrocephalus like your cousin." Her 5-

year-old had *no* idea what hydrocephalus was. He did hear that his mother was confident and happy.

For many teachers, knowledge about a child's syndrome or diagnosis promotes comfort. Turn to the parents for guidance. Ask them:

• What questions do children typically ask about your child?

• What comments have you heard children make around your child?

• What words do you use to describe your child's condition to other kids?

• What words do you use to describe your child's condition to other adults?

We sent a letter to our son's teachers and the families of children in the class at the beginning of each school year (until he was in fourth grade) explaining his syndrome, giving examples of questions and ways to answer them. (He was born with Apert syndrome, which affected the bones of his face, head, hands, and feet. At birth, he had mitten fingers and no forehead bone. His mouth is open because he has to breathe through it. He's had many operations. He's a typical kid who looks and sounds different.)

You will sometimes meet parents who are shy or who refuse to publicly discuss their child's disability. You need to respect their privacy and coping methods.

The cultural norms about disability are in flux. Everyone agrees that pointing is rude. But I deeply believe that children (and adults) need to stare—but to stare respectfully, for a short time and with a smile. It's very helpful to ask questions of a third party, such as the parent, in a private moment. Here is a typical conversation I've had with preschool children:

Me: Do you have a question you want to ask me about Nate?

Child: Why is his head big?

Me: He was just born like that. I love his head.

Child: I was born with curly hair.

Me: I see that both you and Nate play on the slide.

If you want to ask the person with a disability about his or her disability, get to know the person first and then begin with "Do you mind if I ask . . . ?"

There are always challenging children who struggle with issues of their own relating to difference. If a child keeps asking questions and harping on differences in a negative or scared way, you need to set limits. Say, "You can ask one question but no more. Then you need to build with blocks." If a child bullies, it is important to address that behavior separately.

What should we teach children about difference?

1. It is healthy to notice difference.

2. Different does not mean bad.

3. It is OK to be curious but not to be mean.

The whole point is getting to know each other. After we have noticed our differences, our similarities are just waiting to be discovered.

Best wishes for an inclusive year!

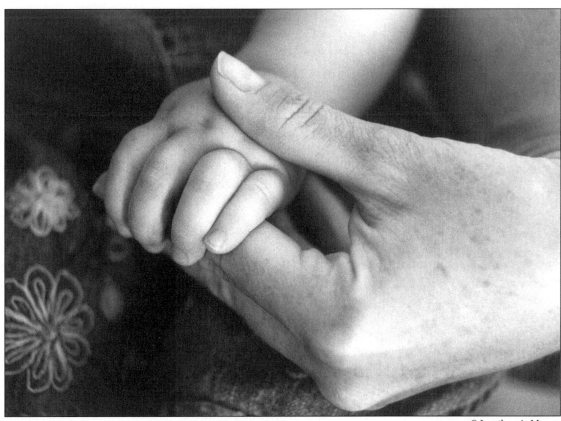

© Jonathan A. Meyers

Linda L. Flynn and Judith Kieff

36

Including *Everyone* in Outdoor Play

Outdoor play has benefits for all children. It offers young children many unique opportunities to develop physical, cognitive, communication, and social skills. When playing outdoors, children often experience a sense of freedom that encourages them to become involved in interactive games that foster language and create authentic opportunities for problem solving (Rivkin 1995). A child's motor development and manipulative skills are enhanced by the spaciousness of outdoor areas and the availability of large equipment for climbing and sliding (Pepler & Ross 1981; Myers 1985; Poest et al. 1990). Outdoor play tends to stimulate greater use of words and more complex language than that used indoors (Tizard, Philps, & Plewis 1976).

The flexibility of outside play permits children greater freedom to interact with peers (Boulton & Smith 1993), which provides opportunities for the development of positive social skills and emotional fitness (Frost, Wortham, & Reifel 2001). In addition, children experience sensory stimulation through access to

natural play materials such as sand, water, grass, dirt, living things, and, of course, fresh air (Olds 1987). Thus, outdoor play promotes children's development and interaction among peers.

Children with a wide range of abilities participate in outdoor play. With typically developing children, learning through outdoor play experiences comes easily and naturally. However, for children with special needs learning through play may take on a different meaning (Merchant & Brown 1996). For example, some children with special needs may lack concentration skills and the initiative to begin and sustain an activity or play with peers (Hughes 1998; Buchanan & Cooney 2000). These difficulties are particularly significant during outside play, which inherently has multiple distractions. The outdoor environment is a wonderful place to engage in fantasy play; however, children with special needs may find it more difficult to sustain dramatic play than their peers. Children with special needs may process information more slowly than typically developing peers (Li 1985).

Because of these characteristics, as well as an array of others, a child with special needs may tend to isolate himself from the other children during outside play. Teachers must provide supports to enhance the level of play with peers.

Teachers must actively support inclusion

Often special and regular education teachers are challenged to facilitate the inclusion of children with special needs in activities outside. Clearly, the role of the teacher and the addition of modifications to support positive inclusive experiences for children are critical (Jones & Rapport 1997). Children with special needs may have unique characteristics that require attention to individual needs and learning styles. They may need both environmental and social supports in the form of adaptations or modifications to take optimal advantage of outside learning activities.

Adaptations may range from extremely simple to complex. Adaptations may include not only physical modifications of the environment but also techniques used by teachers to interact and communicate with children during outdoor activities. All children should be able to have fun outside, participate in activities with each other, and achieve learning goals through environmental modifications as needed.

The purpose of this article is, first, to share information about specific guidelines to outdoor play that are important when children have special needs. Second, we describe talking points or questions that guide the decision-making process about which types of adaptations might be most helpful for a particular child.

Guidelines for inclusive outdoor play

Teachers who address children's needs through individual adaptations should follow a set of guidelines to ensure that the outside experience is positive and promotes learning. These guidelines are critical for *all* children but become especially important when children have special needs.

• **Reflect on the quality and quantity of multisensory activities available to children.** Multisensory experiences include those activities that address the senses of touching, smelling, seeing, tasting, hearing, and moving. A child who has compromised sensory input such as blindness, hearing loss, or physical limitations will not be able to use all of the senses available to typically developing children. This child will need to use the senses that are available to understand and explore the outside environment.

For example, teachers may think at first that a riding toy is not appropriate for a child who is blind or has low vision because of her inability to see where she is going. However, when a multisensory approach is applied, a beeper is placed on the back of the tricycle of another child and the child who is blind plays "follow the leader" with the child whose tricycle has been adapted. With a simple modification and the selection of an appropriate peer, the child who is blind can independently participate in this outside activity. Multisensory activities are good for all children to facilitate their learning but are mandatory for children with certain disabilities.

• **Promote independence for all children.** Children with special needs may have conditions that interfere with their ability to participate independently during outside play. They may be accustomed to adults making decisions for them and to receiving help from adults even though they are capable of completing a task independently through the use of adaptations.

For example, a child who has weak muscle tone and wants to work at the outside woodworking center might ask an adult to hold the nail or help grasp the hammer. If the teacher adds golf tees and Styrofoam to the center, the child will then be able to hammer independently.

Modifications of activities and materials to ensure independence are imperative to the child's success in outdoor play.

• **Use cooperative learning groups.** When children are clustered together into small groups and work collaboratively, the teacher can promote interaction among them. Children with special needs often require teachers to initiate and facilitate social interactions and development of meaningful relationships with nondisabled peers. For cooperative learning groups to be successful, the teacher must ensure that the child with special needs has a specific role in the activity and that the child understands the procedures to conduct the activity. Then, the teacher can facilitate interaction and communication among all of the children.

For example, consider the sandbox area on the playground. The theme in the sandbox is an archeological dig, and a group of children are engaged in discovering fossils and other relics. Two children are digging, one child has the job of recording, and another child categorizes the findings. To participate, a child who has low muscle tone and difficulty with grasping objects can wear an adapted glove with Velcro on the palm so that he can successfully hold a digging trowel with Velcro attached to the handle. By including a simple adaptation, the child with a physical challenge can independently, actively participate in the group project.

The outdoor environment is a prime location to organize cooperative learning groups as the noise level often increases when children are working together rather than completing activities individually. Children can use their "outside" voices and have fun learning together.

Questions to Consider about a Child's Abilities and Needs

• What are the child's current abilities related to movement, cognition, communication, and social interaction?

• What components of the outdoor environment are particularly pleasing or interesting to the child?

• What motivates the child to explore his environment and interact with others?

• Which children in the class have similar interests to the child and could play in cooperative learning groups?

• What tends to overstimulate or even frighten the child?

• What barriers currently exist that impede the child's access to materials, equipment, and/or peers?

• What are the current goals for the child regarding cognitive, physical, social-emotional, and communication development?

• What opportunities does the existing playground—and routines related to playground use—offer for the development of these current goals?

• What easy or inexpensive changes should be made to equipment or playground routines to enhance the opportunities for the child to fulfill identified goals, interact with peers, and have fun?

• What extensive or complex changes should be made to equipment or routines to enhance opportunities for the child to fulfill identified goals, interact with peers, and have fun?

These guidelines can be helpful for both outside and inside environments. However, teachers and other staff often do not extend the inside curriculum into the outside playground. While the concept of play is highly regarded by early childhood regular and special educators, play outside is frequently neglected as a means to achieving functional and academic goals for children (Fewell & Kiminski 1988). These three guidelines should be at the forefront in the decision making processes of planning, organizing, and adapting the outdoor environment. The guidelines are critical to the successful inclusion of children with special needs.

Talking points to guide decision making on appropriate adaptations

The next step in developing appropriate adaptations for children with special needs is to gather specific information about each child. An inventory of the child's likes, dislikes, skills, and challenges is necessary to ensure that interventions match the child's learning needs and abilities.

This information should come from a broad range of perspectives. A team of individuals who are familiar with the child should be brought together. This team could include some, but not necessarily all, of the following individuals: family mem-

Planning Guide for Outdoor Play Adaptations
Examples from Two Children

Activities	Child who is blind	Child who has autism
Transition to playground	Upon entering playground, give child verbal directions about where friends and equipment are located; use sighted guide (peer or teacher) to help child move to area of choice.	Prior to entering playground, tell child he is going to the playground next; give him a ball to carry outside and repeat "We are going outside now."
Gardening	Orient child to garden area verbally and physically; describe other children's activities (watering, digging) and offer choices for participating.	Create a physical boundary around garden area (fence or other physical structure); establish for child a specific area in which to dig, plant, and water.
Water table	Tell child which materials are in water table, where materials are located, which friends are present, and what they are doing.	Model ways to use materials and describe what you are doing or what child is doing.
Balls	Use adapted ball with beeper noise inside; place ball under child's hands rather than pulling child's hands to ball.	Communicate rules and boundaries clearly when playing with balls and repeat in different ways, as needed.
Climbing equipment	Alert child to any potential safety concerns (bumping head) and describe the location of possible danger.	No modification necessary (but monitor activity for safety).
Sandbox	Tell child which materials are available and who is playing; be aware of potential need to facilitate child's entering and maintaining play with peers.	Limit number of toys/ materials available to those specifically of interest to child.

bers, child care provider, speech and language therapist, physical and occupational therapist, teacher, classroom aide, nurse, and program administrator. Whether the team consists of two members or five members, it is imperative that the strengths and needs of the child be carefully considered when designing adaptations that will foster the child's participation in outdoor play activities. *Note that not all modifications are appropriate for all children with special needs.*

Talking points or questions to consider about individual children are listed in the box "Questions to Consider about a Child's Abilities and Needs." Again, as was stated in the discussion about guidelines, many of these questions can be used to facilitate learning and interaction with peers during inside activities, but they were designed specifically for extending the inside curriculum to the outside environment.

Parents, teachers, and other team members should all respond to these questions about the child with special needs. The information gathered can then be used to foster a greater understanding of how to best use outdoor space, equipment, and materials to benefit the child's overall physical, cognitive, communication, and emotional development. The three guidelines previously described—multisensory experiences, independence, and cooperative learning groups—are important elements to consider in the decision making process when planning, implementing, and evaluating the outside environment and interaction with peers.

Specific adaptations to meet individual needs

To benefit fully from outdoor play, children with special needs must overcome unique obstacles. Adapta-

Outside play can allow children a level of comfort and freedom not found in the classroom, which in turn builds confidence and a sense of well-being.

tions or interventions are sometimes necessary. Caregivers should determine these modifications according to each child's individual skills, challenges, and learning needs. Children with low-incidence disabilities such as blindness, hearing loss, and autism, as well as those with physical limitations and cognitive delays, often require modifications in materials and teacher interactions to ensure them the opportunity to participate with their peers to the maximum extent possible.

Conclusion

The outside environment provides a wonderful opportunity to create learning activities and support peer interactions for children with special needs. Many children with special needs tend to participate physically before participating verbally, so the outdoors is a particularly important component of the daily routine for

them. Outside play can allow children a level of comfort and freedom not found in the classroom, which in turn builds confidence and a sense of well-being. For children with special needs to benefit fully from the outside environment, adaptations must be identified and created by teachers and other team members. Adaptations open the door to opportunities for learning, interaction with peers, increased independence, and more active participation in outside play experiences.

References

Boulton, M., & P. Smith. 1993. Ethnic, gender partner, and activity preferences in mixed-race schools in the U.K.: Playground observations. In *Children on playgrounds,* ed. C. Hart, 210–38. Albany, NY: SUNY Press.

Buchanan, M., & M. Cooney. 2000. Play at home, play in the classroom. *Young Exceptional Children* 3 (4): 9–15.

Fewell, R., & R. Kiminski. 1988. Play skills development and instruction for young children with handicaps. In *Early intervention for infants and children with handicaps: An empirical base,* eds. S. Odom & M. Karnes, 141–58. Baltimore, MD: Brookes.

Frost, J., S. Wortham, & S. Reifel. 2001. *Play and child development.* Upper Saddle River, NJ: Merrill.

Hughes, F.P. 1998. Play in special populations. In *Multiple perspectives on play in early childhood education,* eds. O.N. Sarracho & B. Spodek, 171–93. Albany, NY: SUNY Press.

Jones, H.A., & M.J.K. Rapport. 1997. Research-to-practice in inclusive early childhood education. *Teaching Exceptional Children* 30 (2): 57–61.

Li, A.K.F. 1985. Toward more elaborate pretend play. *Mental Retardation* 23 (3): 131–36.

Merchant, C., & C.R. Brown. 1996. The role of play in inclusive early childhood settings. In *Topics in early childhood education: Playing for keeps,* ed. A.L. Phillips, 127–39. St. Paul, MN: Redleaf.

Myers, G.D. 1985. Motor behavior in kindergartners during physical education and free play. In *When children play,* eds. J.L. Frost & S. Sunderlin., 151–55. Wheaton, MD: Association for Childhood Education International.

Olds, A. 1987. Designing spaces for infants and toddlers. In *Spaces for children: The built environment and child development,* eds. C. Weinstein & T. David. New York: Plenum.

Pepler, D.J., & H.S. Ross. 1981. The effects of play on convergent and divergent problem solving. *Child Development* 52 (4): 1202–10.

Poest, C.A., J.R. Williams, D.D. Witt, & M.E. Atwood. 1990. Challenge me to move: Large muscle development in young children. *Young Children* 45 (5): 4–10.

Rivkin, M.S. 1995. *The great outdoors: Restoring children's right to play outside.* Washington, DC: NAEYC.

Tizard, B., J. Philps, & I. Plewis. 1976. Play in preschool centers: II. Effects on play of the child's social class and of the educational orientation of the center. *Journal of School Psychology and Psychiatry* 17 (October): 265–74.

VII

Educating in a Religiously Diverse World

Does nurturing the foundations of children's faith or spiritual development have a place even in nonsectarian early childhood programs? In this section, authors offer perspectives for thinking about faith in young children's lives and describe the kinds of program experiences that may be valid for children regardless of their families' religious backgrounds (Myers & Martin). Although consideration of religious diversity issues should go far beyond the holiday dilemma, there is no doubt that for many of us holidays are where the rubber hits the road. As a result, many early childhood educators have thought a lot about how to approach holidays, and authors in this section share their perspectives, experiences, and suggestions for practice (Neubert & Jones; Derman-Sparks & the A.B.C. Task Force). On holiday-related decisions and a host of other questions related to religion, teachers clearly need to communicate with families openly and respectfully. We need to begin by finding out how families see religious identity relating to their children's participation in the program and then cooperate in working out solutions that both parents and staff are comfortable with (Gartrell).

Barbara Kimes Myers and Mary Pat Martin

37

Faith Foundations for All of Our Children

On Monday afternoon a small group of 4-year-olds and their teacher chat as they munch on cheese and crackers in their public school early childhood classroom. Talking about the weekend, Sam says, "We went to church." His teacher responds, "Tell us about that." Sam sings a little song that he has just learned. "Pretty," affirms his teacher. Sam adds that at church he learns about God. "What is God?" Cassie wants to know. Several children respond: "God is up in heaven." "God watches you." "God is at church."

As the discussion continues the teacher comments that different people believe different things about God. Cory stands up and firmly commands, "Stop!" Immediately the conversation ends, and everyone looks at Cory. Waving his hands dramatically, Cory explains, "I want to tell you about God." Then he takes his right hand and places it over his heart and continues, "God is love and lives in your heart—inside of you. God is in you all the time." Cory seems clear, definite, sure. He sits down and confidently reaches for another cracker as the group switches to the topic of Marco's new puppy.

✂

Young children think about and try to make sense of issues related to faith and formalized religion within their own understandings of the world. Like Sam, Cory, and their friends, they may bring religious words and symbols into our early childhood programs whether we want them to or not. While not all 4-year-olds have direct experience with religious institutions, those who have not will pick up on the language of formalized religion used by those who have. As early childhood professionals we are keenly aware that when we work in secular programs, it is inappropriate for us to advocate any specific religious belief. The division between church and state that lies at the heart of the United States Constitution is not part of the repertoire of knowledge and behaviors of our youngest citizens, however, and if we are to work with the whole child as we say we do, then we must consider the faith dimension of their lives.

We cannot separate what we see as religious experiences, somehow wrap them up, and put them on a shelf for children to take home at the end of the day, nor can we assume that faith is absent from the lives of children whose families are not associated with any formalized religion. In fact, just as the foundations of reading, writing, math, science, and other areas of curriculum are formed in the early years of life, so are the foundations of adult faith. Unfortunately there is little in professional early childhood courses or literature that prepares us for the important work of facilitating the formation of faith foundations or of responding appropriately to comments that children make.

The purpose of this article is

• to provide a framework for early childhood professionals to think and talk about faith and institutionalized religion within the social context of young lives, and

• to suggest ways that issues related to faith can be appropriately addressed in nonsectarian early childhood programs.

Faith

Addressing faith in the lives of young children is not an easy task, nor is it a new concern. Throughout the history of the United States, philosophers, psychologists, educators, and theologians have wrestled with issues related to dimensions of faith in the lives of children. The works of Erik Erikson, John Dewey, and James Fowler have been especially helpful for early childhood professionals.

Erikson (1963) views faith as coming out of the basic first trust relationship with the mother. According to Erikson, young children grow within communities of persons who share a sense of faith, and children acquire their sense of faith through interactions with the important adults within their communities. Fowler (1981) also describes a broad view of faith. He sees a sense of faith as permeating a person's or a group's way of "moving into the force field of life." Fowler draws on the work of Paul Tillich (1958), who stresses the need of all humans for faith in something (God, philosophy, science, theories, or other persons, places, or things).

Reflecting on the works of Erikson and Fowler, the authors view children's sense of faith as encompassing all areas of development and fueling their movement from what is known to what is not yet known (Phenix 1974; Berryman 1985; Myers & Myers 1987). As we in the field of child development and early childhood education well know, all of learning involves such movement.

Dewey also viewed all humans as needing a sense of faith. His distinction between the terms *religion* and *religious* is a help as we search for deeper insights. For Dewey (1934), *religion* is the formal expression (words, symbols, and dogma) of a specific community's system of beliefs, while *religious* describes the quality of the experiences underlying the words, symbols, and dogma of particular religion.

As early childhood professionals we can understand the distinction Dewey makes between *religion* and *religious,* for we are well aware that experiences form the foundation for the spoken and written word. When we consider the written word *apple,* for example, we know that children learn about apples through experiences like holding, biting, smelling, and picking apples. Such activities allow children to form mental images related to apples (Myers & Myers 1992). Persons who share the apple-related experiences provide the word *apple,* which can be used to talk about (and later write and read about) what in the English language is termed *apple.* Apples become a part of what George Kelly (1955) has described as the *personal construct system* of each child because children's experiences with apples are different. What is commonly shared is the language (verbal and nonverbal) that is used to communicate about the experiences—"participatory knowledge." Kelly suggests that such knowing "takes place in a participation, an immersion in the very being of the world in which we are living." Sloan (1989) stresses that "it is knowing that comes through activity."

As adults we have abstract definitions of faith that are often shaped by our religious traditions. While children do not yet understand or have use for such abstract definitions, the claims that our traditions make within our adult lives often inform the ways we help children make sense out of their experiences (Lang 1983). A Hindu child and a Christian child, faced with the same experience, might be led to understand that experience differently by adults who do not have similar traditions of faith.

In quality early childhood programs that are supported by a specific religious group, that group's language can be part of naming the experiences provided for young children as long as the activities and other experiences are congruent with the meanings that the group's traditions assign to the words and symbols used. In the United States, however, such language is viewed as so powerful that it is reserved for each individual faith community to teach the formal words, symbols, and dogma of its faith to its children. This point makes the issue of faith in the lives of young children complex in programs that are supported with public funds.

As we mentioned earlier in this article, we know that teaching the trappings of any specific religion is not the task of a nonsectarian program; however, every early childhood program should provide experiences for all children that are foundational to their sense of faith.

Our task

As early childhood professionals we must step away from any dogmatic faith stance as prescribed by a particular religious tradition and encourage an openness to experiences, mediated by a hopeful presence within a hospitable environment. Because we know that parents are the most important persons in the lives of young children, this reaching out must include working in partnership with families to provide care and early education for children. In such a role we are challenged to stand with children and sometimes even their families as foundations of faith are developed.

We would like to suggest four ways in which we can intentionally provide this support. The first is by reflecting on our own faith and the faith of others as we make decisions related to our professional world. The second is by setting up the environment, including how we plan and manage transitions. The third focuses on a sense of wonder, and the fourth involves looking at ways in which we interact with children and their families that embody respect and support self-esteem. Each of these areas is examined briefly below.

Reflecting on faith stances: Ours and others'

We examine our own faith because sensitivity to that faith causes us to be more aware of the faith that we find in children, their families, and others with whom we work. We are responsible for knowing and modeling the values and beliefs central to our own religious/faith tradition. If we believe in cooperation, generosity, and sharing, then we practice these attributes within the settings in which we work. If we believe in being compassionate and caring, we model these values by listening, having patience, and accepting other people's feelings, opinions, and ways of being unique. If we believe in justice and peacemaking, we act according to our beliefs by having guidelines for the resolution of conflicts with other staff members and with parents and by having appropriate guidelines for helping children develop skills in conflict resolution. We do this in child development and early childhood education to encourage such attributes in appropriate ways in the children we teach and care for.

In addition to reflecting on our own faith stance, we need to reflect on our understandings of the faith stances of others. This reflection can help us understand their strengths. Reflection on the faith of others also helps us better understand our own attitudes and beliefs about different faiths. We might ask, "Do I accept differences? Do I *value* differences? If I am bothered by another person's faith stance, what might be getting in the way of my understanding and acceptance?"

© Marilyn Nolt

The last part of reflection is to know who we are in the context of the center or school in which we work. We might ask, "Do I understand the mission of this program? Is it consistent with my own beliefs about the role of an early childhood professional and with my own personal faith stance? Does my belief system 'fit' here?" There is only so much that we can do with or give to young children if we are working in a center that is not a match for us.

When we find ourselves in a situation in which we are being asked to work with children in a way that conflicts with our own beliefs, we need to ask ourselves, "What is going on here? What are the conflicting areas? Can I work within the mental constructs of those with authority over me and maintain my integrity? Would my being confrontational be

helpful in this situation? Are the persons for whom I work familiar with the knowledge base of early childhood care and education? If not, are there ways that I can help educate them? What are the possibilities for all of us here to grow?" If the possibilities seem nonexistent, then we might have to ask, "What do I need to do to find a position in which I can work with others for children?"

The development of the foundation of children's faith is a shared task—shared with others with whom we work and with children's families. The ways in which we work with families to help children move from the known world of their families to the (for the young child) unknown world of the early childhood setting can be an important component of a child's faith foundation.

Children bring their fears, concerns, joys, and questions into our classrooms as their worlds expand.

Setting up the environment

Another part of our role in supporting faith foundations in children is setting up the environment into which children come each day. Most important here is providing children a sense of security and safety by having staff, schedules, space, and materials that are consistent and predictable. When consistency falls short, as it sometimes will, we lean more heavily on predictability.

There is a specific time when a child initially enters an early childhood program and a time when that child will leave the program. A child also enters and leaves a program on an ongoing basis. It is important that we work with parents during children's initial entrance into our programs so that there is not too much "newness" for any child all at once. We can also intentionally support each parent and child during the regular separations and reunions that occur, keeping in mind the uniqueness of each parent-and-child relationship.

A child's entering a new setting involves the child's moving into what Fowler terms "the force field of life." There are other ways in which we ask children to move from the known into the unknown. In fact, given the limited experiences of young children, adults are constantly asking them to be involved in this process.

Children bring their fears, concerns, joys, and questions into our classrooms as their worlds expand. When they assume new roles, such as brother or sister or stepchild or friend, or when they go to what, for them, are new places, such as hospitals, a relative's or friend's house, or the dentist's office, they are asked to move beyond the borders of their known experience. The ways in which we set up our environment and the relationship we nurture with young children can support their mastering these transitional events of their lives; thus, through what we make available in the classroom, they can trust enough to move further out into the world of new experiences.

Another important part of providing a trustworthy place to be and learn is our keeping of promises to the children, staff, and parents, such as, "I will make sure you get the red truck when Sandra is finished with it," "I will look for those mittens when I'm locking up tonight," "I will have the bulletin board finished by Friday," and "I will take good care of you for your mom while she is at work."

When children belong and are settled into our program and know that they are all right, valued, and capable, it is important that we be flexible and allow time to share a sense of wonder with them.

Supporting a sense of wonder

It is the end of a long day—5:15 P.M. One tired teacher is dragging two trikes to the toy shed. Kalitia is running by. "Look!" she suddenly screams. The teacher looks at her. Kalitia is turned straight west and is pointing. The teacher looks west into a most incredibly glorious sunset. It is magnificent! She is speechless. She goes over to Kalitia. They just stand there . . . very still . . . in awe . . . sharing a special moment together.

Another time for wonder is present when we come in from the playground a few minutes later than scheduled because children are busy watching a worm move slowly into the wet earth after a rainfall. We can ask questions that invite wonder and that can encourage movement into what is yet unknown to the children: "I wonder where the worm will crawl?"

Other situations for wonder exist. "I wonder what will happen when we add salt to the paint?" "I wonder what will happen if we take the snow inside and put it in our water table?" Thus children further learn that they are persons who can think about the world beyond what is already known, that there is always more to learn. In the September 1991 issue of *Young Children*, Haiman suggests ways that we, as adults, can "provide an atmosphere in which wonder can flourish in children" (53). Deep inside children know that "this is a safe place and I am capable of functioning competently within it." The foundations of faith are there. With the help of important others along the way, children can continue to move into the world.

Enhancing self-esteem

In our verbal and nonverbal interactions, we also intentionally work to enhance self-esteem, which means that we offer children hope about themselves. We say to each child "you are worthy" by letting them know that we are glad to be with them. We say "you are capable" when we support their competence. And we say "you belong here" when we let them know that they are a part of the center. In these ways we intentionally deal with what Wagner (1974) suggests are the three parts of self-esteem: a sense of worth, a sense of competence, and a sense of belonging.

A further aspect of enhancing self-esteem is to value and celebrate differences. Here we build on the work of Louise Derman-Sparks and the A.B.C. Task Force in *Anti-Bias Curriculum* (1989), which informs children about their own culture, introduces them to other cultures, and encourages them to respect each culture. It also recommends helping children recognize and take action against unfair behavior practiced toward someone because of his or her identity. The times of sharing joy in uniqueness might include a child's birthday or special religious occasion or a new event in a child's life.

We can give recognition for life and do it in such a way that all of the children (and staff) can participate, including those children whose religious beliefs do not include or may even prohibit celebrations. For a child's birthday, a parent might come and tell the child's life story, a song might be sung about the child, or baby pictures of the child might be shown. We can work with parents to find acceptable ways to acknowledge occasions for which we want to show recognition and gratitude, ways that will include all of the children and staff.

Any time there are differences in religion to discuss, it is helpful to work out with the parents what words are acceptable to use in teaching other children about the religion. It is important that staff and parents are clear about which words are being used and why. It is also important for us to have some specific words to use that are comfortable for us and that fit with our center's philosophy. Some phrasing that we have found helpful includes

• "This is how Joey's family has Thanksgiving."

• "Sarah's family observes Passover. Sarah, would you like to tell us what you do at your house for Passover?"

• "Some African American families observe Kwanzaa. John's mom and dad have come to tell us about Kwanzaa and what their family has been doing."

• "Most Muslim people observe Ramadan. Leila brought a book about it to share with us."

• "People believe different things about Santa Claus. Some people believe like Jamie, and others believe like Tiffany. Each belief is right and OK for that person."

We can give simple historical backgrounds for the religious observances that children talk about or know about or that we want to introduce to them. We can ask the parents to share in class what the observance means historically and to their own family. Activities such as books, stories, songs, games, special foods, or handcrafts might be shared. We can take the time to listen to a child talk about his formal religious experiences.

As a child shares something from her religion, the words we use should give support and value to the child and her family. We can let the words be the basis of teachable moments, whether they be Sonia teaching everyone in the block area to "genguect" (genuflect) or Marcus teaching Hebrew words that he is learning for the lighting of the Menorah candles. These are learning opportunities for everyone.

Conclusion

Colleagues have pointed out to us that there is nothing new in what we are saying—that the points we make to support the development of a

© Elaine M. Ward

We can seize the teachable moment to help children learn about religious differences or to nurture the foundations of faith.

References

Berryman, J. 1985. Children's spirituality and religious language. *British Journal of Religious Education* 7 (3): 126.

Derman-Sparks, L., & the A.B.C. Task Force. 1989. *Anti-bias curriculum: Tools for empowering young children.* Washington, DC: NAEYC.

Dewey, J. 1934. *A common faith.* New Haven, CT: Yale University Press.

Erikson, E. 1963. *Childhood and society.* New York: Norton.

Fowler, J. 1981. *Stages of faith: The psychology of human development and the quest for meaning.* San Francisco, CA: Harper.

Haiman, P.E. 1991. Viewpoint. Developing a sense of wonder in young children: There is more to early childhood education than cognitive development. *Young Children* 46 (6): 52–53.

Kelly, G.A. 1955. *The psychology of personal constructs.* New York: Norton.

Lang, M. 1983. *Acquiring our image of God: Emotional basis for religious education.* New York: Paulist.

Myers, B.K., & W. Myers. 1987. Transcendence in the preschool: Supporting the relationship between the preschool and the church. *British Journal of Religious Education* 9(3): 148–51.

Myers, B.K., & W. Myers. 1992. *Engaging in transcendence: The church ministry and covenant with young children.* Cleveland, OH: Pilgrim.

Phenix, P. 1974. Transcendence and the curriculum. In *Conflicting conceptions of curriculum,* eds. E.W. Eisner & E. Vallance, 122. Berkeley, CA: McCutchan.

Sloan, D. 1989. Educating for a public vision. *The Chicago Theological Register* 79 (1): 7.

Tillich, P. 1958. *Dynamics of faith.* New York: Harper & Row.

Wagner, M. 1974. *The sensation of being someone.* Grand Rapids, MI: Zondervan.

sense of faith are the very points that are central to any quality program for young children. We could not agree more.

In nonsectarian early childhood settings, we do not use the words of any formalized religion to name the experiences that children have. We do, however, provide experiences that can help form the foundations for the children's faith. Children also bring the language of their families' faith stance into our programs whether we want them to or not.

When we can accept these facts, we need not shy away from or perhaps even deny the events in which children bring religious language and elements of faith into our center. We can seize the teachable moment to help children learn about religious differences or to nurture the foundations of faith. Perhaps all of us can learn from the children we work

with. Brian and Daniel taught their teacher an important lesson:

Daniel and Brian are nose to nose. Daniel—although at 4½ years old the same age as Brian—is several inches shorter, so he has to look up as they speak or, like now, raise voices at each other. Quite an intense discussion is going on. The teacher, knowing that each of these two good friends can stand on his own, watches. She hears the word "God." She moves a little closer, curious. They are having a debate about who knows the real God. Is it Daniel, who knows God from synagogue? or is it Brian, who knows God through the Holy Spirit in his Pentecostal church? The teacher cannot hear all that is said. The discussion is heated. At some point these two wise children, realizing that there is no resolution and accepting the fact that they disagree, grin at each other, and run off to play together.

Reprinted from *Young Children* 48 (2): 49–55. Copyright © 1993 NAEYC.

Holiday Activities in an Antibias Curriculum

Excerpted from *Anti-Bias Curriculum*

When early childhood curriculum uses holidays as the primary source of activities about cultural diversity, children do not learn about the common tasks that all people do in culturally different ways. Focusing on holidays is what may be called "tourist curriculum": Children visit a culture by participating in a few activities and then go home to their regular classroom life. This leads to stereotyping and trivializing a culture—"All people do is dance, wear special clothes, and eat."

Early childhood teachers must rethink *why* they use holiday activities. What do children learn? What purposes do such activities serve? As one preschool teacher said with relief, "When I stopped doing holidays every month I found I had so much more time to do other things!"

If used sparingly, holiday activities can contribute to antibias curriculum. One, they are fun to do and children get involved. Two, participating in celebrations and rituals helps build a sense of group collec-

tivity. Especially in child care centers, re-creating the home experiences of preparing for holidays can enhance children's feeling of being part of a close-knit group. Three, holidays are a part of our society's cultural life. Learning about holidays in school can broaden children's awareness of their own and others' cultural experiences if they are *thoughtfully used as part of a more inclusive curriculum about cultural diversity.*

Guidelines

1. Use holiday activities as part of many other kinds of activities about a cultural group. Ask yourself: What is the purpose of teaching about this holiday? Is it developmentally suitable to my group of children? Is it related to their lives? If not, why am I introducing it?

2. Set holiday activities in the context of people's daily life and beliefs by connecting them to specific children and families. With kindergarten children, include holidays that honor

struggles for justice and relate these holidays to children's own experiences with unfairness.

3. Establish the distinction between learning about another person's holiday rituals and celebrating one's own holiday. Invite children to participate as "guests" in a holiday activity not part of their culture. Encourage the children whose holiday it is to share feelings as well as information.

4. Honor every group that is represented in your classroom (children and staff). Do not treat some holidays as "exotic" and others as regular. Everyone is "ethnic": Everyone's traditions come from specific ethnic or national groups (including national holidays such as Thanksgiving and Christmas).

5. Do not assume everyone from the same ethnic group celebrates holidays the same way. Make sure that any differences in how each family celebrates are evident and respected.

6. Demonstrate respect for everyone's traditions throughout the curriculum.

The kindergarten had spent a few days getting ready for and then celebrating Passover. During the Seder ceremony, the meaning of matzo was explained and Esther, one of the Jewish children, explained that she could not eat bread during the whole week of Passover. The next day, cake was served at a birthday celebration for another child. A student teacher gave Esther a piece of cake in violation of the Passover week requirement. She explained later that she felt sorry for Esther because Esther was being deprived of the cake and would feel left out. Luckily, the teacher noticed the pained, conflicted expression on Esther's face and intervened: "Esther, do you know that cake is made with leavened flour and that you can't eat it?" (Esther nodded her head yes.) "Let's freeze your piece and you can eat it after Passover." Esther relaxed, gave her cake to the teacher, and went off to play.

7. Plan strategies for working with the children whose families' beliefs do not permit participation in holiday celebrations. Include the child's parents in creating satisfactory alternatives for the child within the classroom.

8. Be sensitive to the possibility that families with very low incomes may find certain holidays stressful because of the enormous amount of commercialization and media pressure to consume. Stores' advertising of Halloween costumes, media and store emphasis on eating special foods at Thanksgiving, and the commercial equation of love with expensive and numerous gifts at Christmas time are prominent examples.

In the classroom, challenge these pressures by focusing on meaningful ways to celebrate holidays without spending money. Emphasize that homemade costumes and gifts are very special because they are unique and made with each person's wonderful ideas and with love. Make Halloween costumes and Christmas gifts at school—using these times to encourage and support children's creativeness. Talk about the underlying meaning of holidays as times when your family and other people you care about come together to enjoy each other. Critique the way TV and stores make it look like the important thing is to buy, buy, buy!

Don't solve the commercialization problem through charity. Many poor families deeply resent the once-a-year Thanksgiving or Christmas "box." Open up discussion with parents about ways they have found to celebrate holidays and the pressures they experience. Explain how you challenge the commercialization of holidays in your curriculum, and explore with parents how to find and make inexpensive toys and holiday decorations and how to have inexpensive celebrations.

Reprinted from L. Derman-Sparks and the A.B.C. Task Force, *Anti-Bias Curriculum: Tools for Empowering Young Children* (Washington, DC: NAEYC), 86–87. Copyright © 1989 Louise Derman-Sparks. Reprinted with permission.

A World of Difference

Karen Neubert and Elizabeth Jones

39

Creating Culturally Relevant Holiday Curriculum

A Negotiation

In the effort to develop multicultural curriculum, holidays are the first thing teachers think of. Let's enrich our program with celebrations from different cultures, and that way we'll learn about them—by eating their foods, singing their songs, enacting their rituals. However well intended, this approach often results in "tourist curriculum"—a quick visit to the unfamiliar, then home again to events taken for granted (Derman-Sparks & the A.B.C. Task Force 1989).

Staff at Pacific Oaks Children's School approach holiday celebrations with care. Ours is a large school in metropolitan Los Angeles, enrolling some 250 children, from infancy to nine years, in seven programs differentiated by age of children and length of day. Its families are culturally diverse, and most are successful in mainstream America. Within the overall antibias, culturally relevant philosophy of the school, staff for each program make their own curriculum decisions. *No* holiday is celebrated without critical thought guided by questions such as, What universal values does the holiday represent? What cultural tradition?

Is it developmentally appropriate in terms of children's ability to understand it? Does the holiday promote stereotypes? Has it been commercialized? Will children learn all about it outside our school? As an example of one response to these questions, our winter celebrations typically include Hannukah and Kwanzaa but not Christmas, except as it is represented in Las Posadas, the Mexican/Southwestern reenactment of Mary and Joseph's finding no room at the inn.

The decision to celebrate el Día de los Muertos

Similarly, there is an alternative from the Mexican tradition to the usual fall emphasis on Halloween. El Día de los Muertos—the Day of the Dead—honors the ancestors, inviting back their souls to be among us for a time of family reunion. It is both a celebration of love and a frank acknowledgment of the reality of death, right down to the bones. The celebration of el Día de los Muertos described in this article was seen as

appropriate by staff of the primary and preschool programs for these reasons:

1. It was initiated at the request of a member of the school community to whom it was personally important. Manuel Gonzales Briones, who worked on the maintenance staff, grew up in Oaxaca. Missing el Día de los Muertos celebrations of his childhood, he wanted to share his holiday with the school's children. He understood its tradition and was skilled in its art and craft. "People in the social environment" of a school are a significant potential source of emergent curriculum (Jones & Nimmo 1994, 127).

2. This holiday tradition is shared by some families and teaching staff, as well as by many residents in the surrounding metropolitan area. In the multilingual, multicultural Los Angeles area, Spanish is heard frequently and Mexican holidays are publicly celebrated.

3. It was an age-appropriate project for the primary class of 6- to 9-year-olds. By inviting younger children to their celebration, the older children created a wide-age community event

tine has great significance for young children and shouldn't be continually interrupted by special events—either those loved by the adults in the program or those selected in the name of multiculturalism. Tacking on superficial versions of other people's holidays is one of the most common forms of tourist curriculum (Derman-Sparks & the A.B.C. Task Force 1989; Jones & Derman-Sparks 1992).

The challenge is, rather, to select a few holidays to explore in depth during the school year and let the others go for the present, as far as school is concerned. Mainstream holidays and those celebrated by children's families will become part of children's lives without the school's investment in them beyond acknowledgment by staff of what children and parents choose to talk about and share from home (Bisson 1992; Carter & Curtis 1994, 141–49).

Our decision to celebrate el Día de los Muertos took all these issues into account. It generated good experiences for many of the children and adults involved. It raised more issues as well.

What happened?

When Manuel suggested to Karen, the school's artist in residence, celebrating el Día de los Muertos in Children's School, Karen decided that she really wanted to do it, for Manuel and for everyone. She talked to Janice and Robyn, the teachers of the primary children (the oldest children in the school), and found them supportive. Manuel agreed to come in on his day off, for several weeks, to work with the children.

Manuel met with the children during their lunchtime outdoors. He told them about his family's celebration when he was a child in Mexico, and he showed them pictures in the book *The Skeleton at the Feast*

while publicly documenting their work (Edwards, Gandini, & Forman 1993).

4. This celebration offers an alternative to Halloween, a holiday that has generated continuing staff dialogue over the years. A heavily commercialized mainstream holiday, Halloween is a mixture of northern European pre-Christian and Christian traditions. It perpetuates the witch stereotype historically exploited to suppress the power of wise women. It transforms fear into fun: masks, costumes, and candy create a good time for all (except the under-4s, who recognize the fearful when they see it). Many adults love Halloween, remembering it as one of the pleasures of their own childhoods.

El Día de los Muertos comes from a parallel tradition, not part of the U.S. mainstream but very significant in our region of the country and in neighboring Mexico. It mixes indigenous and colonial roots and, like Halloween, transforms fear into fun. It differs from Halloween, however, in its focus on the generations of the family and on the memory of those who have passed on (Luenn 1998). This focus may lend itself more to developmentally appropriate curriculum and to teaching *caring* as a value than does any aspect of Halloween.

This is not at all to say that all schools should celebrate el Día de los Muertos or give up Halloween. In our school, our decision to celebrate it illustrates the process of paying careful attention to a number of criteria in developing any curriculum emphasis, including holidays. Holidays should never *take over* curriculum planning; the day-to-day rou-

A World of Difference

(Carmichael & Sayer 1992). Did they think it would be a good idea to make *calaveras* and *papeles picados* for an altar at school? They were enthusiastic. What will we need? Teachers made a list and went shopping for supplies.

An entire morning was devoted to preparation for the celebration. Manuel, working with half the class at a time, taught the children how to make the *calaveras*—skulls modeled from a paste of flour and powdered sugar, fragrant with vanilla. Karen helped Manuel while Kris, Karen's assistant from Art Studio, and teachers Janice and Robyn worked with the rest of the children on *papeles picados*—traditional designs cut into large, brilliantly colored sheets of tissue paper.

The skulls, layered on trays, rested in the refrigerator over the weekend. Then, during another long morning's work session, they were painted with food coloring.

El Día de los Muertos is a day of memories. Whom do we remember? Whom shall we honor with our altar? We consulted the school's director, who immediately thought of Florence, beloved librarian of Children's School who had died three years earlier. We also missed Brandy and Paz, the school's dog and cat. And Jose, another maintenance staff member, had recently lost John, his pet pigeon that flew 10 miles a day to be with him at work. Sorrowfully the children created drawings, clay sculptures, and stories about John. These and the photographs we had of Florence and of the animals could go on the altar.

Using cardboard boxes and tissue, an altar was constructed in the reception room of the Children's School office (which, with the adjacent hall, is regularly used as a children's art gallery). Karen and Kris provided candles, flowers, candies, and nuts. Manuel hung *papeles picados* he had made and arranged

marigolds, the traditional flower, and incense. He came in very early Monday morning, October 31, with hot food—sweet and hot *tamales* and *pan dulce*. He explained that the candies and favorite foods were for the children, and that the aroma would draw the spirits back for an evening. He also hung two glittery cardboard purple-plumed skeletons outside the office door. Karen was concerned that the store-bought skeletons would seem commercial when we were emphasizing children's work. She discussed them with Manuel. "It's OK, Karen, don't worry," he said.

An invitation had gone out earlier from Art Studio and the primary class to the preschool and kindergarten classes, and the day was scheduled for visits by interested children. Depending on their own interest, teachers devoted more or less energy to preparing children for their visit. Children came in small groups with an adult. Manuel was present, his beautiful *papeles* suspended from the ceiling, his face glowing, his joy tangible. The candles flickered and the scent of marigolds, *pan dulce*, candies, and *tamales* filled the small darkened room. The children—most of them—were awed and respectful, rising to the occasion, as children will, at an event that is clearly a significant time of love and sharing for the adults in their lives.

To whom was it important?

Janice and Robyn, the primary teachers, saw the celebration as age-appropriate for their 6- to 8-year-olds in terms of their relationship with Manuel, their personal experiences with death, and an ongoing curriculum emphasis in their program.

Janice: Making cutouts, working with clay and sugar dough, building the altar, children had lots of time to discuss the whole experience. And it happened

in the context of our year's curriculum: we're reading creation myths from different cultures. Talking about creation leads to ideas about death, spirituality, soul, and questions of symbolism: Is it OK to have different beliefs? We've talked a lot about Native Americans, whose spirituality is related to the heavens and the planets. We've been talking about solstice. . . .

The altar the children built is dedicated to Florence and to the animals. It's not just artistic. Many children in the group have experienced [a loved one's] death recently. El Día de los Muertos introduces them to a ritual by which people acknowledge death.

Janice's negative feelings about previous Halloween events in this classroom made her particularly open to a new idea.

Janice: I hated the haunted house we used to do; it was all about horror and ugliness (and it scared the younger kids we invited to it). El Día de los Muertos is more respectful; it focuses on loved ones, not on fear. I like the thought of my loved ones being around me.

Remembering loved ones was also the focus for those staff and parents whose family traditions were validated by this celebration. Preschool staff who took children to visit the altar commented.

Judy: (Latina) I was so happy to find that you were doing el Día de los Muertos. It's part of my tradition. I had two grandmothers; one was Mexican and the other was Indian—"Somos indios [we are Indians]," she always said. When I was a child, I sometimes didn't comprehend the different things they said about the world, but I followed them and believed all that they showed and told me. I now have an enriched life because of them.

We had an altar in my house all year 'round, with candles and flowers and pictures of all of us. For el Día de los Muertos the pictures of the living family members were removed and it became

One reason we make art is to tap into our collective experience—to connect.

an altar for those we remembered. My grandfather's hat stayed on the altar all year, but for el Día de los Muertos, my mother bought a new hat in his memory. His favorite foods—tortillas and pizza—went on the altar with the hat. The altar was for my baby sister too, who died when she was a few days old; it welcomed her soul back among us.

My mother wouldn't put representations of skulls on the altar. She didn't think children's thoughts should be focused on death.

When my dog died, and I cried, my mother said, "We'll put his picture on the altar." My grandmother disapproved; she didn't think a dog belonged on the altar. But my mom knew how much I loved my dog, and his picture went up there. Having an altar at Children's School was very emotional for me. When I told the children about my family and dog, I brushed away tears. The altar reminded and refreshed my vivid memories, and it was beautiful to be validated.

Lissa: (Anglo) I visited the altar with the children, and we talked about what we saw. There's an article with good background information; I read that. Sara sang songs in Spanish with us. Mateo's family were delighted when they learned we were having el Día de los Muertos; they brought calaveras to share.

Who questioned it?
Adult conflicts

Elizabeth: (Anglo, married to a Latino) My husband's family celebrates el Día de los Muertos, and I wanted the children to be respectful. I was worried about some of the 3-year-olds; I wanted them to understand that we weren't just going to get candy. I insisted that one child wait for a later turn, even though his

family is Mexican; he was sounding too grabby.

Sheila: (Latina) There are some grabby little kids in Mexico too; they have to be socialized into how to behave. When I went with some children we were trying to be respectful and quiet, but there was a mix-up between the sweet and the hot tamales, and Matthew got a hot one by mistake. "Pepper! Where's the trash?" he yelled. But his friend, whose family likes hot food, ate Matthew's leftovers and asked for more.

Rhonda: (an African American preschool teacher who brought a different perspective to staff reflection on the experience) I didn't know how I could talk about it with the children if I didn't understand it myself. And I was worried; I thought maybe it was about calling up the spirits. Would Jesus like it? In my church we don't do Halloween; that's Devil's Day. It's important in my family to do what's right.

At the public school there were alternative activities this year for children not participating in Halloween, so those were what my 6-year-old niece did, but her older brothers did what they weren't supposed to do. They got in trouble when she told at home!

Here at school, though, I know we're trying to help children learn about each other. So I took two children to see the altar, and it was nice. Jake's mom asked me about it because he was out and missed it, and I tried to explain it to her. For myself, I can choose what to celebrate.

Karen: (entered the discussion to comment) Our Japanese students have taught me about Obon, and I've heard Akiko talking with Manuel about the similarities between their two holidays. Obon lasts for a week in August, and it's about respecting and honoring the dead. It is believed that one's ancestors visit in spirit.

Rhonda: (thoughtfully) It sounds like we all celebrate the same things in different cultures. My nephew just passed—he was only a child—and we held hands and sang Happy Birthday on his birthday to remember him.

Other adults with strong religious values reacted differently. In the primary class one boy's mother wouldn't let him participate in making sugar skulls, an activity that offended her Christian views. The staff arranged for the child to visit kindergarten during this activity. He accepted his mother's limits, although he was concerned about being left out of something fun.

Another parent who was Christian, reacting to the skeletons Manuel had hung outdoors and to the use of the word *altar*, called other parents to try to organize a protest. "It's Satanism," she insisted.

"Did you read the explanation of el Día de los Muertos that Manuel and Karen wrote?" she was asked.

"No, I saw enough to know that it's Satanism," she replied.

Finally, asking, "Am I the only one with this issue?" she withdrew her child from the school.

A former teaching staff member of Latina (though not Mexican) heritage was greatly offended by the presence of the altar at the school, insisting that el Día de los Muertos is a family ritual, not a public event. "This is not an art exhibit!" she repeated to Karen, suggesting that the altar be taken down. Karen, unsure whether she should comply, felt as though her own deepest values were being attacked.

Karen: It was as if creating an art installation trivialized the tradition. For me, art is not trivial. One reason we make art is to tap into our collective experience—to connect. And we discover the similarities among our images. I loved a nighttime photo from Obon that showed candles in paper bags floating down the dark river, representing the souls going *home. I thought of Mexican luminarias —also candles in bags—and of all the ways light can be held and carried.*

A culture's celebrations often have religious roots, and religious differences have been a major source of conflict throughout history. Celebration inspires all the arts, and these can bring different people together in mutual appreciation of beauty. But does the participation of outsiders take away from the deeper meanings of the event? Can rituals traditionally celebrated only by believers, or within the intimacy of the family, be made public? Can we learn to understand each other?

Children's misunderstandings

The rituals by which adults create symbolic meanings to be celebrated in community are often difficult for children to understand. The events honored by such rituals are those hard for adults to understand too; they are mysteries to be wondered at and mythologized. Young children find meaning through relationship: These are important events for the people who love me. We do them together.

The presence of adults for whom a celebration is personally meaningful (a crucial criterion for our staff in choosing which holidays to celebrate) does not, however, ensure that children will not experience confusion. In early childhood, confusion is a frequent state of being. Daily reality, as well as the depiction of both fantasy and reality that children see daily on television, can be relied on to generate continual misunderstandings.

In preparation for el Día de los Muertos, Elizabeth asked her small group of preschoolers what they knew about death. "A dead tree might not be dead. When you walk past it, it might move." "And princes

make you feel better." "When I'm sick and my mom kisses me, I feel better."

As the conversation turned to the foods that would be on the altar, it became evident that some children thought those foods were what caused someone to die. Clearly the film version of *Snow White* was a compelling source of misinformation for many children.

Misinformation and excitement stirred children's imaginations. One small child was overheard in late afternoon after dark, as he was being hurried toward the parking lot by his father: "Dad! Did you see it, see in there?" He pointed toward the room where the altar was. Dad, glancing in that direction, responded: "Um-hmm. OK, let's go now." Child: "Dad, Dad, that's where they make the dead people!"

Karen and the primary children, who created the altar, had fond memories of the animals and of Florence, their librarian who read them stories and expected them to be good listeners. On the other hand, many of the younger children had no such memories. Some were particularly confused by the photograph of the

black-and-white cat Paz, who looked just like Paca, the school's new cat. "Why is Paca up there? He didn't die."

Conflict maintenance

Wherever initiative by adults and children is encouraged, many unpredictable consequences follow. The disagreements, small and large, that arise among us are part of our learning to live together—part of *conflict maintenance* (a term used by Cirecie Olatungi, New Orleans site coordinator for the Culturally Relevant Anti-Bias Education Leadership Project).

The airing of genuine differences among people is a source of continuing growth and learning—and conflict. Many of us are in the habit of dealing with conflict through denial; if we don't name it, perhaps it will go away. Death, the focus of el Día de los Muertos, is also handled through denial in much of European American culture; we lack meaningful rituals for confronting the unknowable. In contrast, el Día de los Muertos's cheerful depiction of

The airing of genuine differences among people is a source of continuing growth and learning—and conflict.

skeletons may seem pagan, ironic, or simply unpleasant, but it is accompanied by open acknowledgment of loss and sadness and love.

Doing things (including holidays) "the way we've always done them" may be educationally unsound in a diverse and changing world. Many choices will be available to our children, whether we like it or not. Making intelligent choices requires information as well as a values base. "I don't want to learn about it," was the reaction of one parent from a strong religious faith. In contrast, "I want to know about things," was the reaction of a teacher from a similar faith background. While affirming her own values, she took professional responsibility for learning more in order to be helpful to children, and she was able to recognize and appreciate the fact that different cultures celebrate similar events in different ways.

Trying new things requires us to stretch, to gather new information, to experience the disequilibrium that Dewey, Piaget, and Vygotsky insist is essential to cognitive and social development. Comfortable teachers with all their holiday boxes ready to go are quick to complain about "politically correct" efforts to re-examine familiar ways of doing things. "Why do people have to rock the boat? It used to be so nice around here." Nice, of course, for those comfortable with the tradition. Those who weren't had long since learned to remain silent.

The way we do things reflects our values, examined or unexamined. If we examine our habitual practices in a conscious effort to be true to our values, there will be conflict. In a diverse community where differences are out in the open, conflict comes with the territory (Jones & Nimmo 1995). When we name our differences, we often get defensive about them; if I feel that your differences threaten who I am and what I believe, I will move to defend my own rightness. Through healthy conflict maintenance and free expression we are able to learn and practice skills of conflict resolution. These are some of the most important skills we teach our children as well. Free expression is nonverbal as well as verbal. An altar is a nonverbal construction—a sculpture, if you will. (Wherever free expression has been suppressed, the arts as well as speech are targeted.)

Good curriculum is significant; it raises issues to be grappled with by adults and children alike. Multicultural curriculum isn't just nice. It's about genuine differences among people and the biases accompanying those differences, as well as about discovery of the commonalities we share. At Pacific Oaks Children's School, our experience with the culturally relevant curriculum provided by el Día de los Muertos has been complicated and fruitful.

◌

A year later Manuel died quite suddenly, near the time of el Día de los Muertos. An altar in his memory, spontaneously created by adults on staff, graced the school's front hall for some weeks.

References

Bisson, J. 1992. *Celebrating holidays in the anti-bias early childhood education program.* Pasadena, CA: Pacific Oaks Occasional Papers.

Carmichael, E., & C. Sayer. 1992. *The skeleton at the feast: The Day of the Dead in Mexico.* Austin, TX: University of Texas Press.

Carter, M., & D. Curtis. 1994. *Training teachers: A harvest of theory and practice.* St. Paul, MN: Redleaf.

Derman-Sparks, L., & the A.B.C. Task Force. 1989. *Anti-bias curriculum: Tools for empowering young children.* Washington, DC: NAEYC.

Edwards, C., L. Gandini, & G. Forman, eds. 1993. *The hundred languages of children: The Reggio Emilia approach to early childhood education.* Norwood, NJ: Ablex.

Jones, E., & L. Derman-Sparks. 1992. Meeting the challenge of diversity. *Young Children* 47 (2): 12–18.

Jones, E., & J. Nimmo. 1994. *Emergent curriculum.* Washington, DC: NAEYC.

Jones, E., & J. Nimmo. 1995. *Collaboration, conflict and change.* Pasadena, CA: Pacific Oaks Occasional Papers.

Luenn, N. 1998. *A gift for Abuelita.* Flagstaff, AZ: Northland.

Daniel Gartrell

40

Bridging Differences

Excerpted from *What the Kids Said Today*

In building connections with families, teachers face the uncertainty that comes with cultural differences. Whether due to ethnic, religious, or lifestyle factors, differences can and sometimes do make building teacher-parent relations difficult. The teacher's ability to become a learner in such situations, to be open to the experience of the parent, is essential. Mary Beth, an experienced kindergarten teacher, recalls her experience with a family that other teachers found difficult to work with due to the family's religious beliefs.

As Mary Beth so bravely models in this anecdote, teachers can regard family cultural differences not as obstacles or burdens but as sources of learning and mutual appreciation. In the encouraging classroom, all children feel they have a place, because they know that their families have a place as well.

❧

In my first year, a veteran teacher told me to "watch out" for a certain family. Their younger child was to be in my kindergarten class. The family were Jehovah's Witnesses. As part of

their faith, the family taught their children not to salute the flag or celebrate birthdays and holidays. This teacher told me that in the previous year the parents had become irate when they were not told of a Halloween party in the classroom of the older child, even though their child had not participated. The teacher then tried to let the family know of upcoming events, but she felt they remained distant and uncooperative. There were instances when the older child, now a third-grader, had been made fun of by classmates. The parents had reported these incidents, but the teacher apparently told the family there was not much she could do.

I remembered going to school, when I was in fourth grade, with a child of this faith. I remembered thinking how hard it must be for him to be left out of important school events. I took this teacher's comments as a personal challenge, and decided to work hard to get along with this family. It was my practice to send home notes of introduction to each family before school began and then continue with "happygrams" home on a rotating basis for

each member of my class. I made sure this child went home with at least one complimentary note every week. This was not a hard task. I enjoyed the child's pluckiness. (I read each note to her just to make sure it would get delivered.) I called the home a few times as well, but always got an answering machine. I left messages that I hoped the parents would find friendly.

Other teachers told me not to expect this family to attend the fall parent conference, but the mother did come. I was very pleased to see her, and she seemed rather surprised at my reaction. I decided to let her bring up the religion issue. My job was to let her know how well her daughter was doing in my class. Well, she did bring it up. I told her I was interested to hear about her faith (because I was). She told me about the flag salute, and I said not to worry—we wouldn't be doing the flag salute until close to the end of the year because I didn't think the children could understand it. She smiled at this.

About birthdays, I told her what I told all the parents: I preferred that the children had parties at home, but

© Nancy P. Alexander

we let the children wear a "birthday crown" for the day if that was okay with the parents. She said no crown for Wilma, but otherwise she liked what I did. About holiday activities, I asked her what she would like me to do, and we had quite a conversation about that. I was very surprised when she said Wilma could stay in the classroom if I could figure out a way to have her fit in without participating. That year, I kind of downplayed the holidays, explaining to parents who asked that not all

of the children in the class celebrate all holidays. I did more with the ideas behind the holidays—for instance, why should we be thankful?—rather than do pageants and crafts, a practice I still use today.

What I am still the proudest about with this family had to do with the flag salute. Before we started doing the flag salute in April, I had three parents come in to discuss with the class what saluting the flag meant to them. One was Wilma's mom, and she did a fine job of explaining why

Wilma would stand up (out of respect for the class), but wouldn't be doing the rest. (I had previously told the other two parents what Wilma's mom would say, and they were okay with this.) That whole year, I never remember any of the children making fun of Wilma—they liked her, just as I did.

Reprinted from D. Gartrell, *What the Kids Said Today: Using Classroom Conversations to Become a Better Teacher* (St. Paul, MN: Redleaf), 50–51. (www.redleafpress.org) Copyright © 2000 Daniel Gartrell. Reprinted with permission.

A World of Difference

VIII

Growing as Culturally Responsive Educators

The most challenging part of educating in a diverse society is not responding to what children do or parents say. It is acknowledging that we, too, view the world through our own cultural lens, then *acting* on that knowledge. That is the challenge this final set of readings presents us with—to consider our own development as antibias educators. Where do we start, and what kinds of experiences and resources contribute to our growth (Derman-Sparks #43; Unten)? Essential to becoming an effective antibias educator—although by no means easy or quick—is reflecting on our cultural assumptions and perspectives, identifying and owning our biases, and then working to change them (Derman-Sparks #42; Marshall). As we grow in these vital ways, we begin to alter our teaching and relationships with families, as these readings all describe. A next step may be to see oneself as a change agent in addressing institutional biases—biases that often are deeply embedded in institutions' systems and practices (Phillips).

To be truly culturally responsive, we must continually challenge ourselves to reevaluate and rethink our practice.

Hermine H. Marshall

41

Cultural Influences on the Development of Self-Concept

Updating Our Thinking

Why is it that some children try new things with enthusiasm and approach peers and adults with confidence, whereas other children seem to believe that they are incapable of succeeding in many situations? . . . What can we learn from research that will allow us to help children approach new situations and other people with confidence?

—H.H. Marshall (1989)

In that 1989 article I assumed along with many early childhood educators that approaching new situations with confidence indicated a child's strong self-concept; hesitation and hanging back could indicate lack of self-esteem. In my review of research on the development of self-concept written at that time, the notion that children's behavior is influenced by their cultural background had only begun to enter the research literature and thinking of early childhood educators. I pointed out briefly that cultural values can affect self-esteem and different cultures may value and encourage different behaviors. For instance, taking personal control, important in dominant American culture, might not be valued in other cultures. Yet I indicated that autonomy and initiative are behaviors to look for as reflecting positive self-concept. I implied that children who lacked these traits might have low self-esteem.

The last decade has seen an increase in research on child development in different cultures. Awareness of this research has enhanced early childhood educators' sensitivity to how perspectives may vary in cultures that are different from the culture of individual educators as well as the dominant culture. Culture impacts not just which behaviors are valued and displayed but also our interpretations of these behaviors.

As a result of this decade of research, it has become clear that what many of us have taken for evidence of self-esteem is influenced by our cultural perceptions. It is important, therefore, to revisit some of the issues related to self-concept development in light of a more sophisticated understanding of cultural influences. To this end, as educators we need to increase our awareness that our perceptions, actions, and interactions and those of children derive their meanings from the cultures in which they are embedded.

Constructing a view of self

Children construct their views of self "by participating in interactions that caregivers structure according to cultural values about the nature of human existence" (Raeff 1997). In Western cultures, striving toward *independence* and individuality and asserting oneself are seen as important accomplishments (Markus & Kitayama 1991). As a consequence, Westerners perceive children who are outgoing and eagerly explore new situations as demonstrating competence and having a positive self-concept, especially compared to children who do not appear to seek out and actively participate in these situations.

In contrast, Eastern cultures place greater emphasis on maintaining harmonious, *interdependent* relationships. Markus and Kitayama (1991) note that interdependent views are also characteristic of many African, Latin American, and southern European cultures. (See also Greenfield 1994.) In cultures influenced by Confucian and Taoist philosophies, self-restraint and control of emotional expressiveness is considered an indication of social maturity (Chen et al. 1998). Asserting oneself may be seen as a sign of immaturity (Markus & Kitayama 1991). Children who are shy, reticent, and quiet are likely to be considered competent and well behaved by parents and teachers in the People's Republic of China (Chen et al. 1998; Rubin 1998). These children—whom North American teachers from the dominant culture might see as inhibited and lacking in self-confidence—have a positive view of themselves and of their social relationships.

Similarly, in other cultures where interdependence or "relative enmeshment" (Garcia Coll 1990) are seen as ideal mature relationships, interdependency and interpersonal dependency are likely to be fostered between young children and their mothers. When asked about desirable child behavior, mothers from Latino cultures, such as Spanish-speaking Puerto Rican mothers, are likely to focus on respectfulness, a concept which assumes appropriate interrelatedness. In contrast the Anglo mothers in one study focused on autonomy and active exploration, reflecting more independent values (Harwood 1992). Moreover, some cultures such as traditional Navajo cultures expect children to observe before attempting to try things (Bacon & Carter 1991). For these children too, standing back and observing rather than exploring should not be taken as an indication of low self-esteem.

Nevertheless, although Chinese parents tend to value interdependence and cohesion and may minimize the development of individuality within the family, Taiwanese and immigrant Chinese parents seem to encourage independence so

that children will be able to succeed in the larger society (Lin & Fu 1990). Likewise, some Mexican immigrant families may begin to approve of their children's independent thinking related to school topics as they become more acculturated (Delgado-Gaitan 1994).

In addition, in Eastern cultures (Markus & Kitayama 1991) and Latino cultures (Parke & Buriel 1998), primary concern centers on other people and the self-in-relationship-to-other rather than self alone. Most people in these cultures value developing empathetic understanding and attention to the needs of others. These behaviors serve to maintain harmonious relationships more than would attending to meeting one's own needs.

These contrasts should not be taken to mean that independence and interdependence are mutually exclusive (Raeff 1997). Both independent and interdependent tendencies are common to human experience. People in Western cultures value relationships and cooperation as well as independence. "Every group selects a point on the independence/interdependence continuum as its cultural ideal" (Greenfield 1994, 4).

The impact on socialization and development

Varieties of both independence and interdependence affect socialization and development. Consequently we should be aware that how children see themselves in relationship to others is also a part of their self-concept. Educators need to expand their views of what is considered important to self-concept beyond the typical notions of autonomy, self-assertion, self-enhancement, and uniqueness and include characteristics such as empathy, sensitivity to others, modesty, cooperation, and caring as well.

Although it is important to be aware that our perceptions and interpretations of behavior are influenced by the culture(s) in which we were raised and in which we reside and that the meaning of behavior may vary for different cultures, we must be careful not to assume that just because children or families are from a specific ethnic or racial group they necessarily share a common cultural experience. There are differences within cultures and within families. Other factors impinge on how children are raised and the meanings accorded to behavior, such as the family's countries of origin, the length of time immigrant families have been in the United States, the degree of acculturation the family has experienced, educational background, and social status (Delgado-Gaitan 1994; Killen 1997; McLloyd 1999).

Some children and families experience the influence of multiple cultures. This is particularly true when parents are from different ethnic, racial, or cultural groups. In these families parents may bring values from two or more cultures to their views and practices in raising children. Regardless of children's apparent ethnic or cultural background, it is important for teachers to be sensitive to *individual* children and family members and to how a family's beliefs, attitudes, and values may affect children's behavior.

Attempting to understand what each family values as important behaviors and watching for these behaviors may provide clues to the meaning of children's actions for that family and child. It is important to recognize and affirm behaviors valued by the home culture. It is also essential to provide opportunities for children to learn behaviors that are valued by the Western culture (Delpit 1988). Children who are able to maintain comfort with behaviors that are valued in their home as well as those valued in the wider society may be most likely to have positive views of themselves in both cultural contexts.

What does this mean in practice?

My earlier research on self-concept development describes a number of ways to influence self-concept. These include helping children (1) feel they are of value, (2) believe they are competent, (3) have some control over tasks and actions, (4) learn interpersonal skills. Also noted as important is becoming aware of your expectations for children. The particular techniques for each of these recommendations remain valid today (see Marshall 1989).

Beyond these fundamentals, the following steps are based on a more sophisticated awareness of cultural and individual variations in values and behaviors. Using them as a guide will increase your sensitivity to the values and practices of the families whose children are in your care and enable you to support the development of positive self-concepts.

1. Be aware of the ways your own culture influences your expectations of children. Think about how you were raised, your family values. What behaviors were encouraged? How did your family make you feel proud? Talk to friends or other teachers about their upbringing. Within your own community, there are likely variations in what families value and in the bases for positive self-concept. This reflection and knowledge may help you begin to expand your awareness of the indications of positive self-concept.

2. Consider the cultural backgrounds of the children in your setting and their community. Observe how children approach new

© Jonathan A. Meyers

tasks, relate to other people, and react to praise. This may raise some questions. Be a good listener. If you teach at the primary level, chat with the children before and after school or at lunchtime. Be careful that surface appearances do not influence your perceptions or interactions. Gather more information about the cultural and ethnic groups represented in your class (as noted below).

3. Learn about the cultures from which the children in your program or school may come. Read about the values and child rearing practices of these cultures. Talk to community leaders or people you know who have greater knowledge of these cultures.

Contact community-based organizations, such as the National Council of La Raza (NCLR). Inviting representatives of such organizations to talk to teachers in your setting may

be helpful. Still, do not assume that this general information is sufficient. Further understanding of the cultural background of *particular* children in your class will be necessary since, in every cultural and ethnic group, individual and generational differences are likely.

4. Use your basic knowledge of the culture to talk with each family about its values and practices. Learn what families think is important to consider for their children. You might share with them what you have been learning about their culture or cultures. Explain that you recognize that every family is different and that you would like to know what they think and what they value as important. Asking about the families' methods for teaching and learning may be useful. Discuss what happens if children raise questions or explore on their own and how

In all cases, showing respect for ways of interacting that derive from the home culture is critical to the support and development of a child's self-concept.

children and adults show respect. It is important to accept what family members say as valuable information to consider and avoid letting your own values and methods stifle communication.

5. Build on what you have learned from each family. Provide opportunities for children to learn in a variety of ways. For example, children might learn by observing first, trying things out on their own, or by doing tasks with a partner or group of peers. Children need opportunities to demonstrate caring and cooperation.

All children will benefit from enhanced opportunities to learn and interact in a variety of ways. Enlarge your repertoire of responses; some children will find more comfort in nonverbal acceptance—a smile or nod—than praise. In all cases, showing respect for ways of interacting that derive from the home culture is critical to the support and development of a child's self-concept. Practices that are clearly harmful to the child, of course, should not be supported. In such a case, being able to discuss with the family why the practice is detrimental is important (see Gonzalez-Mena & Bhavnagri 2000 [reading #8 in this volume]).

6. Infuse the curriculum and classroom environment with a rich variety of materials from the cultures of your children as well as other cultures. Parents may be able to share songs or stories or bring in something special representing their home culture. Find books and posters that represent the children in your class. Introduce as snacks special treats from the children's cultures. Seeing their ethnic groups and cultures of origin valued will enhance children's self-concepts.

Conclusion

It is not enough to assume that affirming young children's assertiveness, confidence, and independence suffices to support self-concept development. Such qualities as showing respect for and being sensitive to others, learning by observing, and exhibiting humility may also evidence positive self-concept and should be nourished. Acknowledging the contributions and values of all the families whose children are in our care while also supporting children's development of necessary skills to succeed in mainstream America is most likely to enhance the development of children's self-esteem.

References

Bacon, J., & H.L. Carter. 1991. Culture and mathematics learning: A review of the literature. *Journal of Research and Development in Education* 25: 1–9.

Chen, X., P.D. Hastings, K.H. Rubin, J. Chen, G. Cen, & S. Stewart. 1998. Child-rearing attitudes and behavioral inhibition in Chinese and Canadian toddlers. *Developmental Psychology* 34: 677–86.

Delgado-Gaitan, C. 1994. Socializing young children in Mexican-American families: An intergenerational perspective. In *Cross-cultural roots of minority child development*, eds. P.M. Greenfield & R.R. Hocking, 55–86. Hillsdale, NJ: Erlbaum.

Delpit, L. 1988. The silenced dialogue: Power and pedagogy in educating other people's children. *Harvard Educational Review* 58: 280–98.

Garcia Coll, C. 1990. Developmental outcome of minority infants: A process-oriented look into our beginnings. *Child Development* 61: 270–89.

Gonzalez-Mena, J., & N.P. Bhavnagri. 2000. Diversity and infant/toddler caregiving. *Young Children* 55 (5): 31–35.

Greenfield, P.M. 1994. Independence and interdependence as developmental scripts: Implications for theory, research, and practice. In *Cross-cultural roots of minority child development*, eds. P.M. Greenfield & R.R. Hocking, 1–37. Hillsdale, NJ: Erlbaum.

Harwood, R.L. 1992. The influence of culturally derived values on Anglo and Puerto Rican mothers' perceptions of attachment behavior. *Child Development* 63: 822–39.

Killen, M. 1997. Commentary: Culture, self and development: Are cultural templates useful or stereotypic? *Developmental Review* 17: 239–49.

Lin, C.C., & V.R. Fu. 1990. A comparison of child-rearing practices among Chinese, immigrant Chinese, and Caucasian-American parents. *Child Development* 61: 429–33.

Markus, H.R., & S. Kitayama. 1991. Culture and the self: Implications for cognition, emotion, and motivation. *Psychological Review* 98: 224–53.

Marshall, H.H. 1989. Research in Review. The development of self-concept. *Young Children* 44 (5): 44–51.

McLloyd, V. 1999. Cultural influences in a multicultural society: Conceptual and methodological issues. In *Cultural processes in child development*, Minnesota Symposia on Child Psychology, vol. 29, ed. A.S. Masten, 123–26.

Parke, R.D., & R. Buriel. 1998. Socialization in the family: Ethnic and ecological perspectives. In *Handbook of child psychology*, vol. 3: *Social, emotional, and personality development*, 5th ed., ed. N. Eisenberg, 463–552. New York: Wiley.

Raeff, C. 1997. Individuals in relationships: Cultural values, children's social interactions, and the development of an American individualistic self. *Developmental Review* 17: 205–38.

Rubin, K.H. 1998. Social and emotional development from a cultural perspective. *Developmental Psychology* 34: 611–15.

Reprinted from *Young Children* 56 (6): 19–25. Copyright © 2001 NAEYC.

Louise Derman-Sparks

42

Markers of Multicultural/Antibias Education

Creating a program that genuinely reflects a commitment to diversity and equity is an evolving journey. Change is an integral part as staff deepen their understanding and as new children, families, and staff become part of the program. Here are common markers indicating where you are on the multicultural/antibias education journey.

First steps

If these markers describe your program, you have taken only the very first steps on the journey to providing a multicultural/antibias education.

• The classroom environment is reflective of diversity—but only in small amounts and only some kinds of diversity (for example, one African American doll, a few books, a few posters).

• Curriculum focuses on discrete pieces about the cultures of various racial and ethnic groups and overemphasizes traditional life while downplaying current life.

• Multicultural activities tend to be add-ons to the "regular" curriculum (for example, celebrating various holidays but reflecting little of these cultures in the daily curriculum).

• Staff ask families for information about the most visible aspects of their cultures, such as food, music, and holidays, and occasionally ask parents to share special cultural activities. Staff do not learn about or incorporate the underlying aspects of families' cultures, like beliefs and rules about teacher-child interactions and preferred learning styles.

• Home languages of children in the program are occasionally used in songs, finger games, simple phrases (saying good morning, counting from 1 to 10) but are not incorporated into daily classroom life. Communication with and programs for families are presented in English only or occasionally with translation.

• Multicultural/antibias education is interpreted as learning only about others. In programs serving children of color (all ethnic/cultural groups not part of the White, European ethnic groups and who are targets of ra-

cial/cultural prejudice and discrimination), this results in insufficient attention to supporting children's cultural development. In programs serving European American children, this results in insufficient exploration of the cultural differences among their families.

• Staff bring in antibias activities only when a problem first arises from the children, or staff introduce specific antibias activities only occasionally.

• Staff do not take time to explore their own cultural identities and beliefs or to uncover and change their own biases and discomforts with each other.

On the way: Quality markers

Do you recognize these points? If they relate to your program, then you are well on the way to quality multicultural/antibias education.

• Staff actively incorporate their children's daily life experiences into daily curriculum.

• Staff tailor curriculum and teacher-child interactions to meet the cultural, as well as individual, developmental needs of their children, actively using parents' or family caregivers' knowledge about their home cultures.

• Daily classroom life and curriculum incorporate diversity and justice issues related to gender, disabilities, socioeconomic status, and the many ways of being a family, as well as issues related to ethnicity and culture.

• Staff use a variety of strategies to involve parents actively and regularly in the program, including provisions for languages other than English.

• Staff intentionally encourage children's development of critical thinking and tools for resisting prejudice and unfair behaviors directed at themselves or others. Parents and other neighborhood people share what they do to improve the quality of life and social justice in their communities.

• Staff reflect the cultural and language diversity of the children and families they serve and the communities of their centers and schools.

• Staff engage in intentional and regular reflection about their practice and the influences of their cultural backgrounds, and they openly help each other uncover and change biases and hurtful (even if unintentional) behaviors.

Reprinted from *Young Children* 54 (5): 43. Copyright © 1999 NAEYC.

Louise Derman-Sparks

43

Developing Antibias, Multicultural Curriculum

Excerpted from *Reaching Potentials, Volume 1*

Deciding what specific content will best foster multicultural, antibias goals with a particular child or group of children requires a combination of developmental and contextual analysis. In this section developmental issues will be discussed first; followed by a discussion of the sources of multicultural, antibias curriculum necessary for ensuring that curriculum choices are individually appropriate; and finally, the implications of implementing such curriculum in various contexts will be described.

Applying a developmental framework

The simplest and most effective way to apply a developmental framework to making choices about diversity content is to think of the child as the center of a series of concentric circles. Start with a child's experiences of self, and then move outward in concentric circles to family, neighborhood, city, country, and other countries. Simultaneously, move in a time continuum that be-

gins with current experiences, to learning about the immediate past and future, and then to learning about the more distant past and future. This paradigm of development in terms of concentric circles of experience is the best way to ensure developmentally appropriate curriculum content. The question of what constitutes real experiences within each concentric circle is vital, however.

Teachers who explain a lack of diversity content in their curriculum by insisting that young children do not notice or "care" about differences among people seriously *underestimate* developmental realities. All children, including those growing up in racially or ethnically homogeneous communities, are aware of differences among themselves, including gender, physical characteristics, family styles, traditions, religious beliefs, and disabilities, and do have contact with both positive and negative images and messages about various people. Integrating antibias, multicultural curriculum goals into the educational program of all children is therefore relevant, reflects the needs and interests of the children,

and builds upon what children already know. The key is first choosing content that enables young children to explore their own direct experiences of diversity and then introducing new forms of diversity in ways that connect to the children's learning about themselves and their classmates.

On the other hand, it is equally important not to *overestimate* what young children can learn efficiently and effectively and what they need to function capably in their world. Examples of overestimation are including activities that attempt to teach 3- and 4-year-olds about "ethnic groups" before the preschoolers have constructed the concept of *group* beyond their family, introducing content about countries from which their families emigrated in the far past, or expecting that a few activities in one "unit" about a culture are sufficient to foster a disposition of respect for and comfort with diversity in the face of pervasive societal biases.

Antibias curriculum choices must also carefully explore and evaluate what are meaningful critical thinking and activism activities at various

The teacher's increasing self-awareness about her own identity, cultural beliefs, and behaviors and attitudes toward aspects of other people's identities is essential.

ages. If content is unrelated to children's interests and current level of reasoning, then the activities can defeat their purpose, which is to foster problem-solving and decision-making abilities.

The four main objectives of antibias, multicultural education are to foster in each child (1) construction of a knowledgeable, confident self-identity, (2) comfortable, empathetic interaction with diversity among people, (3) critical thinking about bias, and (4) the ability to stand up for herself or himself and for others in the face of bias (Derman-Sparks 1992, 118–21). Achieving these four goals cannot occur in one year of preschool exposure. Activities related to each goal will have to be repeated in many different ways for several years as children construct increasingly complex understandings about themselves and about others.

Implementing antibias, multicultural curriculum means facing the challenge that "curriculum values children's constructive errors and does not prematurely limit exploration and experimentation for the sake of ensuring 'right' answers" (NAEYC & NAECS/SDE 1991, 31). Clearly, young children make many constructive errors as they grapple with figuring out the assorted components of their identity and as they crystalize attitudes toward others. Some of their "errors" reflect developmental ways of thinking; others represent the influence of socially prevailing biases; yet others are a mixture of both. Moreover, some of the "constructive errors" are potentially seriously damaging to a child's self-esteem or positive attitudes to-

ward aspects of human diversity.

When a 4-year-old thinks that a spread-out line of 10 checkers is more than a pushed-together line of 10 checkers, no harm occurs to that child's sense of self and her ability to function in the world at that point in her life, or to other children. Within a year or so, the 4-year-old will construct the principle of conservation that 10 checkers are still 10 checkers no matter how much space they take up. On the other hand, if the same 4-year-old thinks that brown skin is dirty because of lack of experience with dark-skinned people and therefore will not hold the hand of a brown-skinned classmate, harm *does happen* to her classmate and to her own socioemotional growth and ability to function in the world. Furthermore, while adult society will foster and reinforce the child's eventual discovery that 10 equals 10, society may neither encourage nor support the discovery that brown skin is *not* dirty and that refusing to hold a brown-skinned classmate's hand is hurtful, unfair, and unacceptable. In fact, adult society may actually reinforce the child's "constructive error" so that it becomes prejudice.

Effectively handling "constructive errors" about diversity requires thoughtful balancing between respect and understanding of a child's level of reasoning and informed sensitivity to the error's potential for damage to children's socioemotional and cognitive development. Identifying a range of potential damage can help in decision making about which of the following strategies constitutes an appropriate response:

(A) let the "error" stand; (B) find developmentally or culturally appropriate ways to involve the child in concrete experiences that contradict her theory and that can lead to new concepts; or (C) directly communicate why the idea is not acceptable and set limits on its expression.

If a 5-year-old draws a picture of herself as a surgeon operating on a patient and wearing a pink gown and tiara (K. Taus, personal communication, February 20, 1990), then strategy A is most appropriate because this belief does no present harm, and later knowledge of reality will change the belief. On the other hand, if the same child insists that girls can't play with blocks, then a combination of strategies B and C is necessary because this belief is presently harmful to both the child's and other classmates' developing cognitive abilities. If a 4-year-old is afraid to sit in a wheelchair because he thinks he will lose the ability to walk, strategy B seems best—finding the constructive error that underlies the fear and gradually helping the child overcome it. On the other hand, if a preschooler tells another child who uses a wheelchair, "You can't play with us. You're a baby because you can't walk," then it is essential to employ strategy C first, followed by strategy B. If a 3-year-old thinks that people get their skin color from paint, then strategy B seems most effective; if another 3-year-old refuses to hold a classmate's hand because of her skin color, then strategy C followed by strategy B must be used.

Teachers can learn a great deal about children's thinking and reasoning by attending to their "wrong answers." At the same time, every teacher must also attend to the potential harm of societal biases to the children for whom she is responsible and, when necessary, set limits of psychological and emotional safety. This is no different from setting rules about physical safety while encouraging children's large-motor exploration or setting limits on hitting as a way to solve problems while promoting young children's conflict-resolution skills.

Sources of antibias, multicultural curriculum

For curriculum to be developmentally appropriate, it must also be individually and culturally appropriate to each child; therefore, the children, their families, society, and teachers provide important sources of antibias, multicultural curriculum. Following is a discussion of each of these sources.

Children's culturally relevant needs, experiences, interests, questions, feelings, and behaviors. Children are the starting place of curriculum planning. Teachers must be familiar with research about children's construction of identity and attitudes and have a developmental perspective based on the research. Moreover, it is crucial that teachers regularly gather data throughout the year from the children with whom they work about their ideas, feelings, and skills for handling diversity. Data comes from observing children's interactions; listening to and noting questions and comments; and interviewing the children on their ideas about dimensions of diversity, such as gender, race, ethnicity, and disabilities.

Families' beliefs, concerns, and desires for their children. Over the school year teachers must gather information from parents about (1) what they want their children to know about various aspects of their identity, what name the parents use for their ethnic identity, what they believe to be important, how gender roles fit in, and how the parents want their children to handle bias directed against them; (2) what experiences their children have with various aspects of diversity at home and in their community; (3) where families fit on the continuum of assimilation to the dominant culture versus biculturalism; and (4) concerns and disagreements about antibias, multicultural curriculum topics.

Societal events, messages, and expectations that permeate children's environment. Teachers must continually be alert to the visual, verbal, and behavioral messages about human diversity—both positive and negative—that children absorb from TV, radio, movies, books, toys, greeting cards, lunch boxes, other children, extended family, religious or spiritual leaders, and teachers. This means watching children's television, visiting the toy stores and bookstores in children's neighborhoods, and paying critical attention to the images in children's clothing and toys as well as to all the materi-

© Francis Wardle

als placed in the classroom. It is important to remember that children's ideas about themselves and others do not just come from their families, a misconception that many teachers continue to have.

Teachers' knowledge, beliefs, values, and interests. Teachers design daily curriculum by weaving together threads from these four curriculum sources. What issues teachers see and hear from children, parents, and society, and what they choose to act on or ignore, are strongly influenced by their own cultural beliefs, unexamined attitudes, discomforts, and prejudices, as well as by their knowledge of children's development and learning and of societal biases. An essential component of creating appropriate antibias, multicultural curriculum, therefore, is the teacher's increasing self-awareness about her own identity, cultural beliefs, and behaviors and attitudes toward various aspects of other people's identities.

Contextually appropriate content

Having addressed developmental appropriateness by describing a developmental framework, and having examined the sources of curriculum that influence decisions about what is individually appropriate, we now turn to contextual appropriateness. To look at how curriculum choices might work in practice, let us examine three different classroom configurations: classroom A, which is ethnically diverse; classroom B, which is composed of all White European Americans; and classroom C, which is composed of all children of color. For the sake of brevity, this discussion will be limited to content for the four goals of antibias, multicultural curriculum related to race and cultural issues for 3- and 4-year-olds; however, the same proce-

dure would apply to other content areas, such as gender, disabilities, or class, and to other age groups.

Classroom setting A: Ethnically diverse children

In this setting the background of each child provides the content for the teacher to initiate and fuel children's year-long awareness and exploration learning about themselves and each other. This includes activities that enable children to keep developing within their home culture while also beginning to learn how to participate in the dominant European American culture. It is essential to ensure equitable representation of each child's background in the environment and in all activities. If the majority of children come from one racial or ethnic group, with a few children from other groups, it is important to ensure that the "minority" children are not just tokenly represented. Parents may also be concerned that their child will be singled out and become the target of bias if the teacher only highlights their child's differences from the "majority" group.

Once learning about differences and similarities within the group of children has become an ongoing "thread" of the class, much of the content for working on critical thinking and activism will emerge from the comments and interactions of the children as they engage in learning about themselves and each other. In addition, the teacher initiates exploration of key stereotypes coming from the larger society to which preschoolers are exposed, such as Native American stereotypes surrounding Thanksgiving. Content from the children's caregivers that is especially essential in an ethnically diverse setting includes (1) what ethnic identity terms families use (being sensitive to issues that are faced by children in interracial families and children who have been adopted

into racially or ethnically different families); (2) what families want their children to know about their culture; and (3) family socialization values and methods.

The challenge of creating a classroom environment and teaching styles that are culturally relevant to all of the children is heightened in an ethnically diverse setting. Teachers must be prepared to engage in problem solving with families and with other staff to meet both the children's and the families' cultural needs and the teacher's beliefs about curriculum.

Classroom setting B: All White European American children

In this setting the first step remains children's learning about themselves and each other. The physical and cultural differences among European American families will provide sufficient content for this step. The challenge, however, is to use these activities as a context for the next key step—introducing and weaving learning about further physical and cultural diversity into the ongoing daily curriculum. Once awareness of and comfort with differences within the group of children has become an ongoing "thread" of the class, then it is time to enter step two.

What new information regarding cultural diversity to introduce is determined by what other ethnic groups live in the children's wider community, city, or state. For example, if the city has recently gained a sizable Hmong population, learning about Hmong people becomes appropriate. Just as activities based on the children in the class do not talk about "all European Americans" or about Europe of the past, but about Becky and her family now or Jim and his family now, so, too, must these activities focus on individual people and families in the present.

For example, using the persona doll technique (Derman-Sparks & the A.B.C. Task Force 1989), a teacher can introduce two dolls—one girl and one boy—who "are" Hmong. Telling stories about the dolls and their "families," supplemented by children's books, pictures, and objects "brought" by the dolls, offers numerous opportunities to explore physical and cultural learning about kinds of people who are new to the children's experiences, for example, grandparents, a new baby, or teachers and children encountered on the first day of school.

Some content for working on antibias critical thinking and activism skills will arise out of the children's interactions with each other; however, the bulk of content will come from the teacher's initiating exploration of the misconceptions and discomforts children are absorbing from socially prevailing biases in their environment. Potential parental issues in an all-White setting may include parents' objections to children exploring differences (a colorblind view is that "it will teach them prejudice") or objections from parents who hold strong prejudices against specific ethnic groups. Preparing oneself to discuss with and educate parents who hold either of these views is part of contextually appropriate curriculum.

Classroom setting C:
All children of color

This kind of classroom may consist of children from one ethnic group, such as all African American; all Chinese American; or mixed ethnic groupings, such as African American and Mexican American or combinations of various Latino groups.

Since racism makes the task of constructing a knowledgeable, confident self- and group identity much more difficult for children of color, nurturing each child's positive iden-

tity and appreciation of other members of his ethnic group constitutes a primary goal of the curriculum. Activities that teach children ways to identify and resist negative images and messages about themselves and that counter intragroup biases are directly tied to self- and group-concept activities. If the group is ethnically diverse (although still all non–European Americans), then learning about each other becomes the content for goal two—developing comfortable, empathetic interaction with diversity. If the group is ethnically homogeneous, then learning about other "ethnic minorities" proceeds as described for Classroom B. Critical thinking activities address the socially prevailing biases directed at all "minority" groups.

In settings that serve all children of color, a bicultural approach is another aspect of antibias, multicultural curriculum, balancing support for development within the home culture with awareness and exploration about how to act in the dominant European American culture—for example, learning behavioral rules or learning English while continuing to learn the home language. Close collaboration with the children's families is an integral part of this work, using methods such as those described for Classroom A.

Integrating antibias, multicultural planning into the total curriculum

In addition to choosing developmentally appropriate and contextually relevant content for a particular group of children, it is essential to integrate learning about diversity into

all aspects of the program; otherwise, activities still run the risk of falling into the traps of "tourist curriculum." Antibias, multicultural topics are integral to all of the other subjects that comprise early childhood curricula. One practical brainstorming technique for identifying the numerous topic possibilities is "webbing," which takes its name from a spider web image.

The center of the web is the starting point for planning. This can be any number of traditional topics, such as "my body," "families," "the world of work," or an ongoing theme in social studies, science, math, language arts, physical, or health curriculum; a societal event, such as honoring Dr. Martin Luther King Jr. Day; or an issue raised by the children, such as their insistence that a person who is visually impaired cannot work. The next step is brainstorming the many possible antibias, multicultural issues that stem from the subject at the web's center and seeing how the various issues interconnect. The third step is identifying specific content for a particular classroom. This requires doing contextual/developmental analysis: what is meaningful to this group of children, what resources and knowledge the teacher has, and what family issues might arise. Step four is listing possible activities that are developmentally or culturally appropriate for the particular group. The web on the next page shows issues and topics that a group of preschool teachers might generate around the subject of "Families" in steps one and two.

Integrating diversity content into the whole curriculum requires breaking down the false dichotomy

Example of Potential Topics to Include in Antibias Curriculum on Families

Preschool/kindergarten (3- to 6-year-olds)

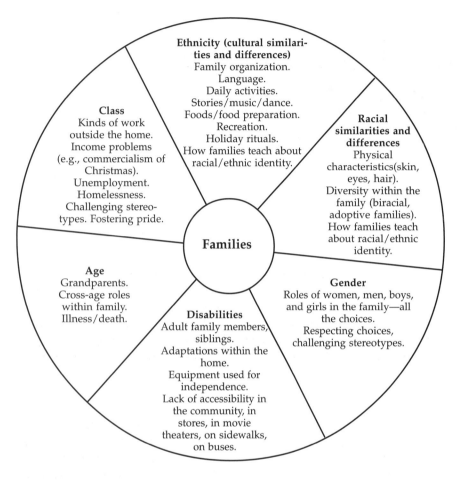

diversity is important, valued, and safe in the classroom, then children will not raise issues. Conversely, if the teacher does not pay attention to children's ideas, interests, and learning styles, then specific diversity content may not be meaningful to them.

To summarize, antibias, multicultural curriculum content must be adapted to the cultural and individual variations of each new group of children if it is to be developmentally and contextually appropriate. Activities that appear in print or that other teachers find effective are not recipes to be strictly copied, but only possibilities. Educators' thoughtful articulation of the reasoning underlying their content choices is nowhere more urgent than in antibias, multicultural curriculum. Fostering children's healthy, positive self-identity and the desire and skills to live comfortably, effectively, and respectfully with the wide range of human diversity is vital to our nation's survival.

References

Derman-Sparks, L. 1992. Reaching potentials through antibias, multicultural curriculum. In *Reaching potentials: Appropriate curriculum and assessment for young children,* Vol. 1, eds. S. Bredekamp & T. Rosegrant, 114–27. Washington, DC: NAEYC.

Derman-Sparks, L., & the A.B.C. Task Force. 1989. *Anti-bias curriculum: Tools for empowering young children.* Washington, DC: NAEYC.

NAEYC and National Association of Early Childhood Specialists in State Departments of Education (NAECS/SDE). 1991. Guidelines for appropriate curriculum content and assessment in programs serving children ages 3 through 8. *Young Children* 46 (3): 21–38.

between the teacher's launching a specific subject versus waiting for the subject to emerge from the children and never mentioning the subject if the children don't. Developmentally/contextually appropriate teaching is a continuous interaction between adults and children, not a one-sided contribution from one or the other. Teachers are responsible for brainstorming, planning, and initiating diversity topics based on their analysis of the children's needs. Teachers create awareness through many methods, such as bringing new materials into the environment and observing children's responses before creating more activities, or reading a book to children and conducting a discussion to uncover their ideas. The teacher's careful attention to children's thinking and behavior leads to modifications and additions to plans. These become new lines on an already existing web or the center of a new web, and the cycle of brainstorming and planning begins anew. If the teacher does not create a material and emotional environment that clearly communicates that

Carol Brunson Phillips*

44

Preparing Teachers to Use Their Voices for Change

It has become a common feeling I believe, as we have watched our heroes falling over the years, that our own small stone of activism, which might not seem to measure up to the rugged boulders of heroism we have so admired, is a paltry offering toward the building of an edifice of hope. Many who believe this choose to withhold their offering out of shame. This is the tragedy of our world. For we can do nothing substantial toward changing our course on the planet, a destructive one, without rousing ourselves, individual by individual, and bringing our small, imperfect stones to the pile.

—Alice Walker,
Anything We Love Can Be Saved

Thankfully, we have reached a time in early childhood education when the commitment to address racial and cultural diversity is pervasive throughout our work. It has become explicit in the position statements of our national organizations, it can be seen in the materials marketed by publishers and manufacturers of educational supplies, and it can be read in the dialogues that occur in publications and heard in the conversations that take place at conferences and meetings. Further, enmeshed in the broad-based national standards both for high-quality practice (Bredekamp & Copple 1997; NAEYC 1998) and for basic and advanced teacher preparation (NAEYC, DEC/CEC, & NBPTS 1996) is the pledge to achieve racial and cultural equity as a necessity for securing the well-being of children.

Yet, while the widespread embrace of equity principles imparts a general sense of progress toward reaching these goals, evidence that the work has been of significant consequence is less widespread. For example, in the National Council for Accreditation of Teacher Education (NCATE) folio reviews, the guidelines that institutions are cited most frequently for not meeting are those related to linguistic and cultural diversity.

Further, a myriad of data on health status, school achievement, family economic status, and other indicators of social well-being (Children's Defense Fund 1996) are consistent in showing that children of color and culturally and linguistically diverse children are failing to thrive. Although many reasons for this failure are offered, the explanation proposed here suggests that while we have done much in the classroom to promote cultural and racial equity through curriculum changes, we have left virtually untouched the institutional infrastructures that produce and reproduce inequities.

Consequently, despite our work to address diversity in ways that benefit children's development, institutional forms of bias—race and cultural bias in particular, for purposes of this article—continue to undermine any real change in the long-term developmental outcomes and life circumstances of these children. (Other forms of bias also threaten development, although they are not discussed here; however, the principles from the lessons we learn about eliminating racial bias can and should be used to address them as well.)

Therefore, removing these institutional constraints must have a higher priority in our work to achieve equity, and ensuring that teachers can be effective to this end may require changing our approach in teacher preparation.

Teacher education: Rethinking the approach

In general, diversity work thus far has helped us largely to learn to regard various cultural and racial backgrounds as potential strengths rather than limitations. That is, we have prepared teachers to acknowledge that the diverse racial and cultural contexts of children and families are important to maintain and emphasize in the educational process.

What remains, however, is to fully prepare teachers to understand in conceptual and practical ways how to eliminate the impact of society's negative responses to diversity insofar as those negative responses countervail against our most avid attempts to ensure the optimal development of children. I am referring not to changing children's attitudes about themselves and the world but rather to identifying and changing school policies instrumental in closing off opportunities and experiences children need to develop fully.

An illustration about a prekindergarten teacher in a public school:

At the end of the school year, my children must be tested and their scores put in their cumulative record. I know that the information is supposed to be used to enhance the instructional climate for each child and help increase his or her chances for school success. However, I also know that there is a controversy raging over cultural bias in standardized tests.

Anticipating the test date, I invite the school psychologist to visit my classroom and have lunch with the children so he will be at ease with them during the testing. I use the opportunity to talk to him about how test scores follow children through their entire school careers and how they contribute to negative expectations for some children, especially Black males.

Then I negotiate with the school psychologist. Instead of his writing the scores in their cumulative files, I suggest he enter the statement "Developmental assessment administered [date]; records on file in Assessment Office." He agrees, and we make plans to work together to make this a school policy.

What approaches can teacher educators use to help teachers understand their roles as clearly as this teacher did? How can teacher education prepare students to recognize developmental obstacles in the social and political settings in which they work and provide them with skills to participate in, if not initiate, the change process?

Studying racism and activism

The goal is to help teacher preparation students see themselves as agents of change in addressing negative responses to race and cultural diversity that exist in institutional practices. One important strategy is to directly explore racism in a way that helps students understand how racism is manifest in its institutional form. Starting with a useful definition of racism is critical.

Racism: an institutionalized system of economic, political, social, and cultural relations that ensures that one racial group has and maintains power and privilege over all aspects of life. Individual participation in racism occurs when the objective outcome of behavior reinforces these relations, regardless of the subjective intent. Consequently, an individual may act in a racist manner unintentionally. (Derman-Sparks & Phillips 1997, 2)

Approaching racism conceptually in this way is very important. For if we regard racism solely as the bad things people do and say, then our work to change racism targets the individual only. When racism is seen, however, as a systemic web of forces that works to preserve social and economic privilege based on race, change requires targeting the mechanisms within institutions that perpetuate the systemic sanctions for the process. Learning about racism in this broadened way shifts the focus away from studying the lifestyles and cultural traits of people of color so people will like each other better, focusing instead on the system of preservation of White privilege and how it operates in the lives of each one of us—those who benefit from it as well as those who don't.

Preparing students to work effectively and with integrity toward effecting change in schools and human services agencies requires a dialogue to help them understand deeply and personally how they are connected to institutional forms of bias. Unlike some lessons that can be taught quickly, helping adult students find their voice to change such conditions requires work over time. The approach suggested challenges teacher educators to devote the time and energy required to carry the learner (and the teacher educator) beneath the surface issues of the larger multicultural movement. It goes to the heart of the conceptual debate about inequality in society to examine how we each have been touched by inequality in our own lives and behaviors.

Such experiences are described in *Teaching/Learning Anti-Racism: A Developmental Approach* (Derman-Sparks & Phillips 1997), which details my work with college students preparing for careers in human services. The book describes the structure and activities of the semester, and it also reveals some overarching lessons for those in teacher preparation who wish to address racism as a core issue in the human development curriculum.

What are those lessons?

Three useful lessons

1. Changing our ideas about racism is a slow process that requires sustained work.

For those who grew up in and now live in a racist society, ideas about race and racism are deep-seated; they are not easily accessed, much less easily changed. Therefore one-workshop formats, such as those often used for inservice training in early childhood education, or one-time lectures fall far short of the effort required. Moreover, changes in behavior are built on changes in conceptual understanding and attitude as well, requiring a multiphase process.

Because racism is ongoing and the subtle messages justifying White privilege are reinforced daily, the work to overcome the influence of these messages on attitudes and behaviors must also be ongoing. It is not possible to be neutral in this process; you are either part of the problem or part of the solution. As long as the forces to reinforce racist relations in society continue to operate, the individual contributes to their perpetuation unless she actively works to eliminate them.

Further, because the change process is a slow one, faculty in teaching/learning settings must not confine permission to deal with the topic to a narrow time and space. Just as we expect teachers to deal with racial name-calling whenever it occurs, we expect teacher educators to actively create a climate wherein racism can be discussed productively whenever the topic comes up. We must learn how to defuse the hysteria around racism and make it a topic people are more comfortable discussing. (*Comfortable* may not be the right word, since tense emotional exchanges do and should arise from time to time.) The overarching concern should be to give teachers-in-training the sense that they are expected (if not required) to be enough at ease with the topic to handle it sensitively, professionally, and effectively.

2. From one racial group to another, the experience of racism is different.

Although this may sound like a simple, logical statement, we often ignore its implications when we work on addressing racism. We want everyone to work together in the same space at the same time, because we think this will contribute to positive interracial relations. Despite the fact that the major consequences of racism are to give privilege to Whites and deny it to people of color, we think that for Whites and people of color to work together and "be on the same page" they must see things in the same way. By failing to acknowledge dual realities, we risk engaging in conversations that distort someone's reality—usually that of the persons of color—and that are superficial and dishonest.

The complicated dynamics that characterize deep engagement in these issues sometimes require separate discussions in which "homogeneous groups" can reflect on the similarities and differences of their experiences. Created around common group identity, homogeneous groups are a useful way for people of color to explore issues such as internalized oppression and for Whites to explore issues such as White privilege. Although separate groups may make it difficult at first for people to feel comfortable (because they are segregated), these groups are useful in creating an environment where free and honest sharing can occur, by lessening the fear of hurting others' feelings or evoking anger or defensive denial.

In separate, homogeneous groups useful discussion can occur about diversity within a group—people having the same extended group identity yet being very different from each other. This concept helps dispel myths and stereotypes (for example, that all Black people are alike), while at the same time it helps students understand that cultural characteristics have important meaning. Either/or thinking often gets in the way of understanding that two different (seemingly opposite) things can be true at the same time.

3. A person goes through stages moving from racist to antiracist consciousness.

Working to directly address racism can be painful and at times seems to yield little progress. It is important, therefore, to understand the dynamics involved in changing consciousness and behavior. It has been argued elsewhere by social scientists that becoming antiracist psychologically and behaviorally results not solely from linear accumulation of facts and information but through a process that transforms consciousness (Terry 1975; Cross 1991; Tatum 1997). Derman-Sparks & Phillips (1997) describe these stages as they appear in adult college students studying human development. Although Whites experience the process differently than do people of color, the end point for all is transformed consciousness about both personal roles and collective strategies in addressing racism in institutions. Briefly, the stages are as follows:

Stage One—Taking stock: Beginning explorations of racism. The informational content narrows students' focus to concrete evidence that society operates in racist ways and creates tension around how they have dealt with this fact. Facing the contradiction between society's creed and deed, Whites initially resist the alarming possibility that they participate in maintaining racism and insist, "I'm not a racist" or "Racism isn't my responsibility."

Students of color readily accept the reality of racism but find open discussions about it very upsetting and enraging. They begin to discover how deeply they have been touched by racism, and they examine how they have managed to bury within their consciousness society's negative views of them.

In this phase the individual in both groups works to uncover how he has managed society's conflicting messages.

Stage Two—Exposing the contradictions. Students examine beliefs and behaviors that have kept them enmeshed in racist and proracist consciousness and behavior. (Explaining the term *proracist*, Derman-Sparks and Phillips state, "Racist behavior and beliefs among the White dominating population have a kind of counterpart in the behavior of populations victimized by racism. We call those behaviors and beliefs proracist rather than racist because the structural dynamics are different" [1997, 25].) They continue to examine personal experiences with racism, their own identity as members of a racial group, and their cross-racial interactions. There is a strong emphasis on exposing the internal inconsistencies in how they understand the nature of the relationship between themselves and society.

For students of color the emphasis is on reexamining their racial group identity, rethinking their relationships to Whites and to society's explanations of racism, and reassessing their relationships to other groups of color.

For Whites the emphasis is on facing institutional racism and how it works to secure for them the position of privilege despite their own actions or lack thereof. Once accepting the idea, they struggle to see their own position in perpetuating the system, evaluate their attitudes toward people of color, and give up

their images of themselves as nonracist.

Stage Three—Transformation to an understanding of self and society. Students engage actively in searching for the knowledge and tools to address the contradictions in society and bring an antiracist perspective to their own work and community life. The informational content gives them practice in channeling emotions and energy toward activities that will result in change.

Students of color work toward (a) reclaiming and affirming their racial group identity, and therefore themselves, where the new identity is based on their group's definition of themselves, not the dominant group's definition; (b) constructing a frame of reference that locates responsibility for the creation and evolution of racism in institutions of the dominant society; and (c) building new relationships with other people of color and with Whites.

White students work to (a) construct a new racial group identity by discarding the false notion of nonracism while seeking to keep what is good and abolish what is bad in European American culture; (b) accept responsibility for racism as a White problem and develop an ability to critique institutional structures; and (c) build real relationships with people of color that are consciously more equitable.

Stage Four—Antiracism as a new beginning: Activism. Acting on the belief that personal and social change are possible and building on a self-perception of having the power and ability to affect systems, students can effectively take an active role to change things. Having the analytic tools to identify institutional constraints also opens doors to institutional solutions (where major constraints to children's development reside). Having found their

voice, energy to raise it comes from having shed racist beliefs.

The considerable energy students have used to contain or repress the tensions racism creates is now available for acting on their own convictions. Along with the opportunity to become more psychologically whole, antiracism education enables students to gain a more realistic sense of self by demystifying the interaction between the individual and the social system (Derman-Sparks & Phillips 1997, 139).

Recognizing these then as three useful lessons, how can we apply them as we reorganize professional preparation to create the activists we want and need in early childhood education?

Teacher preparation: Practical recommendations

Two recent reports, one from Canada and one from the United States, shed light on how we might proceed in early childhood higher education. Both start from the premise that college-level teacher preparation is inadequate in fully preparing students to work with diverse populations of children and parents. From a perspective similar to the one advanced thus far, both reports look at some practical ways to solve this problem.

The Canadian report (Bernhard et al. 1995) evaluates the responsiveness of teacher education to diversity based on the collective institutional desire to produce students who demonstrate a respectful, nonbiased, collaborative, empowering approach to working with children and families. In institutions the intent is to accomplish this by including course content that incorporates a worldview different from the prevailing ethnocentric framework, by making sure students encounter multicultural approaches in both theoretical and practical program components and by addressing diversity issues in core (compulsory) subjects as well as electives.

The second report (Fund 1997) comes from California and documents the work of a group of child development instructors in California community colleges who held an institute based on their desire to restructure course work and experiences in teacher preparation. Focused on understanding the pervasive impact of institutional oppression and internalized oppression on their work, the institute had as its stated vision "the development of networks, skills and understandings for community college instructors to prepare a multicultural, multiracial, multilingual workforce to provide culturally competent care in a rapidly changing, highly diverse society" (Fund 1997, 3). The report contains the proceedings of the nine days of work (three 3-day meetings spread over nine months), during which the group generated ideas for teaching strategies, course revisions, and new approaches to assignments, all building on concrete examples of their college classroom experiences.

The following recommendations are echoed in the two reports:

Examine the ways in which ethnocentrism and racism distort the content of courses; where you can't eliminate them, infuse material that helps students see the biases and limitations

Both groups concluded that teacher education must address the racial and cultural bias in the basic child development database. Bernhard and her colleagues (1995) suggest that rather than infuse cross-cultural studies, perhaps a more promising approach is to question the existence of universal norms or milestones of child development. They argue that this position is

Standard child development courses and texts generally have a universalistic, monocultural approach to development in which a single pattern of milestones is usually presented.

based on the theories of Cole and Cole (1993), Rogoff (1990), and Scribner (1985), which are derived from the framework of Vygotsky and his colleagues.

The report holds that North American standard child development courses and texts generally have a universalistic, monocultural approach to development in which a single pattern of milestones is usually presented. The unfortunate result is that graduates may be left with the impression that culture, race, and language are not associated with fundamental differences but merely linked to colorful customs such as wearing a turban or *kipah*. They recommend an active approach that takes the position that all development occurs in and is influenced by social and cultural contexts.

The California report argues similarly that since there is information missing from the child development database used to generalize about children, instructors should always ask how every course taught lends itself to the additional inclusion of issues of race, class, language, and culture. Moreover, because the conclusions drawn about what is good, healthy, and desirable for children convey only one cultural perspective, it is critical to alert students to the inherent limitations. Further, the report suggests posing profound questions to students (and among faculty), such as "Is there any such thing as The Child?" and "Are there developmental universals? If so, what are they?" These strategies will keep a strong tension between the known and the unknown that helps students to both respect and question the research and thus sends

them into the workplace with the best possible attitude about what they do and do not know.

Acknowledge your own limitations

Both groups concluded that the teacher educator is the starting point for change. For teacher educators to accept that racism and other forms of bias have affected their attitudes and behavior and to be willing to engage in addressing changing themselves is critical to achieving effective interactions with students. The California group proposes posing profound queries for themselves as they work, such as "I fear my own unconscious negative attitudes about groups of people may interfere with my effectiveness as a teacher and as a learner. How can I stay open to this possibility and at the same time teach my students to stay open as well?" and "How has my own development as a learner and then as a teacher been impacted by my experiences with race? How are those experiences shaping my choices in what I teach in this class?"

As members of faculties within institutions, teacher educators should establish consultations among their colleagues to help each other explore these dynamics as well as plan and evaluate the infusion and sequencing of student experiences. Further, collective commitments to self-examination can and should strengthen the active role we play as activists in the process of changing institutions and the early childhood profession. An illustration:

I want to change the way I teach child development and use a textbook that is not ethnocentric in its presentation of cultural influences on development. I finally figured out what that really means. I'm in a position where I can get adoption approval for my choice. But, there is no such textbook in existence. Do I have to write it myself? Do I have to organize a group to lobby/pressure a publisher to commission such a text? What can my colleagues and I do?

Establish a course in which students reflect on their attitudes and experiences based on systematic study of racism and ethnocultural bias in the institutions where we work

Teachers must be able to develop an attitude of equality, humility, and respect for those of other cultures and be willing to elicit and make use of perspectives, feelings, and beliefs of those native to a given culture. This means they must be able to remove themselves and their views from the center of all thought and hold in abeyance their sense of being the expert in a situation.

As part of such courses students should be encouraged to reflect upon their own attitudes and experiences. Further, they must be given the opportunity to understand activism and the critical importance of addressing institutional racism.

The shift in consciousness that should result means moving students through the stages described earlier in the article. In the end they would be able to move beyond analyses of situations that are based on how racism is manifested through individual behaviors to analyses that lead to actions resulting in institutional change. A recent example from the national news illustrates how we get stuck in common dilemmas.

In Riverside County, California, parents in a White community opposed a proposal that their high

school be renamed for Martin Luther King Jr. They stated that the reason for the protest was not that they were racist but that they felt the action would brand the school as a Black school and hurt their children's chances for college. Although it may indeed be racist for parents to take such action, the arena for antiracist activism is not a fight against the parents who don't want the school renamed. Rather, the real combat ground is the college admissions system that responds negatively to applicants from Black schools. The challenge in Riverside is to organize the energies of those parents who are protesting and redirect their voices toward developing some concrete action strategies to eliminate the institutionalized forms of bias in the college admissions system.

Conclusion

Antiracism education is lodged in the belief that becoming an antiracist activist is not so much an end in itself as it is an ongoing process situated in a climate of self-examination, critical thinking, and exploration of collective commitments to participate in institutional change. The challenge to the work to achieve these as part of teacher preparation is to engage in dialogue in careful and directed ways, remembering that what we're aiming for has as much to do with will as with anything else.

We must be cautious not to stop working after we get one piece into place or to feel discouraged by the small scope of our triumphs. For we must keep at it until the consequences of our work to achieve equity give evidence in the larger society that the need no longer exists to dialogue about race. In very profound ways the challenge to transform teacher preparation—a challenge that rests squarely on the

shoulders of teacher preparation staff—is to convince our students and ourselves that each small act toward this end is an important contribution to changing the world in which we live.

References

Bernhard, J.K, M.L. Lefebvre, G. Chud, & R. Lange. 1995. *Paths to equity: Cultural, linguistic, and racial diversity in Canadian early childhood education*. North York, Canada: York Lanes Press.

Bredekamp, S., & C. Copple, eds. 1997. *Developmentally appropriate practice in early childhood programs*. Rev. ed. Washington, DC: NAEYC.

Children's Defense Fund. 1996. *The state of America's children*. Washington, DC: Author.

Cole, M., & S.R. Cole. 1993. *The development of children*. 2d ed. New York: Oxford University Press.

Cross, W.E. 1991. *Shades of Black: Diversity in African-American identity*. Philadelphia: Temple University Press.

Derman-Sparks, L., & C.B. Phillips. 1997. *Teaching/learning anti-racism: A developmental approach*. New York: Teachers College Press.

Fund for the Instructional Improvement of the California Community College's Chancellor's Office. 1997. *Race, class, culture, language: A deeper context for early childhood education (A teaching and curriculum guide from the 1996–1997 Early Childhood Education Curriculum Leadership Institute)*. Available from Michele Richardson, Child Development Training Consortium, Modesto Junior College, 435 College Ave., Modesto, CA 95355; fax 209-575-6989; phone 209-575-6592.

NAEYC. 1998. *Accreditation criteria and procedures of the National Association for the Education of Young Children*. Washington, DC: Author.

NAEYC, Division for Early Childhood of the Council for Exceptional Children (DEC/CEC), & National Board for Professional Teaching Standards (NABT). 1996. *NAEYC Guidelines for preparation of early childhood professionals*. Washington, DC: NAEYC.

Rogoff, B. 1990. *Apprenticeship in thinking: Cognitive development in social context*. New York: Oxford University Press.

Scribner, S. 1985. Vygotsky's uses of history. In *Culture, communication, and cognition*, ed. J.V. Wertsch, 119–45. Cambridge, England: Cambridge University Press.

Tatum, B.D. 1997. *Why are all the Black kids sitting together in the cafeteria? And other conversations about race*. New York: Basic.

Terry, R. 1975. *For Whites only*. Grand Rapids, MI: Earmans.

Annette Unten

45

Weaving the Pieces Together

Excerpted from *In Our Own Way*

To people just starting out in diversity work, I'd like to say this: Make the physical changes first. Change the books in your room, the toys, and the pictures. These are changes you can make right away. That's important. The work you do later will not always be so visible, but there will be a thrill to doing it. In fact, there will be many feelings (fear, excitement, frustration, disappointment, anticipation) because the work is so complex.

I've found that one way to bring antibias teaching into my pre-K classroom is to look for openings rather than trying to create them. For instance, one of my students, Tracy, came in on a Monday and quietly said to me, "Mrs. Unten, I was in a parade this weekend."

"You were?" I said.

"Yeah. It was kind of for Black people. It was a neat parade. It was for Martin Luther King."

"That's wonderful," I said. "Dr. Martin Luther King was a really great man. It's wonderful that you were in a parade for him." Then I added, "You know there were a lot of Black people there because Mar-

tin Luther King was Black and he did so many wonderful things for Black people. He did many wonderful things for White people too. That's something that we should talk about more."

Upon reflection, I realized this little boy thought that this wasn't an event he could share with everyone—maybe he thought he could just talk to Black people about it. So I used our conversation as an opening to read everyone a story about Martin Luther King and his life. It helped Tracy feel comfortable sharing something that had been important to him. That's how it happens.

Here's another example of how I was able to bring antibias teaching into my class by using the openings that the children create. I overheard two Black girls talking in the housekeeping area. One said to the other, "White girls talk like this …" and she mimicked a voice that was slow and kind of sweet.

I listened and then asked, "Simone, how do Black girls speak?"

"Black girls, they … " and she made her speech have much more rhythm.

"That's interesting," I said. "It seems like we speak differently. How do I speak?" So she started imitating me perfectly. (I just wanted to crack up.) We talked about that and then I asked her how the other adult in our room, Mrs. Houchen, speaks. Simone had it down to a science. Then we moved on to different people in our class, particularly a girl named Michelle, who was White. I asked her, "Is that how Michelle speaks?"

"No," she said, "She don't speak like that."

"But I thought that was how White girls speak."

"Well, Michelle don't speak like that. Is she White?" Simone is bright, and as we continued to talk, she began to realize that skin color isn't what makes people speak differently from one another.

That is one of the reasons working in early childhood is so wonderful. You have time to spend together and you can use the openings that the children provide to make diversity discussions a natural part of conversations. In this case, Simone and I sat down to talk and everybody in the housekeeping area kind of listened.

Diversity makes you aware that things are not always as you assume. It challenges your paradigm and makes you grow.

Our conversation became a lesson for many of those children. I think that a lot of things happen in my classroom like that.

Another way to encourage children's growth is to introduce a concept and then let them take it wherever they can. For instance, we talk about skin color because I really believe it's so important. Growing up, nobody ever said anything to me like: "Annette, the color of your skin is just beautiful" or "That brown color is just so pretty." And that contributed to why I always wanted to be White. So I like to tell all the children that their skin color is pretty and just right for them. We draw pictures of ourselves and match skin colors. We talk about different colors of skin. From there, lots of incidents just happen.

For instance, we couldn't find the dolls when school started this year. We finally found a few to put out, mostly little tiny dolls of color. But of the big dolls, I only had one and she was White. Early in the year, one of my students, Antoinette, who is Black, looked up and said, "I was wonderin', Mrs. Unten, why you don't have my dolly out there. You have other people's dollies, but you don't have mine." She had been looking for the Black doll. That's the one she wanted, not the White doll. We looked together and she spotted it way back in the closet. So we got it out and found some clothes for her. It was too important not to.

My job is easier because I have such diversity in my class. We have time to sit together, share, and talk about differences, and most of the time, everyone is represented in some way. In addition, early childhood lends itself to talking about diversity. Children's developmental ages are ripe for growth at this time. They're very, very open. And, over the course of a year, I can see much growth in the ways they treat each other and how they interact. All you have to do in a classroom like mine is offer opportunities through the books that we read and what we show about being accepting of who we are and where we are. For instance, a lot of my children don't have daddies. So every time we read a book or we talk about families, we make sure we show mommies without daddies. That helps children feel accepted. And I believe, when people feel accepted for who they are and are accepting of themselves, they're more willing to accept others who are different.

As I said, I'm hit with diversity every day in countless little incidents that just come up. Diversity is just a part of what we do. It's so natural that it's hard for me to separate antibias work from everything else or to think of what I do that's different.

Every year I ride home on the bus with the children. Seeing where they live helps me to focus, to remember what they have to go home to. The families in our program are really poor. Many have no screens on their windows. Many doors are kicked in. I know when the children come to school in the mornings, many haven't had a warm bed to sleep in. The bus ride pulls me together and reminds me about what I have to do. It reminds me that sometimes the openings I observe are really for my own awareness and growth.

For example, the other day my aide and I were observing the housekeeping area. The children hadn't been using the table, and everything was on the floor—including the food they had set out. My aide wondered why, and that's when it occurred to me that probably the children didn't have a table at home. As every early childhood person knows, what children see at home is often what they model in the housekeeping corner.

About four days later one of the girls, Tracharia, came in with newspapers in her hand. She said, "Here, Mrs. Unten, I have some newspapers to bring to school."

I said, "That's great. What shall we do with this newspaper? Where shall we put it? Shall we put it with the books in the book corner?"

"No," she said. "In housekeeping."

I said, "Okay, that sounds fine to me. Let's put it in housekeeping." I thought Tracharia meant they would read it in housekeeping. No. When it was time for centers, Tracharia spread the newspaper on the floor like a tablecloth so that it would keep the play food clean. These kinds of things happen daily.

Diversity makes you aware that things are not always as you assume. It challenges your paradigm and makes you grow. Over the years, I have had many opportunities. And at the end of each year I sit back and ask myself, What have I learned? What have I gained? How have I grown? And I always come out the winner.

Reprinted from A. Unten, "Weaving the Pieces Together," in *In Our Own Way: How Anti-Bias Work Shapes Our Lives* (St. Paul, MN: Redleaf), 13-18. (www.redleafpress.org) Copyright © 1999 Annette Unten. Reprinted with permission.

A World of Difference

For Further Reading

In the interest of space this list does not repeat the publications from which the readings in this volume were taken.

Akaran, S.E., & M.V. Fields. 1997. Family and cultural context: A writing breakthrough? *Young Children* 52 (4): 37–40.

Atkin, S.B. 1993. *Voices from the fields: Children of migrant farmworkers tell their stories.* Boston, MA: Little, Brown.

Ball, J., & A.R. Pence. 1999. Beyond developmentally appropriate practice: Developing community and culturally appropriate practice. *Young Children* 54 (2): 46–50.

Barbour, C., & N. Barbour. 2001. *Families, schools, and communities: Building partnerships for educating the child,* 2d ed. Columbus, OH: Merrill/Prentice Hall.

Barrera, I., R.M. Corso, & D. MacPherson. 2003. *Skilled dialogue: Strategies for responding to cultural diversity in early childhood.* Baltimore, MD: Brookes.

Beaty, J. 1997. *Building bridges with multicultural picture books: For children 3 to 5.* Upper Saddle River, NJ: Merrill.

Bornstein, M.H. 1991. *Cultural approaches to parenting.* Hillsdale, NJ: Erlbaum.

Boutte, G.S., I. Van Scoy, & S. Hendley. 1996. Multicultural and nonsexist prop boxes. *Young Children* 52 (1): 34–39.

Bowman, B., ed. 2002. *Love to read: Essays in developing and enhancing early literacy skills of African American children.* Washington, DC: National Black Child Development Institute, Inc.

Bromer, J. 1999. Cultural variations in child care: Values and actions. *Young Children* 54 (6): 72–78.

Brown, J.C., & L.A. Oates, eds. 2001. *Books to grow on: African American literature for young children.* Washington, DC: NAEYC. Brochure.

Burchfield, D. 1996. Teaching all children: Four developmentally appropriate curricular and instructional strategies in primary grade classrooms. *Young Children* 52 (1): 4–10.

Byrnes, D.A., & G. Kiger, eds. 1996. *Common bonds: Anti-bias teaching in a diverse society.* 2d ed. Wheaton, MD: Association for Childhood Education International.

Chandler, P.A. 1994. *A place for me: Including children with special needs in early care and education settings.* Washington, DC: NAEYC.

Corbett, S. 1993. A complicated bias. *Young Children* 48 (3): 29–31.

Cornell, C. 1993. Language and culture monsters that lurk in our traditional rhymes and folktales. *Young Children* 48 (6): 40–46.

Creaser, B., & E. Dau. 1995. *The anti-bias approach in early childhood.* Watson, Australia: Australian Early Childhood Association.

Cronin, S., L. Derman-Sparks, S. Henry, & C. Olatunji. 1998. *Future vision, present work: Learning from the culturally relevant anti-bias leadership project.* St. Paul, MN: Redleaf.

Cunningham, B., & L.W. Watson. 2002. Recruiting male teachers. *Young Children* 57 (6): 10–15.

Delpit, L. 1995. *Other people's children: Cultural conflict in the classroom.* New York: New Press.

d'Entremont, L. 1998. A few words about diversity and rigidity: One director's perspective. *Young Children* 53 (1): 72–73.

Derman-Sparks, L., M. Gutierrez, & C. Brunson Day. 1989. *Teaching young children to resist bias: What parents can do.* Washington, DC: NAEYC. Brochure.

Derman-Sparks, L., & C.B. Phillips. 1997. *Teaching/learning anti-racism.* New York: Teachers College Press.

Dickinson, D.K., & P.O. Tabors, eds. 2001. *Beginning literacy with language: Young children learning at home and school.* Baltimore, MD: Brookes.

Dickinson, D.K., & P.O. Tabors. 2002. Fostering language and literacy in classrooms and homes. *Young Children* 57 (2): 10–18.

Diffily, D., & K. Morrison, eds. 1996. *Family-friendly communication for early childhood programs.* Washington, DC: NAEYC.

Dimidjian, V.J. 1989. Holidays, holy days, and wholly dazed: Approaches to special days. *Young Children* 44 (6): 70–75.

Dunn, L., N. Kling, & J. Oakley. 1996. Homeless families in early childhood programs: What to do and what to expect. *Dimensions of Early Childhood* 24 (1): 3–8.

Dyson, A.H. 1997. *What difference does difference make? Teacher reflections on diversity, literacy, and the urban primary school.* Urbana, IL: National Council of Teachers of English.

Edwards, C.P., & L. Gandini. 1989. Teachers' expectations about the timing of developmental skills: A cross-cultural study. *Young Children* 44 (4): 15–19.

Elswood, R. 1999. Really including diversity in early childhood classrooms. *Young Children* 54 (4): 62–66.

Espinosa, L.M. 1995. Hispanic parent involvement in early childhood programs. *ERIC Digest.* ED 382412. Urbana-Champaign, IL: ERIC Clearinghouse on Elementary and Early Childhood Education.

Feeney, S., & N.K. Freeman. 1999. *Ethics and the early childhood educator: Using the NAEYC code.* Washington, DC: NAEYC.

Feng, J. 1994. Asian American children: What teachers should know. *ERIC Digest.* ED 369577. Urbana-Champaign, IL: ERIC Clearinghouse on Elementary and Early Childhood Education.

Field, T.M., A.M. Sostek, P. Vietze, & P.H. Leiderman, eds. 1981. *Culture and early interactions.* Hillsdale, NJ: Erlbaum.

Freeman, M., S. Foster, N. Peddle, & L. Burnley. 1995. God revels in diversity: Converting the faithful to antibias education. *Young Children* 50 (2): 20-25.

Froschl, M., & B. Sprung. 1999. On purpose: Addressing teasing and bullying in early childhood. *Young Children* 54 (2): 70–72.

Garcia, E.E., B. McLaughlin, B. Spodek, & O.N. Saracho, eds. 1995. *Meeting the challenge of linguistic and cultural diversity in early childhood education.* Yearbook in Early Childhood Education, vol. 6. New York: Teachers College Press.

Garcia, S.B., ed. 1994. *Addressing cultural and linguistic diversity in special education: Issues and trends.* Reston, VA: Council for Exceptional Children.

Genishi, C. 2002. Research in Review. Young English language learners: Resourceful in the classroom. *Young Children* 57 (4): 66–70.

George, F. 1990. Checklist for a non-sexist classroom. *Young Children* 45 (2): 10–11.

Gollnick, D.M., & P.C. Chinn. 2002. *Multicultural education in a pluralistic society.* 6th ed. Upper Saddle River, NJ: Merrill.

Gonzalez-Mena, J. 2001. *Foundations: Early childhood education in a diverse society.* 2d ed. Mountain View, CA: Mayfield.

Gonzalez-Mena, J. 2001. *Multicultural issues in child care.* 3d ed. Mountain View, CA: Mayfield.

Greenberg, P. 1992. Ideas that work with young children. Teaching about Native Americans? Or teaching about people, including Native Americans. *Young Children* 47 (6): 27–30, 79–81.

Gutwirth, V. 1997. A multicultural family study project for primary. *Young Children* 52 (2): 72–78.

Harkness, S., & C. Super. 1996. *Parental cultural belief systems: Their origins, expressions, and consequences.* New York: Guilford.

Hart, E.T. 1999. *Barefoot heart: Stories of a migrant child.* Tempe, AZ: Bilingual Press.

Hildebrand, V., L.A. Phenice, M. Gray, & R. Hines. 2000. *Knowing and serving diverse families.* 2d ed. Columbus, OH: Merrill/Prentice Hall.

Hopkins, S. 1999. *Hearing everyone's voice: Educating young children for peace and democratic community.* Redmond, WA: Exchange.

Hunt, R. 1999. Making positive multicultural early childhood education happen. *Young Children* 54 (5): 39–42.

Huntsinger, C.S., P.R. Huntsinger, W-D. Ching, & C-B. Lee. 2000. Understanding cultural contexts fosters sensitive caregiving of Chinese American children. *Young Children* 55 (6): 7–12, 14–15.

Jalongo, M.R. 2003. *Early childhood language arts: Meeting diverse literacy needs through collaboration with families and professionals.* 3d ed. Boston: Allyn & Bacon.

Johnston, L., & J. Mermin. 1994. Easing children's entry to school: Home visits help. *Young Children* 49 (5): 62–68.

Jones, E., & L. Derman-Sparks. 1992. Meeting the challenge of diversity. *Young Children* 47 (2): 12–18.

Jones, E., & J. Nimmo. 1994. *Emergent curriculum.* Washington, DC: NAEYC.

Kabagarama, D. 1997. *Breaking the ice: A guide to understanding people from other cultures.* Boston, MA: Allyn & Bacon.

Kaeser, G., & P. Gillespie. 1997. *Of many colors: Portraits of multiracial families.* Amherst: University of Massachusetts Press.

Katz, L.G., & D.E. McClellan. 1997. *Fostering children's social competence: The teacher's role.* Washington, DC: NAEYC.

Kendall, F.E. 1996. *Diversity in the classroom: New approaches to the education of young children.* 2d ed. New York: Teachers College Press.

Kindler, A.L. 1995. *Education of migrant children in the United States.* ERIC Document Reproduction Services No. 394 305.

Klein, T., C. Bittle, & J. Molnar. 1993. No place to call home: Supporting the needs of homeless children in the early childhood classroom. *Young Children* 48 (6): 22–31.

Kontos, S., & A. Wilcox-Herzog. 1997. Teachers' interactions with children: Why are they so important? *Young Children* 52 (2): 4–12.

Lakey, J. 1997. Teachers and parents define diversity in an Oregon preschool cooperative: Democracy at work. *Young Children* 52 (4): 20–28.

Levin, D. 2003. *Teaching young children in violent times: Building a peaceable classroom.* 2d ed. Cambridge, MA: Educators for Social Responsibility; Washington, DC: NAEYC.

Little Soldier, L. 1992. Working with Native American children. *Young Children* 47 (6): 15–21.

Lynch, E.W., & M.J. Hanson, eds. 1998. *Developing cross-cultural competence: A guide for working with children and their families.* 2d ed. Baltimore, MD: Brookes.

MacNaughton, G. 1999. *Saris and skirts: Gender equity and multiculturalism.* Research in Practice Series, Vol. 6, no. 4. Watson, Australia: Australian Early Childhood Association.

Mangione, P., ed. 1995. *Infant/toddler caregiving: A guide to culturally sensitive care.* Sacramento, CA: Far West Laboratory and California Department of Education.

McAdoo, H.P., ed. 1997. *Black families.* Thousand Oaks, CA: Sage.

McBride, S.L. 1999. Research in Review. Family-centered practices. *Young Children* 54 (3): 62–68.

McCormick, L., & R. Holden. 1992. Homeless children: A special challenge. *Young Children* 47 (6): 61–67.

McCracken, J.B. 1993. *Valuing diversity: The primary years.* Washington, DC: NAEYC.

Meier, D.R. 2000. *Scribble scrabble—Learning to read and write: Success with diverse teachers, children, and families.* New York: Teachers College Press.

Moore, R.C., S.M. Goltsman, & D.S. Iacofano, eds. 1992. *Play for All guidelines: Planning, design, and management of outdoor play settings for all children.* 2d ed. Berkeley, CA: MIG Communications.

Morrison, J., & L. Rodgers. 1996. Being responsive to the needs of children from dual heritage backgrounds. *Young Children* 52 (1): 29–32.

NAEYC. 1993. Educating yourself about diverse cultural groups in our country by reading. *Young Children* 48 (3): 13–16.

NAEYC. 1996. Position Statement. Responding to linguistic and cultural diversity—Recommendations for effective early childhood education. *Young Children* 51 (2): 4–12. Online: www.naeyc.org/resources/position_statements/psdiv98.htm.

NAEYC. 1999. *Involving men in the lives of children.* Washington, DC: Author. Brochure.

NAEYC. 1999. Using NAEYC's Code of Ethics to negotiate professional problems: How do we balance cultural diversity and our own cultural values? *Young Children* 54 (5): 44–46.

Neugebauer, B., ed. 1992. *Alike and different: Exploring our humanity with young children.* Rev. ed. Washington, DC: NAEYC.

Phillips, C.B. 1995. Culture: A process that empowers. In *Infant/toddler caregiving: A guide to culturally sensitive care,* ed. P. Mangione. Sacramento, CA: Far West Laboratory and California Department of Education.

Powlishta, K. 1995. Research in Review. Gender segregation among children: Understanding the "Cootie phenomenon." *Young Children* 50 (4): 61–68.

Ramsey, P., L.R. Williams, & E.B. Vold. 2002. *Multicultural education: A source book.* 2d ed. New York: RoutledgeFalmer.

Rand, M.K. 2000. *Giving it some thought: Cases for early childhood practice.* Washington, DC: NAEYC.

Rogoff, B. 1990. *Apprenticeship in thinking: Cognitive development in social context.* New York: Oxford University Press.

Rogoff, B., C. Mosier, J. Mistry, & A. Goncu. 1993. Toddlers' guided participation with their caregivers in cultural activity. In *Context for learning: Sociocultural dynamics in children's development,* eds. E.A. Forman, N. Minick, & C.A. Stone. New York: Oxford University Press.

Rosegrant, T. 1992. Reaching potentials in a multilingual classroom: Opportunities and challenges. In *Reaching potentials: Appropriate curriculum and assessment for young children,* Vol. 1, eds. S. Bredekamp & T. Rosegrant, 145–47. Washington, DC: NAEYC.

Ross, H.W. 1992. Integrating infants with disabilities? Can "ordinary" caregivers do it? *Young Children* 47 (3): 65–71.

Rothenberg, B.A. 1995. *Understanding and working with parents and children from rural Mexico: What professionals need to know about child rearing.* Menlo Park, CA: Children's Health Council, Center for Children and Family Development Press.

Salmon, M., with S.E. Akaran. 2001. Enrich your kindergarten program with a cross-cultural connection. *Young Children* 56 (4): 30–32.

Sandall, S., & M. Ostrosky. 1999. *Practical ideas for addressing challenging behaviors.* Denver, CO: Division for Early Childhood, Council for Exceptional Children.

Sandall, S., M. McLean, & B. Smith. 2000. *DEC recommended practices in early intervention/early childhood special education.* Denver, CO: Division for Early Childhood, Council for Exceptional Children.

Schlank, C.H., & B. Metzger. 1997. *Together and equal: Fostering cooperative play and promoting gender equity in early childhood programs.* Needham Heights, MA: Allyn & Bacon.

Schon, I. 2002. *Books to grow on: Latino literature for young children.* Washington, DC: NAEYC. Brochure.

Sheldon, A. 1990. Kings are royaler than queens: Language and socialization. *Young Children* 45 (2): 4–9.

Soriano-Nagurski, L. 1998. And the walls came tumbling down: Including children who are differently abled in typical early childhood educational settings. *Young Children* 53 (2): 40–41.

Spillane, C., & M. Crowley. 1996. *Books for boys and girls today: An annotated bibliography of non-sexist books for infants, toddlers, and preschoolers.* Wellesley, MA: Center for Research on Women.

Stonehouse, A. 1991. *Opening the doors: Child care in a multicultural society.* Watson, Australia: Australian Early Childhood Association.

Surr, J. 1992. Public Policy Report. Early childhood programs and the Americans with Disabilities Act (ADA). *Young Children* 47 (5): 18–21.

Tabors, P.O. 1997. *One child, two languages: A guide for preschool educators of children learning English as a second language.* Baltimore, MD: Brookes.

Tertell, E.A., S.M. Klein, & J.L. Jewett, eds. 1998. *When teachers reflect: Journeys toward effective, inclusive practice.* Washington, DC: NAEYC.

Wardle, F. 1990. Endorsing children's differences: Meeting the needs of adopted minority children. *Young Children* 45 (5): 44–46.

Wardle, F. 1993. Interracial families and biracial children. *Child Care Information Exchange* (90): 45–48.

Wardle, F. 1998. Meeting the needs of multiracial and multiethnic children in early childhood settings. *Early Childhood Education Journal* 26 (1): 7–11.

Wardle, F. 1999. *Tomorrow's children: Meeting the needs of multiracial and multiethnic children at home, in early childhood programs, and at school.* Denver, CO: Center for the Study of Biracial Children.

Washington, V. 1996. National Institute for Early Childhood Professional Development. Professional development in context: Leadership at the borders of our democratic, pluralistic society. *Young Children* 51 (6): 30–34.

Wehrly, B., K. Kenney, & M. Kenney. 1999. *Counseling multiracial families.* Thousand Oaks, CA: Sage.

Wellhousen, K. 1996. Girls can be bull riders, too! Supporting children's understanding of gender roles through children's literature. *Young Children* 51 (5): 79–83.

Wheeler, K.A. 1993. *How schools can stop shortchanging girls (and boys): Gender-equity strategies.* Wellesley, MA: Center for Research on Women.

Wickens, E. 1993. Penny's question: "I will have a child in my class with two moms—What do you know about this?" *Young Children* 48 (3): 25–28.

Wolfe, L. 1992. Reaching potentials through bilingual education. In *Reaching potentials: Appropriate curriculum and assessment for young children,* Vol. 1, eds. S. Bredekamp & T. Rosegrant, 139–44. Washington, DC: NAEYC.

Yelland, N., ed. 2000. *Promoting meaningful learning: Innovations in educating early childhood professionals.* Washington, DC: NAEYC.

York, S. 1991. *Roots & wings: Affirming culture in early childhood programs.* St. Paul, MN: Redleaf.

York, S. 1998. *Big as life: The everyday inclusive curriculum,* Vol. 1. St. Paul, MN: Redleaf.

Zeitlen, S.A. 1997. Finding fascinating projects that can promote boy/girl partnership. *Young Children* 52 (6): 29–30.

For Further Reading

For Reflecting, Discussing, Exploring

To the Reader: Use these questions to help you reflect on the materials in this volume, relate them to your own experiences, and apply any new insights and learning to your work as an early childhood educator.
To the Instructor: The questions are likely to be most effective as catalysts for discussion between students in groups of two to four, or as in-class writing questions followed by discussion.

I. Teaching in a Multicultural, Multilingual Society

1. Should a teacher be expected to take responsibility for learning about the culture(s) of the children she is teaching? Why or why not?

2. Kathleen Evans writes, "Both traditional beliefs and the requirements of modern culture can coexist in one person." Do you agree? Do you believe it is possible for a person to be bicultural, living effectively in two cultural and language traditions?

3. What would you do as a teacher to welcome a child and family whose language you don't understand? Have you had any opportunities to do that?

4. How would you react if you observed a mother or grandmother spoon-feeding a 4-year-old boy from your classroom? If you learn that a toddler is always spoon-fed at home, would you spoon-feed her in child care if her mother asked you to?

5. Do you think of children as language-deficient if they come to school not speaking English?

6. We often hear that total immersion into English is the best way to prepare young children for success in an English-speaking society. Do you agree? Why or why not?

7. Do you think schools should support maintenance of children's home language? If so, how?

8. What kinds of differences make you most uncomfortable as a teacher?

9. Have you ever tried using stories or discussions to explain social injustices to children? Did you feel this was effective?

II. Forging a Caring Classroom Community

1. In what ways do building a sense of community and helping children develop empathy foster respect for diversity?

2. Do you think class meetings (as described by Vance and Weaver) would help create a sense of community? Why or why not? Are there some kinds of problems that would be better handled by one or two children rather than by the whole group?

3. How can teachers convey respect for children without losing authority?

4. In the program you know best, what is displayed on the classroom walls and other areas, and why? How do children react to these materials?

5. In the early childhood program you are most familiar with, what conflict resolution strategies are the most effective? Which are most ineffective?

6. How would you deal with a 1½-year-old child who made a statement you found offensive? Would you

react differently if the same comment came from a 4-year-old? If so, how would you respond? Why?

7. How can you help children to better understand the feelings of others? Can you describe a time when a child's insights or lack of understanding surprised you?

III. Building Relationships with All Families

1. In your experience, when do teachers know more than parents? When do parents know more than teachers?

2. If a family member criticizes some aspect of your program, what do you do?

3. Would you call a child's family if he or she was showing behavior problems in the classroom? What would you say?

4. Do you look forward to conferences with parents, or do you dread them? Why?

5. What times of the day/week does your program hold parent conferences, "family nights," or other special events for families? How do you determine such scheduling?

IV. Regarding Social Class and Family Circumstances

1. When you were a child, with whom did you live, and what was your home like? What was your family's social class? When you were in preschool what was your sense of your own family's status and circumstances in comparison to those of other families? Did this view change as you got older?

2. How are the families of the children you teach different from the family you grew up in and the ones you knew best? Do you find this difference difficult in any way?

3. Without using names, describe the home life of a child you know, a way of life that is hard for you to understand or value.

4. For the program you know best, think about four things in the classroom environment or experience that might reinforce social class stereotypes. How could these elements be modified to be more positive for all the children?

5. Is there anything in this program's activities or materials that are intended to counteract societal biases against certain kinds of work? If not, can you suggest some possible additions or changes that would do so?

6. Do you think teaching poor children should be just the same as teaching middle-class children? Why or why not?

7. Is the program you know best responsive to the families' life circumstances, including the hours the adults work, the person(s) who cares for the child, constraints in finances and other resources, and social and financial differences among the various families? Are there ways the program could be more responsive to these realities?

V. Promoting Gender Equity, Respecting Gender Difference

1. Do you agree with the contributors to this section who feel that teachers should be concerned with gender roles, or do you think this perspective is an example of "political correctness"?

2. When you were a child, did you learn that it was important for you to be: cute/good-looking? polite? brave? well-behaved? smart? loving? helpful? What other messages came through to you about what you should be?

3. In your interactions with children, do you convey different expectations with respect to any of the above characteristics?

4. Does it make you uncomfortable to see girls play as soldiers or superheroes (e.g., to yell, run, and shoot)? How about for boys to play with dolls? cook and eat a pretend meal? dress up in girls' clothes in the dramatic play area?

5. At group time in the program you know best, which children talk the most? Which children get the most positive attention from the teacher? the most negative attention?

6. Look at children's books in the classroom or the public library to find some that reinforce traditional gender roles and some that challenge stereotypes. Do you think those that reinforce gender stereotypes should be avoided?

7. What would you say to parents who objected to enrollment of a lesbian-headed family in the program or who told their child not to play with this family's child?

8. If you were the program director and responsible for hiring staff, would you have reservations about hiring a well-qualified man as lead teacher for the preschool class? as infant/toddler caregiver? Do you think you would encounter any parent opposition to hiring men for either of these positions? If so, how would you respond?

VI. Creating an Inclusive Classroom

1. Do you have any hesitations or concerns about having children with disabilities in your program? If so, do some kinds of disabilities cause you particular concern? What positive aspects do you perceive in having an inclusive program?

2. Think in terms of a specific child with a specific physical disability, a child who is just entering your program: what adaptations would be needed both indoors and outdoors?

3. How would you approach the other children in the program about this child's entering the group? approach other families in the program?

4. What would be your response when a child makes a negative comment about another child who has a disability, such as "She looks weird," or "He always spills his food"?

5. If the typically developing children in the program were not interacting much with a child with a disability, what would be your reaction?

VII. Educating in a Religiously Diverse World

1. How do your own religious background and beliefs influence your work with children? Would you consider working in a faith-based early childhood program? Why or why not?

2. What holiday is your favorite (or was your favorite as a child)? Is it appropriate to celebrate that holiday in your early childhood program? Put another way: can you describe several ways of handling the holiday that seem inappropriate to you and several that seem appropriate?

3. Some teachers and directors feel that holiday-related curriculum should be eliminated from early childhood programs. Do you agree? Why or why not?

4. Some people may have feelings against those who practice a particular religion. As an early childhood teacher or director, what actions could you take to help children resist this bias?

5. What events and places create a feeling of awe and wonder for you? What moments of awe and wonder have you shared with children?

VIII. Growing as Culturally Responsive Educators

1. Did your own family experiences teach you to be proud of your culture? Did your schooling teach you to be proud of your culture? Do you respond differently to children who share your background than to others who don't?

2. Have you yourself encountered prejudice or discrimination based on any of the social categories to which you belong? If so, how did you cope with it, and how have your reactions changed over the years?

3. What languages are spoken in your classroom, and by whom (including staff)?

4. Have you ever observed a young child rejecting another person because of color, language, gender, dress, or other characteristic? What happened? What did you do? What do you wish you had done?

5. Do you think that the existence of racism in American society affects you personally? Why or why not?

6. Is it embarrassing for you to talk about race, disability, social class, and other differences? Why or why not? What do you do when children raise one of these subjects?

7. Do you respond to stereotypes you observe in children's play or interaction? Are there some you are more likely to respond to and some less so?